CFA® LEV
EXAM COMPANI ..

The 7city/Wiley study guide to getting the most out of the CFA Institute curriculum

Foreword by Pamela Peterson Drake, PhD, CFA

WILEY

This edition first published 2013 by John Wiley & Sons Ltd

© 2013 7city Learning

Registered office

John Wiley & Sons Ltd, The Atrium, Southern Gate, Chichester, West Sussex, PO19 8SQ, United Kingdom

For details of our global editorial offices, for customer services and for information about how to apply for permission to reuse the copyright material in this book please see our website at www.wiley.com.

Wiley publishes in a variety of print and electronic formats and by print-on-demand. Some material included with standard print versions of this book may not be included in e-books or in print-on-demand. If this book refers to media such as a CD or DVD that is not included in the version you purchased, you may download this material at http://booksupport.wiley.com. For more information about Wiley products, visit www.wiley.com.

Designations used by companies to distinguish their products are often claimed as trademarks. All brand names and product names used in this book are trade names, service marks, trademarks or registered trademarks of their respective owners. The publisher is not associated with any product or vendor mentioned in this book. This publication is designed to provide accurate and authoritative information in regard to the subject matter covered. It is sold on the understanding that the publisher is not engaged in rendering professional services. If professional advice or other expert assistance is required, the services of a competent professional should be sought.

Required disclaimer:
CFA Institute does not endorse, promote, or warrant the accuracy or quality of the products or services offered by 7city Learning or John Wiley & Sons Ltd. CFA Institute, CFA®, and Chartered Financial Analyst® are trademarks owned by CFA Institute.

Certain materials contained within this text are the copyrighted property of CFA Institute. The following is the copyright disclosure for these materials: "Copyright, 2013, CFA Institute. Reproduced and republished from 2013 Learning Outcome Statements with permission from CFA Institute. All Rights Reserved."

Disclaimer: This 7city/Wiley CFA® Level I Exam Companion should be used in conjunction with the original readings as set forth by CFA Institute in their 2013 CFA® Level I Study Guide. The information contained in this Exam Companion covers topics contained in the readings referenced by CFA Institute and is believed to be accurate. However, their accuracy cannot be guaranteed nor is any warranty conveyed as to your ultimate exam success. The authors of the referenced readings have not endorsed or sponsored this Exam Companion.

A catalogue record for this book is available from the British Library.

978-1-118-56034-1 (paperback)   ISBN 978-1-118-56031-0 (ebk)
ISBN 978-1-118-56032-7 (ebk)   ISBN 978-1-118-56033-4 (ebk)

Set in 10/14 pt Times New Roman by Sparks Publishing Services Ltd – www.sparkspublishing.com

Printed in Great Britain by TJ International Ltd, Padstow, Cornwall

CONTENTS

Foreword   by Pamela Peterson Drake, PhD, CFA   vii

How to Use the Exam Companion   ix

STUDY SESSION 1   **Ethics and Professional Standards**   1

Reading 1   Code of Ethics and Standards of Professional Conduct   3
Reading 2   Guidance for Standards I–VII   6
Reading 3   Introduction to the Global Investment Performance Standards (GIPS)   8
Reading 4   Global Investment Performance Standards (GIPS)   11

STUDY SESSION 2   **Quantitative Methods: Basic Concepts**   13

Reading 5   The Time Value of Money   15
Reading 6   Discounted Cash Flow Applications   19
Reading 7   Statistical Concepts and Market Returns   22
Reading 8   Probability Concepts   26

STUDY SESSION 3   **Quantitative Methods: Application**   31

Reading 9   Common Probability Distributions   33
Reading 10   Sampling and Estimation   37
Reading 11   Hypothesis Testing   40
Reading 12   Technical Analysis   45

STUDY SESSION 4   **Economics: Microeconomic Analysis**   49

Reading 13   Demand and Supply Analysis: Introduction   51
Reading 14   Demand and Supply Analysis: Consumer Demand   56
Reading 15   Demand and Supply Analysis: The Firm   58
Reading 16   The Firm and Market Structures   62

STUDY SESSION 5   **Economics: Macroeconomic Analysis**   **67**

Reading 17   Aggregate Output, Prices, and Economic Growth   69
Reading 18   Understanding Business Cycles   74
Reading 19   Monetary and Fiscal Policy   78

STUDY SESSION 6   **Economics: Economics in a Global Context**   **83**

Reading 20   International Trade and Capital Flows   85
Reading 21   Currency Exchange Rates   88

STUDY SESSION 7   **Financial Reporting and Analysis: An Introduction**   **91**

Reading 22   Financial Statement Analysis: An Introduction   95
Reading 23   Financial Reporting Mechanics   98
Reading 24   Financial Reporting Standards   103

STUDY SESSION 8   **Financial Reporting and Analysis: Income Statements, Balance Sheets, and Cash Flow Statements**   **107**

Reading 25   Understanding Income Statements   109
Reading 26   Understanding Balance Sheets   114
Reading 27   Understanding Cash Flow Statements   118
Reading 28   Financial Analysis Techniques   124

STUDY SESSION 9   **Financial Reporting and Analysis: Inventories, Long-lived Assets, Income Taxes, and Non-current Liabilities**   **129**

Reading 29   Inventories   131
Reading 30   Long-lived Assets   135
Reading 31   Income Taxes   140
Reading 32   Non-current (Long-term) Liabilities   144

STUDY SESSION 10   **Financial Reporting and Analysis: Evaluating Financial Reporting Quality and Other Applications**   **151**

Reading 33   Financial Reporting Quality: Red Flags and Accounting Warning Signs   153
Reading 34   Accounting Shenanigans on the Cash Flow Statement   155
Reading 35   Financial Statement Analysis: Applications   156

Study Session 11 **Corporate Finance**   159

Reading 36   Capital Budgeting   161
Reading 37   Cost of Capital   165
Reading 38   Measures of Leverage   170
Reading 39   Dividends and Share Repurchases: Basics   172
Reading 40   Working Capital Management   175
Reading 41   The Corporate Governance of Listed Companies: A Manual for Investors   180

Study Session 12 **Portfolio Management**   183

Reading 42   Portfolio Management: An Overview   185
Reading 43   Portfolio Risk and Return: Part I   187
Reading 44   Portfolio Risk and Return: Part II   192
Reading 45   Basics of Portfolio Planning and Construction   196

Study Session 13 **Equity: Market Organization, Market Indices, and Market Efficiency**   199

Reading 46   Market Organization and Structure   201
Reading 47   Security Market Indices   206
Reading 48   Market Efficiency   209

Study Session 14 **Equity Analysis and Valuation**   213

Reading 49   Overview of Equity Securities   215
Reading 50   Introduction to Industry and Company Analysis   218
Reading 51   Equity Valuation: Concepts and Basic Tools   221

Study Session 15 **Fixed Income: Basic Concepts**   225

Reading 52   Features of Debt Securities   227
Reading 53   Risks Associated with Investing in Bonds   231
Reading 54   Overview of Bond Sectors and Instruments   236
Reading 55   Understanding Yield Spreads   241

Study Session 16 **Fixed Income Analysis and Valuation**   245

Reading 56   Introduction to the Valuation of Debt Securities   247
Reading 57   Yield Measures, Spot Rates, and Forward Rates   252
Reading 58   Introduction to the Measurement of Interest Rate Risk   257
Reading 59   Fundamentals of Credit Analysis   262

STUDY SESSION 17   **Derivatives**   **265**

Reading 60   Derivative Markets and Instruments   267
Reading 61   Forward Markets and Contracts   270
Reading 62   Futures Markets and Contracts   274
Reading 63   Option Markets and Contracts   278
Reading 64   Swap Markets and Contracts   284
Reading 65   Risk Management Applications of Option Strategies   287

STUDY SESSION 18   **Alternative Investments**   **289**

Reading 66   Introduction to Alternative Investments   291
Reading 67   Investing in Commodities   294

Answers to Sample Questions   297

Index   317

FOREWORD

by Pamela Peterson Drake, PhD, CFA

The CFA Level I exam is the first and broadest of the three exams in the CFA Program. The Level I exam is a challenge primarily because of the breadth of the material – candidates preparing for this exam must have a basic foundation in accounting, economics, statistics, corporate finance, and investments. Every candidate comes with a different background and skill set, so the areas a candidate may need to emphasize may differ. But all candidates should be familiar with the readings in the 18 study sessions.

The Ethics topic, which you will see again on Levels II and III, is focused on the Code of Ethics and the Standards of Professional Conduct, but don't forget to look at the CFA Institute Professional Conduct Program, which delineates the process of enforcement with the possible revocation of membership, candidacy, or, in the extreme, the use of the CFA designation. Also, don't overlook the Global Investment Performance Standards (GIPS), which focus on the ethics of reporting investment results. Understand both the "why" and the "how" of reporting results compliant with GIPS.

The Quantitative Methods topic covers financial mathematics, probability, and statistics. While the emphasis of the learning outcomes is on calculations, don't just focus on the mechanical; you will remember and be better prepared to apply the calculations if you understand the math or statistics behind the equations. You'll notice that Technical Analysis is tacked on to Quantitative Methods; you needn't become an expert in Elliott Wave Theory, but you need to know that some practitioners use technical analysis and that there are common approaches to analysis of patterns. Key, however, is recognizing the difference between technical analysis and fundamental analysis.

The coverage of macro- and micro-economics is similar to what you would find in the introductory courses in each, but remember that the focus is on how the analyst will use this knowledge in the analysis of an industry or a company. Therefore, as you read this material, think about the implications for financial analysis. As with all the topics, you also need to think globally, and in the context of Economics this means understanding the benefits of international trade as well as knowing the basics of exchange rates.

The biggest topic in terms of the weight is Financial Reporting and Analysis, which encompasses what we more familiarly refer to as accounting. You need to be familiar with financial statements – how they are constructed and how they are linked to one another – and then focus on specific accounting. This specific accounting sets the stage for the quality of financial statements, which is the closing subject of this topic.

The Corporate Finance topic is broad and encompasses many readings that are a bit out of proportion for its weight in the exam. However, this is material that is covered in a typical principles of finance course, and some of this material overlaps material elsewhere in the curriculum (e.g. financial ratios). Remember that the focus is on financial analysis and think about how investment and financing decision-making by a company affects its value.

Portfolio Management is a topic whose importance grows as you progress through the three levels of exams. At Level I, this topic spans the basics of portfolio theory and asset pricing. But don't forget the wealth planning component, and be sure to consider clients' needs with respect to investment objectives, constraints, and risk tolerance. Be sure to consider how this topic relates to the ethics coverage.

The Equity topic includes descriptive information on markets, as well as the theory and evidence regarding market efficiency. The topic also covers fundamental analysis, which begins with the economy, and extends to the industry, and then finally the company. Keep in mind that some of this material links back to financial reporting and analysis.

The Fixed Income topic is broad, but the emphasis is on the characteristics, valuation, and risks of bonds. Be prepared to describe the different risks associated with bonds, and to perform calculations specific to interest rate risk and the arbitrage-free valuation of a bond.

The Derivatives topic covers the basic definitions and description of futures, forwards, options, and swaps. Key to mastery of this topic is understanding the factors that affect the value of derivatives. Calculations comprise a relatively few learning outcomes in this topic, and the focus of these calculations is on the payoffs from forward rate agreements, the boundaries for the value of puts and call, the profits from option strategies, and the cash flows associated with plain vanilla swaps. It is important to establish a solid foundation in derivatives at this level because you will be seeing derivatives at Level II and Level III in the context of portfolio management and risk management.

The final topic is Alternative Investments, which is a hodge-podge of investments, ranging from hedge funds to commodity funds. You must be able to recite the features of these different investments, with special emphasis on commodities.

The CFA Level I curriculum is broad, and as such it may seem daunting, especially with its emphasis on tools and terminology. To make this manageable, keep in mind as you read through the material that the ultimate goal is the relevance of this material to investment analysis and portfolio management.

HOW TO USE THE EXAM COMPANION

The CFA Institute curriculum forms the basis of the Level I exam and this Exam Companion book aims to bring focus to your studies, making sure that you have access to the most thorough exam prep possible.

This is the only book on the market that references the CFA Institute's curriculum directly. As such, you have a unique guide to help you understand how to navigate the vast amount of information contained within the readings. Our experienced instructors have pooled their knowledge of the CFA exams to give you hints and tips on how best to approach each of the readings and the key information that you need to know from each reading.

HOW YOU SHOULD USE THIS BOOK

We recommend that you should read the Exam Companion section for each of the readings before reading the CFA Institute readings. The Exam Companion will point you to the learning outcome statements that you should spend longest on and those that will place less of a demand on your time.

We have also highlighted key formulae and facts that you will need to learn for each of the readings.

This book doesn't cover all the points that you will need to know, though, and you should not rely on this book alone for your knowledge. As with any practical test, you will need to spend time practising questions and applying your knowledge to different scenarios. 7city's online portal contains thousands of questions for this purpose.

STUDY SESSION 1
ETHICS AND PROFESSIONAL STANDARDS

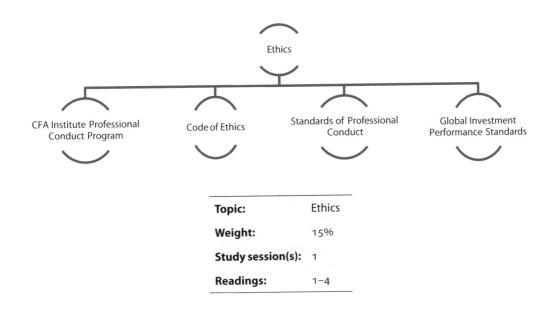

Topic:	Ethics
Weight:	15%
Study session(s):	1
Readings:	1–4

THE BIG PICTURE

Just as ethics are an important part of investment management, analysis, and research, they are an important part of the CFA examination and curriculum. Included along with ethics are the Global Investment Performance Standards (GIPS), which are principles detailing how performance results are measured and reported.

The ethics section is 15% of the syllabus by weighting, yet is often overlooked by delegates who focus on the calculations later in the syllabus. It is a purely written section mostly testing the CFA Institute professional practice handbook, but the questions are usually scenario based and as such can often be quite tricky.

Whereas ethics comprises 15% of the Level I exam, it is 10% of the Level II and Level III exams. In other words, the effort expended to learn about the Code of Ethics, the Standards of Professional Conduct, and GIPS is well worth it – because you will see it again. And again.

CODE OF ETHICS AND STANDARDS OF PROFESSIONAL CONDUCT

Candidates are responsible for not only being able to recite the Code of Ethics and the Standards of Professional Conduct [keywords: describe, state, explain] but also for understanding how the Code and Standards are applied in investment management and research [keywords: demonstrate, distinguish, recommend]. Be sure to practice the application of these to different situations.

Whereas the Code of Ethics provides the broad framework for conduct, the Standards are more specific with respect to how the Code is operationalized for CFA Institute members and CFA candidates. For example, the Code of Ethics states "Place the integrity of the investment profession and the interests of clients above their own personal interests," and the Standards expand on "III. Duties to Clients" with explanations on "Loyalty, Prudence, and Care," "Fair Dealing," "Suitability," "Performance Presentation," and "Preservation of Confidentiality."

The key to the Code and Standards is to remember:

- The Code and Standards apply to both CFA Institute members and CFA candidates
- Always put the client, the profession, and one's employer ahead of oneself
- Be professional, knowledgeable, and objective
- Comply with securities laws

GIPS

The basic idea of GIPS is to facilitate the comparison of investment performance. The beneficiaries of GIPS are investors and investment management firms, with the benefits arising primarily from the clear, understandable, and comparable results. Investment management firms comply on a voluntary basis, but they can also employ a third party to verify their claim on compliance to GIPS. A key element of GIPS is that they form the ethical principles of performance reporting.

Learning Outcome Statements

Application LOS	Knowledge LOS
	1a **Describe** the structure of the CFA Institute Professional Conduct Program and the process for the enforcement of the Code and Standards
	1b **State** the six components of the Code of Ethics and the seven Standards of Professional Conduct
	1c **Explain** the ethical responsibilities required by the Code and Standards, including the sub-sections of each Standard

Knowledge Learning Outcome Statements

1a Describe the structure of the CFA Institute Professional Conduct Program and the process for the enforcement of the Code and Standards

The program is fundamental to the values of the CFA Institute. The key points to note are:

- The program is a model for measuring the ethics of investment professionals globally
- All members and candidates must abide by the Code and Standards
- They are encouraged to notify their employer of this responsibility

Violations of the Code and Standards may result in disciplinary sanctions by the CFA Institute. Sanctions include:

- Revocation of membership
- Revocation of candidacy in the CFA program
- Revocation of right to use the CFA designation

1b State the six components of the Code of Ethics and the seven Standards of Professional Conduct

The Code of Ethics
"Members of CFA Institute and candidates for designation must:

- Act with integrity, competence, diligence, respect, and in an ethical manner with the public, clients, prospective clients, employers, employees, colleagues in the investment profession, and other participants in the global capital markets
- Place the integrity of the investment profession and the interests of clients above their personal interests

- Use reasonable care and exercise independent professional judgment when conducting investment analysis, making investment recommendations, taking investment actions, and engaging in other professional activities
- Practice and encourage others to practice in a professional and ethical manner that will reflect credit on themselves and on the profession
- Promote the integrity of and uphold the rules governing capital markets
- Maintain and improve their professional competence and strive to maintain and improve the competence of other investment professionals"

Standards of Professional Conduct

I. Professionalism
    A. Knowledge of the Law
    B. Independence and Objectivity
    C. Misrepresentation
    D. Misconduct
II. Integrity of Capital Markets
    A. Material Non-public Information
    B. Market Manipulation
III. Duties to Clients
    A. Loyalty, Prudence, and Care
    B. Fair Dealing
    C. Suitability
    D. Performance Presentation
    E. Preservation of Confidentiality
IV. Duties to Employers
    A. Loyalty
    B. Additional Compensation Arrangements
    C. Responsibilities of Supervisors
V. Investment Analysis, Recommendations, and Actions
    A. Diligence and Reasonable Basis
    B. Communication with Clients and Prospective Clients
    C. Record Retention
VI. Conflict of Interest
    A. Disclosure of Conflicts
    B. Priority of Transactions
    C. Referral Fees
VII. Responsibilities as a CFA Institute Member or CFA Candidate
    A. Conduct as Members and Candidates in the CFA Program
    B. Reference to the CFA Institute, the CFA Designation, and the CFA Program

1c Explain the ethical responsibilities required by the Code and Standards, including the sub-sections of each Standard

This simply requires knowledge of the Standards and the Code, ready to apply to scenarios in Reading 2.

Reading 1 sample question
(Answers on p. 297)

The Standard covering "Communication with client and prospective clients" is least likely to require that:

(A) Analysts distinguish between fact and opinion in their reports
(B) Clients must be informed promptly about any changes to the investment process
(C) Analysts always show at least ten years of historic information in their reports

LEARNING OUTCOME STATEMENTS

Application LOS	Knowledge LOS
2a **Demonstrate** the application of the Code of Ethics and Standards of Professional Conduct to situations involving issues of professional integrity	
2b **Distinguish** between conduct that conforms to the Code and Standards and conduct that violates the Code and Standards	
2c **Recommend** practices and procedures designed to prevent violations of the Code of Ethics and Standards of Professional Conduct	

APPLICATION LEARNING OUTCOME STATEMENTS

2a Demonstrate the application of the Code of Ethics and Standards of Professional Conduct to situations involving issues of professional integrity

2b Distinguish between conduct that conforms to the Code and Standards and conduct that violates the Code and Standards

2c Recommend practices and procedures designed to prevent violations of the Code of Ethics and Standards of Professional Conduct

The emphasis in this reading is on applying the Standards to situations that members face, rather than being able to recite the Standards from the handbook. As such, spend your review time here with the case studies and examples that are shown throughout the handbook rather than learning the names and numbers of each Standard.

Within each Standard there are several examples of how the Standard would be applied in specific situations. Make sure you understand each example and the rationale for the conclusions reached. There are then plenty of practice questions at the end of the reading that you should complete.

Reading 2 sample question
(Answers on p. 297)

A discretionary fund manager of an equities fund invests new cash received in T-bills. Is this necessarily a breach of the Code and Standards?

(A) Yes, as it is an equities fund
(B) No, as the T-bills may be a temporary investment
(C) No, as the fund manager is only guided towards, not legally bound to, equity investments

LEARNING OUTCOME STATEMENTS

Application LOS	Knowledge LOS
	3a **Explain** why the GIPS standards were created, what parties the GIPS standards apply to, and who is served by the standards
	3b **Explain** the construction and purpose of composites in performance reporting
	3c **Explain** the requirements for verification

KNOWLEDGE LEARNING OUTCOME STATEMENTS

3a Explain why the GIPS standards were created, what parties the GIPS standards apply to, and who is served by the standards

Why were the GIPS standards created?

Global Investment Performance Standards were devised for the following reasons:

- The investment community had great difficulty making meaningful comparisons on the basis of accurate investment performance data
- Misleading practices hinder comparability
- Representative accounts
- Reporting only top-performing accounts
- Survivorship bias (i.e. ignoring performance of funds that no longer exist)
- Presenting an "average" performance history
- Excluding poor-performing portfolios
- Varying time periods
- Selecting time periods to favor results
- Practitioner-driven set of ethical principles
- Establish a standardized, industry-wide approach for calculating and presenting historical investment results
- Help avoid misrepresentation of performance by investment firms

Who can claim compliance?

- Any investment management firm may choose to comply with GIPS
  - Voluntary compliance
  - Not typically required by legal or regulatory authorities
- Investment firm
  - Must manage assets
- Plan sponsors and consultants
  - Cannot make a claim of compliance

- o   Can claim to endorse the GIPS
- Software vendors
  - o   Cannot be compliant
- Firm-wide process
  - o   Cannot be achieved on a single product or composite
- Two options:
  - o   Comply or do not comply

Who benefits from compliance?

Benefits two main groups:

1   Investment management firms
2   Prospective clients
    - Provide reassurance to prospective clients about track record of the investment management firm
      - o   Record is complete and fairly presented
      - o   Allows global competition for compliant firms
      - o   Investors have a greater level of confidence in integrity of performance management
      - o   Can more readily compare firms

3b Explain the construction and purpose of composites in performance reporting

Composites

Key concepts:

- Required use of composites
  - o   An aggregation of discretionary portfolios into a single group that represents a particular investment objective or strategy
  - o   Must include all actual, fee-paying discretionary portfolios managed in accordance with the same investment objective or strategy
- Firms cannot choose portfolios to include or exclude
- Establish criteria on an ex-ante basis (before the fact, not after)

3c Explain the requirements for verification

Verification
- Firms are responsible for their claim of compliance and for maintenance of the claim
- Firms self-regulate
- Firms may voluntarily hire an independent third party to verify claim
- Primary purpose
  - o   Provide assurance that a firm has adhered to the GIPS on a firm-wide basis
  - o   Verification
  - o   Entire firm; not on specific composites
- Has the firm complied with all the composite construction requirements of GIPS on a firm-wide basis?
- Are the firm's processes and procedures designed to calculate and present performance results in compliance with the GIPS standards?
- Performed only by qualified independent third parties

Reading 3 sample question
(Answers on p. 297)

Abraham Management was established five years ago and has complied with GIPS in presenting information about the performance of its assets under management for this time. The firm has commissioned its internal audit department to test whether the firm has complied with composite construction criteria firm-wide and has the policies and procedures to calculate performance in accordance with GIPS. It put a note on its marketing materials stating "Abraham Management have complied with GIPS standards and have had the compliance verified." Abraham Management is:

(A) in full compliance with GIPS
(B) in violation of GIPS because it has not presented at least ten years' information
(C) in violation of GIPS because the firm cannot provide its own verification

Introduction to the Global Investment Performance Standards

STUDY SESSION 1 READING 4

LEARNING OUTCOME STATEMENTS

Application LOS	Knowledge LOS
	4a **Describe** the key features of the GIPS standards and the fundamentals of compliance
	4b **Describe** the scope of the GIPS standards, with respect to an investment firm's definition and historical performance record
	4c **Explain** how the GIPS standards are implemented in countries with existing standards for performance reporting, and describe the appropriate response when the GIPS standards and local regulations conflict
	4d **Describe** the nine major sections of the GIPS standards

KNOWLEDGE LEARNING OUTCOME STATEMENTS

4a Describe the key features of the GIPS standards and the fundamentals of compliance

4b Describe the scope of the GIPS standards, with respect to an investment firm's definition and historical performance record

4c Explain how the GIPS standards are implemented in countries with existing standards for performance reporting, and describe the appropriate response when the GIPS standards and local regulations conflict

4d Describe the nine major sections of the GIPS standards

Note that the examinable portion of Reading 4 is actually very short. There is a large optional section, denoted with blue lines, that is not examinable. The key to this reading is to memorize the main components of the GIPS framework. These are listed in detail in the early part of the reading before the optional section.

Following the optional section is a set of sample disclosures – these provide an excellent interactive way of committing the GIPS rules to memory.

Reading 4 sample question
(Answers on p. 297)

Ames Capital is a global financial services firm incorporated in the United States of America. Each overseas branch of the firm operates through separate legal entities under the name Ames Capital except for in Europe where the company operates through a single subsidiary called Europa Wealth. Europa Wealth has head offices in Geneva but branches in 15 other European countries. For the purposes of GIPS compliance the definition of the firm includes:

(A) all legal entities called Ames Capital only
(B) all legal entities called Ames Capital and the head office of Europa Wealth
(C) all legal entities called Ames Capital, the head office of Europa Wealth and all of Europa Wealth's branches

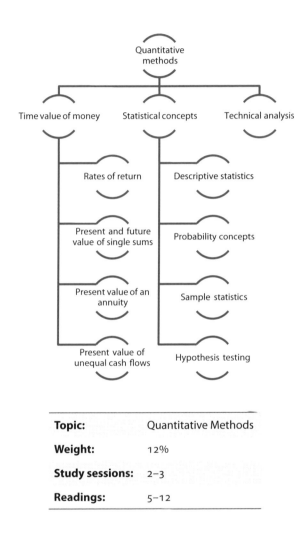

Topic:	Quantitative Methods
Weight:	12%
Study sessions:	2–3
Readings:	5–12

THE BIG PICTURE

Investment managers must be prepared to grapple with both valuation and uncertainty, the latter requiring a working knowledge of probability and statistics. The Quantitative Methods segment of the curriculum covers these, plus the topic of technical analysis. With the exception of technical analysis, candidates must be familiar with and understand the underlying concepts [keywords: define, distinguish, identify, explain], but also – and this is most important – apply the many tools and concepts developed in these readings [keywords: calculate, solve, demonstrate]. The majority of the learning outcomes in this topic pertain to the application of these many tools and concepts.

Though candidates are expected to use the time value of money functions in the BAII or the HP12C calculator, knowing the concepts behind the math will help you remember the calculations, verify your answers, and figure out how to work a problem that doesn't fit neatly in the calculator functions.

In addition to being able to calculate the present value and future value of a single amount, an annuity, and a series of uneven cash flows (i.e. net present value), candidates need to be able to solve for the rate of return (i.e. the internal rate of return (IRR)) and must be aware of the potential problems when applying IRR.

Setting the stage for applications of performance measurement in Level II and Level III, candidates must be able to calculate returns, both money-weighted and time-weighted. And setting the stage for returns in the context of fixed income, candidates must be able to calculate different yields: the bank discount yield, the holding period yield, the money-market yield, and the bond-equivalent yield.

The key to mastery of these learning outcomes is practice, practice, practice.

STATISTICAL CONCEPTS

Ultimately, when we view market prices or behavior, we look at samples and infer from these samples whether we are looking at a sample mean, comparing means, or looking specifically at a sample variance. Before one can infer anything, there must be an understanding of probability, sampling, and hypothesis testing. You must be able to select the appropriate test statistic to use in a particular situation.

You should recognize that just because something is statistically significant, it does not mean that it is economically significant. For example, a test of a trading rule may produce statistically significant results that are not economically meaningful once you consider transactions costs.

TECHNICAL ANALYSIS

Despite the emphasis on efficient markets throughout the CFA curriculum, candidates must have a working knowledge of what technical analysis is, be able to identify common indicators from a basic description or from a chart, and be able to describe specific technical analysis approaches. Keep in mind that you don't have to become an expert in technical analysis, but you do need to recognize its existence, know the common approaches, and be able to distinguish it from fundamental analysis.

Quantitative Methods is an important area and the first two readings are particularly crucial. They rely heavily on being familiar with your calculator (although strangely the readings are very careful not to mention calculator use). You can save valuable time by being speedy on your calculator so it is vital you go through the calculator tutorial on the 7city portal. This is not for "normal" calculator functions but the time value of money buttons on the third row of the Texas Instruments BAII or the top row for the Hewlett Packard 12C.

In addition this reading looks at interest rate manipulation and jargon, which are important for your understanding of later studies.

LEARNING OUTCOME STATEMENTS

Application LOS	Knowledge LOS
5c **Calculate** and interpret the effective annual rate, given the stated annual interest rate and the frequency of compounding	5a **Interpret** interest rates as required rates of return, discount rates, or opportunity costs
5d **Solve** time value of money problems for different frequencies of compounding	5b **Explain** an interest rate as the sum of a real risk-free rate and premiums that compensate investors for distinct types of risk
5e **Calculate** and interpret the future value (FV) and present value (PV) of a single sum of money, an ordinary annuity, an annuity due, a perpetuity (PV only), and a series of unequal cash flows	5f **Demonstrate** the use of a timeline in modeling and solving time value of money problems

APPLICATION LEARNING OUTCOME STATEMENTS

5c Calculate and interpret the effective annual rate, given the stated annual interest rate and the frequency of compounding

It is crucial that you understand these terms and how to calculate one or the other. The assumption about the stated annual interest rate in particular will be used throughout your studies.

Example

A three-year investment has an interest rate (yield) quoted of 6% but interest is paid quarterly:

Quoted (stated) "nominal" rate = 6% annual rate (always assume annual unless told otherwise)

Period rate = 6% × ¼ = 1.5% per quarter

Compound rate (effective annual rate or EAR) given by:

(1 + period rate) no of periods in year = (1 + EAR)

So (1 + EAR) = 1.015⁴ = 1.06136 and EAR = 6.136% p.a.

Notice in Section 3.2, the reading also discusses continuous compounding (i.e. the compounding period is infinitely small). You won't use this much in your studies (derivative valuations at Level II mostly) but you're meant to know it and it might give the odd question. Don't spend too long worrying about it if you're puzzled: it's not worth the time. Using the example above, there is no period rate – we go straight from quoted to EAR:

$(1 + EAR) = e^{\text{stated rate}} = e^{0.06} = 1.0618$ so EAR = 6.18% p.a.

(e^x is a button on your calculator – underneath LN)

It is less common in questions, as it is less useful in practice, but you should be able to see how to go the other way, i.e. from EAR to quoted rate.

Example

EAR = 12.68%, compounded monthly

$(1 + \text{period rate})^{12} = 1.1268$

$(1 + \text{period rate}) = 1.1268^{1/12} = 1.01$ so period rate is 1% per month

Quoted rate = 1% × 12 = 12%

If EAR = 5.127%, compounded continuously

$(1 + EAR) = 1.05127 = e^{\text{quoted rate}}$

Quoted rate = LN (1.05127) = 0.05, i.e. 5%

5d, e Solve time value of money problems for different frequencies of compounding; calculate and interpret the future value (FV) and present value (PV) of a single sum of money, an ordinary annuity, an annuity due, a perpetuity (PV only), and a series of unequal cash flows

There is a good likelihood that you will get some questions on these areas; they are also used elsewhere in the Level 1 syllabus so you will score in Corporate Finance, Fixed Income and Financial Reporting and Analysis as well if you get to grips with this.

There are lots of examples in the reading to take you through this, and it is a good idea to make sure you follow the numbers used to demonstrate the techniques, rather than trying to memorize formulae.

An annuity is when we have a series of identical cash flows at regular intervals of time; although we could find the present value by using the formula, it is often easier to use the financial calculator you are allowed in the exam. The reading is careful not to mention calculator use as this might endorse a particular model, but it is crucial you practice these calculations. Our website has a step-by-step guide to using the Texas BAII which will save you time on these questions. It is particularly useful when trying to find the discount rate (I/Y) when we have the cash flows, but we could find PV, FV, periodic cash flow, number of periods or yield, given the other values. The calculator (third row of buttons for these calculations) will easily cope with regular annuities or annuities due by switching between 'END' and 'BGN' modes. Without the calculator some of these would be a very longwinded calculation so you *must* be familiar with how to use it. [Caution: Be sure to toggle back to "END" when you finish an annuity problem.]

If there are unequal cash flows for a finite number of periods (i.e. not an annuity), we must discount or compound each one individually before adding them. Again, this can be quicker on your calculator using the second row this time. This really comes into its own when trying to find the yield (this is the IRR and comes in the next reading).

KNOWLEDGE LEARNING OUTCOME STATEMENTS

5a, b Interpret interest rates as required rates of return, discount rates, or opportunity costs; explain an interest rate as the sum of a real risk-free rate and premiums that compensate investors for distinct types of risk

This is going to be of more use in Corporate Finance, in which we look at the return investors require. Here it's enough to notice that the return required by any investor is made up of three parts:

The risk premium can be sub-divided into risk relating to:

- Default (default risk premium)
- Loss if sold quickly (liquidity premium)
- Sensitivity of value (maturity risk)

This return required is the rate used by an investor to discount any future cash flows to give the present value. An investor that uses the money for immediate consumption is forgoing this return; it could, therefore, be viewed as an opportunity cost.

5f Demonstrate the use of a timeline in modeling and solving time value of money problems

It's difficult to see how this would be tested in its own right. It's a useful technique to make sure we get the time between cash flows right and hence discount or compound by the correct number of periods.

Reading 5 sample questions
(Answers on p. 298)

1   A repayment mortgage of $120,000 is taken out over 20 years. What is the annual repayment required at the end of each year if the rate of interest is fixed at 6.5%?

(A) $6,390.00
(B) $10,111.13
(C) $10,890.76

2   Jennifer takes out a 25-year loan for $10,000. The loan is repayable via 25 annual installments, due at the year end. The interest on the loan is 6% per annum. Which of the following is closest to the interest due for the second year and the amount of the loan outstanding at the end of the second year?

(A) $589 and $9,625 respectively
(B) $600 and $9,818 respectively
(C) $782 and $9,625 respectively

This carries on from Reading 5 and looks at the present value and yield of an investment with uneven cash flows. Again, the calculator is crucial (the second row this time) and again the reading makes no mention of it (calculating the IRR without the calculator would be a nightmare).

The money-weighted and time-weighted rates of return are favorite exam topics (and are used in later levels) so you should make sure you can both calculate them and remember which is which.

LEARNING OUTCOME STATEMENTS

Application LOS	Knowledge LOS
6a **Calculate** and interpret the net present value (NPV) and the internal rate of return (IRR) of an investment	6c **Calculate** and interpret a holding period return (total return)
6b **Contrast** the NPV rule to the IRR rule, and identify problems associated with the IRR rule	6e **Calculate** and interpret the bank discount yield, holding period yield, effective annual yield, and money market yield for US Treasury bills and other money market instruments
6d **Calculate** and compare the money-weighted and time-weighted rates of return of a portfolio, and evaluate the performance of portfolios based on these measures	6f **Convert** among holding period yields, money market yields, effective annual yields, and bond equivalent yields

APPLICATION LEARNING OUTCOME STATEMENTS

6a, b Calculate and interpret the net present value (NPV) and the internal rate of return (IRR) of an investment; contrast the NPV rule to the IRR rule, and identify problems associated with the IRR rule

The NPV is an application of what has been seen in Reading 5. If an investment opportunity has various cash flows (some positive, some negative), find the PV of all of them and sum (including the initial investment as a negative amount). If the NPV is positive, it is worthwhile as the investment adds value.

The IRR is the discount rate which gives a zero NPV, i.e. the NPV of the future cash flows exactly matches the investment; this is the yield, or yield to maturity, of an investment. If this exceeds the return required, it is worthwhile.

Both of these can be calculated using the second row of the Texas Instruments BAII Plus calculator (see the guide on the website), and you should practice until you are fairly confident as it will save you a lot of time (particularly the IRR) in the exam. These two also crop up in Corporate Finance.

There are some technical problems with the IRR result, which makes NPV safer (you should learn these as they are likely factual questions).

6d Calculate and compare the money-weighted and time-weighted rates of return of a portfolio, and evaluate the performance of portfolios based on these measures

These are important in assessing the performance of a portfolio and the performance of an investment manager over a time period that includes changes to the amount available for investment. You need to be comfortable with calculating both of these for the exam:

Money-weighted rate of return (MWRR) calculates the IRR of the cash flows.

Time-weighted rate of return (TWRR) divides it up into small periods (a period starts or ends when money is received into or paid out of the portfolio). It then calculates holding period returns (HPRs) for each small period and produces a geometric average. For example, if there were three small periods:

$$(1 + \text{TWRR})^3 = (1 + \text{HPR}_1) \times (1 + \text{HPR}_2) \times (1 + \text{HPR}_3)$$

or

$$\text{TWRR} = \sqrt[3]{\left(1+\text{HPR}_1\right)\times\left(1+\text{HPR}_2\right)\times\left(1+\text{HPR}_3\right)} - 1 = \left[\left(1+\text{HPR}_1\right)\times\left(1+\text{HPR}_2\right)\times\left(1+\text{HPR}_3\right)^{1/3}\right] - 1$$

For assessing the manager, we would prefer the TWRR as the MWRR will be biased towards those periods when the most money was invested (but the amount invested is not usually under the control of the manager).

KNOWLEDGE LEARNING OUTCOME STATEMENTS

6c, e, f Calculate and interpret a holding period return (total return), the bank discount yield, holding period yield, effective annual yield, and money market yield for US Treasury bills and other money market instruments; convert among holding period yields, money market yields, effective annual yields, and bond equivalent yields

There's a little bit of repetition from the last reading here, but some new terminology is introduced as well.

Suppose a $100,000 investment is available for 48 days that will return $100,800 at the end of that period.

$$\text{Holding period return} = 800 / 100{,}000 = 0.8\%$$

$$\text{Quote in money market as } 0.8\% \times 360/48 = 6\%$$

$$\text{Effective annual yield (EAY / EAR)} = 1.008^{365/48} - 1 = 6.246\%$$

A discount instrument pays the face value at maturity and can be bought for less than face value before then:

$$\text{Bank discount yield} = 800 / 100{,}800 \times 360/48 = 5.95\%$$

(i.e. income as a percentage of the end value then annualized)

A bond equivalent yield is similar to the money market yield but is always simply annualized from a compounding period of six months (by doubling). To express a yield as a bond equivalent yield, compound the rate from its "true" compounding period up to six months and then double the result to annualize it.

Reading 6 sample questions
(Answers on p. 298)

1   A T-bill with a face value of $100,000 and 130 days until maturity is selling for $98,200. The money market yield is closest to:

(A) 1.83%
(B) 4.99%
(C) 5.08%

2   Ms Anne Niven, fund manager of X Limited, wants to invest $5 million for 120 days. The bank discount yield on 120-day Treasury bills is 3%. What is the price paid for each bond if the face value of each T-bill is $100,000?

(A) $99,000
(B) $99,013
(C) $99,031

After the crucial Readings 5 and 6, this will produce fewer questions in the exam, as it sets the context for sampling and hypothesis testing. However, you should make sure you can calculate the means and standard deviations, as well as the coefficient of variance, Sharpe ratio, and Chebyshev's inequality.

LEARNING OUTCOME STATEMENTS

Application LOS	Knowledge LOS
7e **Calculate** and interpret measures of central tendency, including the population mean, sample mean, arithmetic mean, weighted average or mean, geometric mean, harmonic mean, median, and mode	7a **Distinguish** between descriptive statistics and inferential statistics, between a population and a sample, and among the types of measurement scales
7g **Calculate** and interpret 1) a range and a mean absolute deviation and 2) the variance and standard deviation of a population and of a sample	7b **Define** a parameter, a sample statistic, and a frequency distribution
7h **Calculate** and interpret the proportion of observations falling within a specified number of standard deviations of the mean using Chebyshev's inequality	7c **Calculate** and interpret relative frequencies and cumulative relative frequencies, given a frequency distribution
7i **Calculate** and interpret the coefficient of variation and the Sharpe ratio	7d **Describe** the properties of a data set presented as a histogram or a frequency polygon
7m **Explain** the use of arithmetic and geometric means when analyzing investment returns	7f **Calculate** and interpret quartiles, quintiles, deciles, and percentiles
	7j **Explain** skewness and the meaning of a positively skewed or negatively skewed return distribution
	7k **Describe** the relative locations of the mean, median, and mode for a unimodal, nonsymmetrical distribution
	7l **Explain** measures of sample skewness and kurtosis.

APPLICATION LEARNING OUTCOME STATEMENTS

7e, m Calculate and interpret measures of central tendency, including the population mean, sample mean, arithmetic mean, weighted average or mean, geometric mean, harmonic mean, median, and mode; explain the use of arithmetic and geometric means when analyzing investment returns

Most of these should be familiar to you from your school days (even if you need a little reminder!). Read through Section 5; as long as you can follow the examples, don't worry too much about the formulas.

Make sure you are happy with:

- The weighted mean covered in Section 5.4.1 (Example 6 is the best to follow what's going on)
- The geometric mean (we saw this in Reading 6 with the time-weighted rate of return) in Section 5.4.2 (again, if you can follow Example 7, you're fine)
- The harmonic mean, which you probably haven't come across, which is in Section 5.4.3. This seems a bit weird, but don't spend too much time on this page

Section 10, at the end of the reading, has a page and a half on the uses of geometric and arithmetic means, which is worth looking through as long as you don't get bogged down and can make a brief summarized list.

7g Calculate and interpret 1) a range and a mean absolute deviation and 2) the variance and standard deviation of a population and of a sample

The important areas in Section 7 are not the range and mean absolute deviation (MAD) but the variance and standard deviation. Make sure you understand Section 7.3, which explains:

Variance is the average of the squared differences from the mean

Standard deviation = $\sqrt{\text{(variance)}}$

The *sample* variance and standard deviation are described in Section 7.4 and many people find this confusing. The point is that we could calculate the variance of 20 results as if it was the entire population. However, if we intend to use this to estimate the variance of the entire population from this sample, we have a problem. What if this sample of 20 items was more closely grouped around its mean than items in the population are grouped around the population mean? We might have picked a sample that was unrepresentatively concentrated around its mean.

We therefore increase our estimate of the population variance by dividing by 19 instead of 20. This is called a *sample variance* (i.e. this means it's an estimate of the population variance from the sample). The standard deviation is, as usual, the square root of the variance.

The idea of using a sample to infer something about the population reappears in Readings 9 and 10.

7h, i Calculate and interpret the proportion of observations falling within a specified number of standard deviations of the mean using Chebyshev's inequality; calculate and interpret the coefficient of variation and the Sharpe ratio

These are three very useful little formulas, which you should take on board:

- Chebyshev (7.6): for any distribution, the proportion within k standard deviations of the mean is at least $(1 - 1/k^2)$
- Coefficient of variation (7.7): CV = standard deviation / mean
- Sharpe ratio (7.8): (mean return − risk-free rate) / standard deviation

KNOWLEDGE LEARNING OUTCOME STATEMENTS

7a, b Distinguish between descriptive statistics and inferential statistics, between a population and a sample, and among the types of measurement scales; define a parameter, a sample statistic, and a frequency distribution

These are definitions which you may be asked; you can find them covered in the two pages of Sections 2.1, 2.2, and 2.3.

7c, d Calculate and interpret relative frequencies and cumulative relative frequencies, given a frequency distribution; describe the properties of a data set presented as a histogram or a frequency polygon

The description of these in Section 3 looks quite involved. You are probably better skimming this and going straight to Table 6, which shows absolute, relative, cumulative absolute, and cumulative relative frequency.

Histograms and frequency polygons are in Section 4, and again it will probably make more sense if you look at Figures 1–4.

Questions are likely to be fairly factual or very easy calculations.

7f Calculate and interpret quartiles, quintiles, deciles, and percentiles

You should read through Section 6, but don't spend too long on this as you're not likely to get many questions on this area in the exam.

7j, k, l Explain skewness and the meaning of a positively skewed or negatively skewed return distribution; describe the relative locations of the mean, median, and mode for a unimodal, nonsymmetrical distribution; explain measures of sample skewness and kurtosis

This is covered in Sections 8 and 9 and goes into quite a bit of detail. The LOS in this area only want you to:

- Explain skewness and understand positive vs negative
- Explain relative location of mean, median, and mode in a skewed distribution (first page of Section 8)
- Explain (not calculate) measures of skewness and kurtosis (note that the normal distribution has kurtosis of 3 or excess kurtosis of 0)

Reading 7 sample questions
(Answers on p. 299)

1   A fund has lost the following amounts over the past four years. Which of the following is closest to the geometric mean?

20%, 10%, 11%, 15%

(A) 13.9%
(B) 14.1%
(C) 15.1%

2   For negatively skewed data, which of the following is most likely to be true?

(A) The mean will be greater than the median which will be greater than the mode
(B) The mode will be greater than the mean which will be greater than the median
(C) The mode will be greater than the median which will be greater than the mean

Although you need to look through this to get an understanding of the building blocks of probability distributions, which in turn are used in sampling, you are not likely to get many questions on this reading. Covariance and correlation are important but primarily in the context of risk in a portfolio and they are better explained in the readings for Portfolio Management.

The most important techniques to grasp are the use of the tree diagram, covered in LOS 8j, and Bayes' formula, covered in LOS 8n.

LEARNING OUTCOME STATEMENTS

Application LOS	Knowledge LOS
8j **Explain** the use of a tree diagram to represent an investment problem	8a **Define** a random variable, an outcome, an event, mutually exclusive events, and exhaustive events
8n **Calculate** and interpret an updated probability using Bayes' formula	8b **State** the two defining properties of probability and distinguish among empirical, subjective, and a priori probabilities
	8c **State** the probability of an event in terms of odds for and against the event
	8d **Distinguish** between unconditional and conditional probabilities
	8e **Explain** the multiplication, addition, and total probability rules
	8f **Calculate** and interpret 1) the joint probability of two events, 2) the probability that at least one of two events will occur, given the probability of each and the joint probability of the two events, and 3) a joint probability of any number of independent events
	8g **Distinguish** between dependent and independent events
	8h **Calculate** and interpret an unconditional probability using the total probability rule
	8i **Explain** the use of conditional expectation in investment applications
	8k **Calculate** and interpret covariance and correlation
	8l **Calculate** and interpret the expected value, variance, and standard deviation of a random variable and of returns on a portfolio
	8m **Calculate** and interpret covariance given a joint probability function
	8o **Identify** the most appropriate method to solve a particular counting problem, and solve counting problems, using the factorial, combination, and permutation notations

APPLICATION LEARNING OUTCOME STATEMENTS

8j, n Explain the use of a tree diagram to represent an investment problem; calculate and interpret an updated probability using Bayes' formula

The use of a tree diagram is the way to answer most of the questions you might get in probability; make sure you can follow the figure below.

Bayes' formula is covered in Section 4.1 and allows us to refine our probabilities in the light of further information. If you can understand the following you're probably OK on this.

Example
100 boxes of eggs are sold through two shops, P and Q; 40 were sold by P and 60 by Q. Of the eggs sold by P, 20% of the boxes had at least one bad egg in them, while of those sold by Q, 10% of the boxes had at least one bad egg in them.

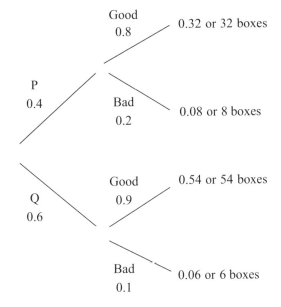

I buy a box of eggs:

If I buy from P, what is the probability there is a bad egg in the box?

$$\text{Probability (bad / P)} = 0.2$$

What is the probability that I bought from Q and that all the eggs are good?

$$\text{Probability (Q and good)} = \text{probability (Q)} \times \text{probability (good / Q)} = 0.6 \times 0.9 = 0.54$$

You can see that it is much easier and clearer with a diagram, rather than trying to remember formulae.

Suppose I am given a box of eggs by a friend and don't know which shop it came from. What is the probability it came from P?

Probability (P) = 0.4

Now suppose I use the eggs and find that at least one was bad. What is the probability it came from P? (This is Bayes' formula in action.)

Probability (P) = probability (bad and P) / probability (bad) = 0.08 / (0.08 + 0.06)

= 8/ (8 + 6) = 8/14 = 0.57

KNOWLEDGE LEARNING OUTCOME STATEMENTS

8a, b, c, d, e, f, g, h, i Define a random variable, an outcome, an event, mutually exclusive events, and exhaustive events; state the probability of an event in terms of odds for and against the event. State the two defining properties of probability, the multiplication, addition, and total probability rules, and the use of conditional expectation in investment applications. Distinguish among empirical, subjective, and a priori probabilities, between unconditional and conditional probabilities, and between dependent and independent events. Calculate and interpret 1) the joint probability of two events, 2) the probability that at least one of two events will occur, given the probability of each and the joint probability of the two events, and 3) a joint probability of any number of independent events; calculate and interpret an unconditional probability using the total probability rule

This goes on for 23 pages in Section 2 and unless you love probability, you are likely to drown if you don't use the following approach:

• Remember that exam questions in this area are infrequent so don't spend too long on it
• Look at the summary at the back of the reading to see if what you actually need to know makes sense
• Review the examples in Section 2 (it's usually much easier to follow once there are some numbers to play with)
• Have a go at the questions at the back of the reading. If these seem to go OK, don't spend any more time on it

8k, l, m Calculate and interpret covariance and correlation given a joint probability function, the expected value, variance, and standard deviation of a random variable and of returns on a portfolio

You have seen variance and standard deviation before. The expected value (EV) is the weighted average of returns using the probabilities as weights.

The important part is covariance and correlation:

Covariance measures how closely connected two variables are by seeing how much of the time they are both above or both below their respective means. A high covariance means they move together for much of the time, but is challenging to interpret because it is in squared units (e.g. if the unit of measure is €1, then the covariance is in terms of $\in^2$). Correlation is a standardized version of covariance, bound by -1 (perfect negative correlation) and $+1$ (perfect positive correlation).

However, the explanation in Section 3 is highly mathematical and difficult to follow. You would be using your time much more productively if you left this until you have covered Portfolio Management. Once you have read about covariance and correlation in Study Session 12, this should make more sense and you'll be able to see what is going on.

8o Identify the most appropriate method to solve a particular counting problem, and solve counting problems, using the factorial, combination, and permutation notations

Read through 4.2 but try not to get confused by these three pages. The main reason it's here is not to provide exam questions but to make sure you have seen factorials before we get to the Binomial Distribution in Reading 9.

Reading 8 sample questions
(Answers on pp. 299 and 300)

1. A committee is interested in selecting three directors from a pool of 12 to head a special task force on money laundering. How many different groups of directors could be selected?

    (A) 210
    (B) 215
    (C) 220

2. Given the following data:

    - covariance: 36
    - standard deviation Kansas wheat: 16
    - standard deviation Canadian hard wheat: 9

    which of the following is closest to the correlation coefficient between Kansas and Canadian hard wheat?

    (A) 0.25
    (B) 1.44
    (C) 3

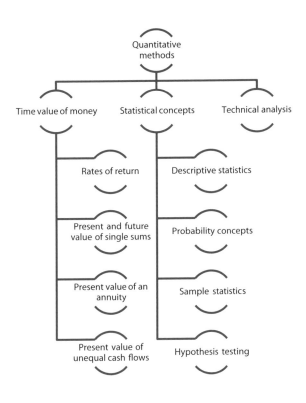

Topic:	Quantitative Methods
Weight:	12%
Study sessions:	2–3
Readings:	5–12

You need to be familiar with a normal distribution for sampling and hypothesis testing, so it's well worth taking the time to master it. In addition, don't ignore the binomial distribution or the uniform distributions (both discrete and continuous) as they do get tested (and often using the cumulative distribution functions).

You won't get normal distribution tables in the exam but will be provided with a small relevant extract in questions that need it.

LEARNING OUTCOME STATEMENTS

Application LOS	Knowledge LOS
9e **Define** a discrete uniform random variable, a Bernoulli random variable, and a binomial random variable	9a **Define** a probability distribution and distinguish between discrete and continuous random variables and their probability functions
9f **Calculate** and interpret probabilities given the discrete uniform and the binomial distribution functions	9b **Describe** the set of possible outcomes of a specified discrete random variable
9g **Construct** a binomial tree to describe stock price movement	9c **Interpret** a cumulative distribution function
9h **Calculate** and interpret tracking error	9d **Calculate** and interpret probabilities for a random variable, given its cumulative distribution function
9j **Explain** the key properties of the normal distribution	9i **Define** the continuous uniform distribution and calculate and interpret probabilities, given a continuous uniform distribution
9k **Distinguish** between a univariate and a multivariate distribution, and explain the role of correlation in the multivariate normal distribution	9o **Explain** the relationship between normal and lognormal distributions and why the lognormal distribution is used to model asset prices
9l **Determine** the probability that a normally distributed random variable lies inside a given interval	9p **Distinguish** between discretely and continuously compounded rates of return, and calculate and interpret a continuously compounded rate of return, given a specific holding period return
9m **Define** the standard normal distribution, explain how to standardize a random variable, and calculate and interpret probabilities using the standard normal distribution	9q **Explain** Monte Carlo simulation and describe its major applications and limitations
9n **Define** shortfall risk, calculate the safety-first ratio, and select an optimal portfolio using Roy's safety-first criterion	9r **Compare** Monte Carlo simulation and historical simulation

APPLICATION LEARNING OUTCOME STATEMENTS

9e, f, g, h Define a discrete uniform random variable, a Bernoulli random variable, and a binomial random variable; calculate and interpret probabilities given the discrete uniform and the binomial distribution functions; construct a binomial tree to describe stock price movement, and calculate and interpret tracking error

These deal with the two discrete probability distributions (uniform and binomial) in the syllabus.

The discrete uniform distribution (all possible outcomes have the same probability) is dealt with in 2.1. If there are n possibilities between a and b, then

- Probability $(x = r) = 1/n$ if $a \leq r \leq b$, otherwise probability $(x = r) = 0$
- Questions are very keen on *cumulative* probability distributions:
  $F(r) =$ probability $(x \leq r)$

The binomial distribution is in 2.2 and gradually builds up to the general formula (Formula 1). It is worth skimming through but the LOS is really about application, so make sure you can follow Example 4.

Binomial trees are demonstrated at the end of the section and are fairly obvious if you go straight to Figure 2.

9j, k, l, m Explain the key properties of the normal distribution; distinguish between a univariate and a multivariate distribution, and explain the role of correlation in the multivariate normal distribution; define the standard normal distribution, explain how to standardize a random variable, and calculate and interpret probabilities using the standard normal distribution; determine the probability that a normally distributed random variable lies inside a given interval

There won't be a huge number of questions on the normal distribution itself, but it is worth making sure you are comfortable with using it as it will appear in other readings (such as 10 and 11).

Section 3.2 does a reasonable job of taking you through what you've probably forgotten from school. It does get a little excited about portfolio distributions and a density function in Equation 3, but all you need for LOS 9k is that a portfolio return can be assumed to be normally distributed if the individual assets are normally distributed but the standard deviation will depend on the individual standard deviations and the correlations between assets.

The test is whether you can do the questions at the back of the reading (the LOS are mostly about application apart from the three bullet-pointed characteristics), so if you're feeling relatively confident, go straight to them after checking out the three defining characteristics at the start of this section.

9n Define shortfall risk, calculate the safety-first ratio, and select an optimal portfolio using Roy's safety-first criterion

These get used quite a bit in questions and are easy to apply – make sure you know them:

- Shortfall risk = risk that portfolio return is below an acceptable level
- Roy's safety-first ratio:
  (expected portfolio return – minimum acceptable return) / standard deviation of portfolio
- the optimal portfolio is the one with the highest safety-first ratio

Section 3.3 gives more detail but the above addresses the LOS.

KNOWLEDGE LEARNING OUTCOME STATEMENTS

9a, b, c, d Define a probability distribution and distinguish between discrete and continuous random variables and their probability functions; describe the set of possible outcomes of a specified discrete random variable, and interpret a cumulative distribution function; calculate and interpret probabilities for a random variable, given its cumulative distribution function

All of these are run through in the three pages of Section 1. They are mostly definitions or comparisons, which are easy marks if they come up. Although the cumulative distribution function is covered in some detail here, it is usually tested in the context of uniform distributions, which are covered later in the reading.

9i Define the continuous uniform distribution, and calculate and interpret probabilities, given a continuous uniform distribution

This is the only continuous distribution in the syllabus apart from the normal distribution. Notice that you only have to define it and use it (usually quite simple questions), so don't get bogged down. Key points are:

- There is a constant probability between two values, a and b, and a probability of zero outside these values
- Being a continuous variable, we can only talk about the probability of x taking a value *in a range*
- Probability $(p \leq x \leq q) = (q - p) / (b - a)$
- The cumulative function will gradually increase to 1 as x approaches b. So
- $F(x) = (x - a) / (b - a)$ or *1 if $x \geq b$ or 0 if $x \leq a$* (favorite question area)
- Mean $= (a + b) / 2$ and variance $= (b - a)^2 / 12$

9o Explain the relationship between normal and lognormal distributions and why the lognormal distribution is used to model asset prices

The reading goes into more depth in 3.4 than you need, so don't lose sight of the LOS. The main points are:

- A stock price (for example) has a minimum of zero so it is not normal (should have a minimum of $-\infty$) and is skewed (positively as the "hump" is to the left, and the "tail" to the right)
- New price / old price (= 1 + return) is called *lognormal* because LN (new / old) is normally distributed
- (New / old) is lognormal, skewed and runs from 0 to $+\infty$; LN (new / old) is normal, symmetrical and runs from $-\infty$ to $+\infty$

9p Distinguish between discretely and continuously compounded rates of return, and calculate and interpret a continuously compounded rate of return, given a specific holding period return

You've already seen this in Reading 6, so there's no need to go through it again. Try the questions at the end of the reading.

9q, r Explain Monte Carlo simulation and describe its major applications and limitations; compare Monte Carlo simulation and historical simulation

Notice the LOS in this area are only explain, describe, and compare. Monte Carlo simulation uses random number generation to simulate numerous possible outcomes and their likelihood. Example 11 (with Table 8) demonstrates it quite well.

Reading 9 sample question
(Answers on p. 300)

A Bernoulli random variable has which of the following characteristics? The probability of success:

(A) rises with each trial
(B) stays the same with each trial
(C) decreases with each successful trial

Often we cannot examine the whole population (if we're looking at daily price changes, for example, there are an infinite number of days in the future which we can't examine), so we have to look at a sample and infer what the population parameters are likely to be.

There will probably be numerous questions in this area, and it is also needed for the next reading on Hypothesis Testing, so you should spend some time becoming familiar with how a sample can give a confidence interval for the population mean and practicing the technique.

LEARNING OUTCOME STATEMENTS

Application LOS	Knowledge LOS
10e **Explain** the central limit theorem and its importance	10a **Define** simple random sampling and a sampling distribution
10f **Calculate** and interpret the standard error of the sample mean	10b **Explain** sampling error
10g **Identify** and describe desirable properties of an estimator	10c **Distinguish** between simple random and stratified random sampling
10h **Distinguish** between a point estimate and a confidence interval estimate of a population parameter	10d **Distinguish** between time-series and cross-sectional data
10i **Describe** the properties of Student's t-distribution and calculate and interpret its degrees of freedom	10k **Describe** the issues regarding selection of the appropriate sample size, data-mining bias, sample selection bias, survivorship bias, look-ahead bias, and time-period bias
10j **Calculate** and interpret a confidence interval for a population mean, given a normal distribution with 1) a known population variance, 2) an unknown population variance, or 3) an unknown variance and a large sample size	

APPLICATION LEARNING OUTCOME STATEMENTS

10e, f, g, h Explain the central limit theorem and its importance; calculate and interpret the standard error of the sample mean; identify and describe desirable properties of an estimator, and distinguish between a point estimate and a confidence interval estimate of a population parameter

You do not have to be able to prove the Central Limit Theorem, but you should understand what it says and why it's important. It is stated in 3.1.

If we have a population with a mean of μ and a variance of σ^2 (standard deviation = σ), then we could pick a sample of size n (with a sample mean and a standard deviation of s); if we picked all the possible samples of the same size, n, we would have lots of sample means. The central limit theorem says that if $n \geq 30$, then these sample means are distributed normally with a mean = μ and a standard deviation = $\sigma / \sqrt{n}$.

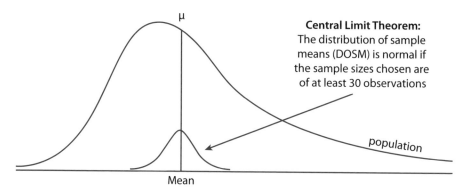

Central Limit Theorem: The distribution of sample means (DOSM) is normal if the sample sizes chosen are of at least 30 observations

The standard deviation of this "distribution of the sample means" is called the Standard Error of the Mean. This is because, using a sample, we could estimate the population mean as being the same as the sample mean (a "point" estimate) but this is not likely to be correct. A better statement might be:

$$\mu = \text{sample mean} \pm \text{margin of error}$$

As the distribution of the sample means is normal, we can be 95% confident, for example, that

$$\mu = \text{sample mean} \pm 1.96 \text{ standard deviations}$$

However, the standard deviation of this distribution (the standard error) = $\sigma / \sqrt{n}$

$$\text{So } \mu = \text{sample mean} \pm 1.96 \, \sigma / \sqrt{n}$$

Lastly, in most cases if we don't know μ, we're unlikely to know σ so we can use an estimate based on the sample standard deviation (s) in which we used (n − 1) rather than n to calculate the variance (see Reading 7):

$$\mu = \text{sample mean} \pm 1.96 \, s / \sqrt{n}$$

10i, j Describe the properties of Student's t-distribution and calculate and interpret its degrees of freedom; calculate and interpret a confidence interval for a population mean, given a normal distribution with 1) a known population variance, 2) an unknown population variance, or 3) an unknown variance and a large sample size

These are discussed in 4.2 and it is essential that you know the conclusions. In summary these are:

If we want confidence intervals for μ

- If the sample size is large (≥ 30)
  Sample mean $\pm z \, \sigma / \sqrt{n}$ (or sample mean $\pm z \, s / \sqrt{n}$ if σ is not known)
  (where z = 1.96 for example for a 95% confidence level)

- If the sample size is small (≤ 30) but population is normal and σ is known
  Sample mean ± z σ / √n
- If the sample size is small (≤ 30) but population is normal and σ is not known
  Sample mean ± t s / √n
- If the sample size is small (≤ 30) and population is not normal
  These techniques cannot be used

Notice:

- Increasing the sample size will decrease our margin of error (or narrow the confidence interval) which is common sense as well
- t is the statistic of the Student's t-distribution; it is similar to the normal distribution but is more cautious (fatter tails) and there is a different result depending on the *degrees of freedom* (here the degrees of freedom = (n – 1)) so the smaller the sample size, the lower the degrees of freedom and the larger the t-statistic and the larger the margin of error calculated.

KNOWLEDGE LEARNING OUTCOME STATEMENTS

10a, b, c, d Define simple random sampling and a sampling distribution, and distinguish between simple random and stratified random sampling, and between time-series and cross-sectional data; explain sampling error

These are defined in the six pages of Section 2. You should read through them, but notice that the LOS requires only definitions or to be able to state the differences between simple random and stratified random sampling and between time-series and cross-sectional data.

10k Describe the issues regarding selection of the appropriate sample size, data-mining bias, sample selection bias, survivorship bias, look-ahead bias, and time-period bias

This LOS will lead to factual questions in the exam. Read Section 5 and make sure you understand the broad idea of each one. There's no need to learn huge amounts of detail.

Reading 10 sample question
(Answers on p. 300)

A random sample of 70 listed Brazilian stocks has been found to have an average return of 14.6% with a variance of 92.73690. Assuming Brazilian stock returns are normally distributed, the 90% confidence interval for the true average returns of these companies is closest to:

(A) 10.7066% to 18.49340%
(B) 12.34402% to 16.85598%
(C) 12.7066% to 16.49340%

This is a use of sampling, in that we have a hypothesis about the population and then we use a sample to see whether the hypothesis is likely to be true or not. It may seem rather pedantic at first but it's worth working at it, as you will get a number of questions in the exam, not only on the results but also on the various stages. As before, you won't get tables for normal distribution, Student-t, X^2, or F, but will be given extracts when you need them in particular questions – this makes it a little easier.

It also appears at Level II, so you are getting double points if you master it here!

LEARNING OUTCOME STATEMENTS

Application LOS	Knowledge LOS
11a **Define** a hypothesis, describe the steps of hypothesis testing, describe and interpret the choice of the null and alternative hypotheses, and distinguish between one-tailed and two-tailed tests of hypotheses	11d **Distinguish** between a statistical result and an economically meaningful result
11b **Explain** a test statistic, Type I and Type II errors, a significance level, and how significance levels are used in hypothesis testing	11e **Explain** and interpret the p-value as it relates to hypothesis testing
11c **Explain** a decision rule, the power of a test, and the relation between confidence intervals and hypothesis tests	11j **Distinguish** between parametric and nonparametric tests and describe the situations in which the use of nonparametric tests may be appropriate
11f **Identify** the appropriate test statistic and interpret the results for a hypothesis test concerning the population mean of both large and small samples when the population is normally or approximately distributed and the variance is 1) known or 2) unknown	
11g **Identify** the appropriate test statistic and interpret the results for a hypothesis test concerning the equality of the population means of two at least approximately normally distributed populations, based on independent random samples with 1) equal or 2) unequal assumed variances	
11h **Identify** the appropriate test statistic and interpret the results for a hypothesis test concerning the mean difference of two normally distributed populations	
11i **Identify** the appropriate test statistic and interpret the results for a hypothesis test concerning 1) the variance of a normally distributed population, and 2) the equality of the variances of two normally distributed populations based on two independent random samples	

Quantitative Methods: Application

APPLICATION LEARNING OUTCOME STATEMENTS

11a, b, c Define a hypothesis, describe the steps of hypothesis testing, describe and interpret the choice of the null and alternative hypotheses, and distinguish between one-tailed and two-tailed tests of hypotheses; explain a test statistic, Type I and Type II errors, a significance level, and how significance levels are used in hypothesis testing; explain a decision rule, the power of a test, and the relation between confidence intervals and hypothesis tests

Hypothesis testing seems a bit weird until you get used to the approach, but it's worth the effort as the questions can be quite straightforward and ask for particular aspects of the approach (e.g. what would H_0 be) as well as the conclusions of a calculation.

Everything you need to know is summed up in the steps outlined at the bottom of the first page of Section 2. The rest of the section then explains each of the elements.

If you get bogged down, it is worth going straight from the summary in Section 2 to Example 1 and Example 2 in Section 3.1, which show it in action. Then go back and read through Section 2.

Notice:

- H_0 is always assuming that nothing has changed / everything is fine
- Alpha is the significance level – it is the risk we assume of rejecting a true H_0
- We then examine a sample to see if it's so unlikely to have come from the population as stated in H_0, that H_0 is probably wrong
- The "test statistic" for normal distributions (z) and Student's t-distribution (t) both represent the number of standard deviations the sample mean is from the assumed population mean
- Remember this is using the distribution of sample means so the standard deviation is $\sigma/\sqrt{n}$ or estimated using $s/\sqrt{n}$
- So test statistic = (sample mean $- \mu$) / $\sigma/\sqrt{n}$
- If this test statistic exceeds, for example, 1.96, this suggests the result is so far away that the H_0 assumption about μ is probably wrong
- Questions are very keen on Type I and Type II errors:
  Type I = sample was very unlikely so we rejected H_0, but it was actually right although we didn't know it
  Type II = sample was not unusual enough to reject H_0, but it was actually wrong although we didn't know it

The smaller we try to make the possibility of making a Type I error, the larger the possibility of making a Type II error.

11f Identify the appropriate test statistic and interpret the results for a hypothesis test concerning the population mean of both large and small samples when the population is normally or approximately distributed and the variance is 1) known or 2) unknown

Section 3.1 shows how the idea of hypothesis testing is applied. The calculations are the same as you have seen in sampling in Reading 10 but are simply framed in a different way.

- If the sample is large
  Test statistic: $z = $ (sample mean $- \mu$) $/ (\sigma / \sqrt{n})$
- If sample is small but population is normal
  Test statistic: $t = $ sample mean $- \mu) / (\sigma / \sqrt{n})$

If we don't know σ (less likely in hypothesis testing as we have an assumed μ in H_0) we can use the sample standard deviation, s.

Notice that a 5% significance level is "easier" to get a significant result with a one-tail test than with a two-tail test as all the 5% is on one side rather than being split with 2.5% above and below the mean.

11g, h Identify the appropriate test statistic and interpret the results for a hypothesis test concerning the equality of the population means of two at least approximately normally distributed populations, based on independent random samples with 1) equal or 2) unequal assumed variances; identify the appropriate test statistic and interpret the results for a hypothesis test concerning the mean difference of two normally distributed populations

This is the hardest part of the reading. We want to check if the means of two populations are the same so we pick a sample from each. The principle is the same, in that H_0 we will normally assume that there is no difference (i.e. $\mu_1 = \mu_2$) and then compare the two sample means to see if there is a significant difference:

$$\text{Test statistic} = t = \text{(sample mean 1} - \text{sample mean 2)} / \text{standard deviation}$$

The problem is in the standard deviation of this distribution and the degrees of freedom:

If we assume the population variances are the same

$$\text{Standard deviation} = (s^2 / n_1 + s^2 / n_2)^{\frac{1}{2}} \text{ where } s^2 = [(n_1 - 1)s_1^2 + (n_2 - 1)s_2^2] / (n_1 + n_2 - 2)$$

$$\text{Degrees of freedom} = (n_1 + n_2 - 2)$$

If we do not assume the population variances are the same

$$\text{Standard deviation} = (s_1^2 / n_1 + s_2^2 / n_2)^{1/2}$$

Degrees of freedom = well, just have a look at Equation 9!

The good news is that this exam is not really about whether you can memorize this sort of formula, so if you need it they will probably give you the degrees of freedom, for example. The other thing to realize is that often the test statistic is so large or so small that the conclusion is obvious without going any further.

Don't give up after 3.2 though, as there is a much simpler bit at the end in 3.3. If the two samples are the same size and individual items in each can be paired up, it is much easier. It's back to a test of a single mean but we are looking at a single sample of differences with H_0 assuming that the mean of all these differences is zero.

11i Identify the appropriate test statistic and interpret the results for a hypothesis test concerning 1) the variance of a normally distributed population, and 2) the equality of the variances of two normally distributed populations based on two independent random samples

These are nowhere near as bad as you might think.

The tests of variances are in Section 4:

- A single variance (i.e. testing whether the variance of a population is as we assume in H0) uses χ^2:
  Test statistic $= \chi^2 = (n-1) s^2 / \sigma^2$
  If it exceeds the value in the table ($(n-1)$ degrees of freedom) it is a significant result (i.e. the sample variance is significantly different from the population variance assumed)
- Checking whether the variances of two populations are equal uses F
  Test statistic $= F = s_1^2 / s_2^2$ (put the bigger s on the top)
  If it exceeds the value in the table (degrees of freedom $= (n_1 - 1)$ and $(n_2 - 1)$ for numerator and denominator) then the variances would appear to differ significantly

KNOWLEDGE LEARNING OUTCOME STATEMENTS

11d Distinguish between a statistical result and an economically meaningful result.

The statistical decision consists simply of rejecting or not rejecting the null hypothesis based on the calculations. The economic decision takes into account all issues relevant to the decision, such as transactions costs.

11e Explain and interpret the p-value as it relates to hypothesis testing.

This is worth a quick look (at the end of Section 2) but the syllabus and questions generally use a test statistic approach rather than p-value. Rule to follow: if the p-value is less than the level of significance (i.e. α), then we reject the null hypothesis.

11j Distinguish between parametric and nonparametric tests and describe the situations in which the use of nonparametric tests may be appropriate

This is covered in Section 5; you only need the difference between parametric and nonparametric tests and the situations in which nonparametric might be appropriate. This is all covered in the first two paragraphs; the rest is examples.

Reading 11 sample question
(Answers on p. 300)

An analyst suspects that the average PE ratio for an index is at the most 15. She finds that the average PE and standard deviation of a sample of 40 is 16.5 and 7 respectively. What is the value of the test statistic?

(A) 1.65
(B) 1.69
(C) 1.36

This is almost entirely factual, rather than calculation based, but you don't have to memorize everything. The LOS are focused on explaining and describing the principles of different charting techniques, as they are widely used (despite being told there's no evidence they work in the reading on efficient markets!).

LEARNING OUTCOME STATEMENTS

Application LOS	Knowledge LOS
12a **Explain** the principles of technical analysis, its applications, and its underlying assumptions	12c **Explain** the uses of trend, support, and resistance lines and change in polarity
12b **Describe** the construction of and interpret different types of technical analysis charts	12d **Identify** and interpret common chart patterns
12e **Describe** common technical analysis indicators: price-based, momentum oscillators, sentiment, and flow-of-funds	12f **Explain** the use of cycles by technical analysts
12g **Describe** the key tenets of Elliott Wave Theory and the importance of Fibonacci numbers	12h **Describe** intermarket analysis as it relates to technical analysis and asset allocation

APPLICATION LEARNING OUTCOME STATEMENTS

12a, b Explain the principles of technical analysis, its applications, and its underlying assumptions; describe the construction of and interpret different types of technical analysis charts

Technical analysis is described in Section 2 and typical charts in Section 3.1. You should know enough to distinguish technical analysis from fundamental analysis, and to be able to briefly describe a line, bar, candlestick, or a "point and figure" chart.

12e Describe common technical analysis indicators: price-based, momentum oscillators, sentiment, and flow-of-funds

You need to be able to describe these rather than calculate them, so read 3.4 in enough detail so that you could distinguish between price-based indicators (such as moving averages and Bollinger Bands) and momentum oscillator indicators (such as ROC, RSI, and MACD).

Sentiment indicators are well worth noting (put/call ratio, options volatility index (VIX), margin debt, and shorting interest), as are the flow-of-funds indicators in 3.4.4 (make sure you grasp what is going on in the TRIN and what a value above or below 1 suggests).

12g Describe the key tenets of Elliott Wave Theory and the importance of Fibonacci numbers

This suggests that prices move in waves, which are themselves comprised of smaller waves. It is described over three pages in Section 4. The heights of the waves are frequently linked by Fibonacci ratios. It's probably not worth trying to memorize the exact pattern of the waves described.

KNOWLEDGE LEARNING OUTCOME STATEMENTS

12c, d Explain the uses of trend, support, and resistance lines and change in polarity; identify and interpret common chart patterns

3.2 describes the idea of a trend and support (stops the decline in a price) and resistance (stops the rise in a price) levels. 3.3 looks at chart patterns: reversals such as head and shoulders, double and triple tops and bottoms, and continuation patterns such as triangles, rectangles, flags, and pennants. It is unlikely that you will be asked to identify detailed patterns in the exam but you should be able to describe them and follow the reading when it demonstrates them.

Notice that for a head and shoulders:

Price target (i.e. price at which to buy after a short sale) = neckline – (head – neckline)

And for a reverse head and shoulders:

Price target (i.e. price at which to sell for a long position) = neckline + (neckline – head)

12f Explain the use of cycles by technical analysts

Apart from the length of the cycles described in 3.5 (54 years, 18 years, 10 years, and presidential term) and the fact that the longer the cycle the smaller the sample size in which to base any conclusions, it is probably not worth spending much time on this area.

12h Describe intermarket analysis as it relates to technical analysis and asset allocation

This looks at equities, bonds, currencies, and commodities as well as sub-sectors and different national stock markets in the belief that all these markets are interrelated. The analysis is then used to spot trends before they arrive in a specified market.

Reading 12 sample question
(Answers on p. 301)

In the context of technical analysis the principle states that once a support level is breached, it becomes a resistance level that is known as the:

(A) change in polarity principle
(B) wave principle
(C) divergence principle

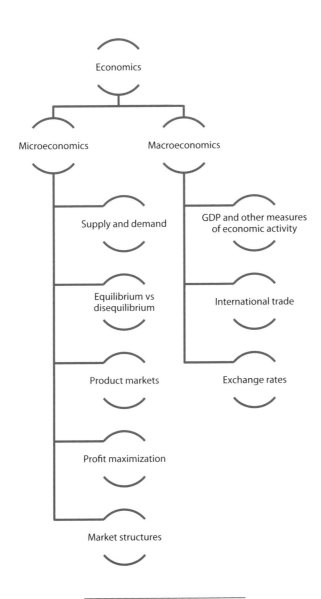

Topic:	Economics
Weight:	12%
Study sessions:	4–6
Readings:	13–21

THE BIG PICTURE

You will see Economics on all three levels, with Economics integrated with Portfolio Management by the time you get to Level III. But at Level I, Economics consists primarily of the basic principles of both microeconomics and macroeconomics. Microeconomics is the study of how individuals and firms make decisions, whereas macroeconomics is the study of the overall economy.

MICROECONOMICS

The readings in Study Session 4 cover the basics of supply and demand, in general terms, and from the perspectives of the consumer and the firm. Following naturally from supply and demand are the concepts of equilibrium and non-equilibrium prices, imbalances, and the consequences of governmental regulation.

The coverage of product markets includes the perspective of both the consumer and the firm. From the perspective of the individual consumer, you should understand the interaction of utility, indifference curves, and budget constraints. From the perspective of the firm, you should understand the concepts of total, marginal, and average revenues and costs, as well as profit maximization.

With respect to different market structures, you must be able to describe these structures (e.g. perfectly competitive, monopoly), and relate each structure to elasticity of the demand for the product, costs, and profits. In addition, you need to know what measures are typically used in measuring market concentration and be able to identify a structure.

MACROECONOMICS

Study Sessions 5 and 6 shift the focus to macroeconomics. Study Session 5 focuses on measures of economic activity and monetary policy, whereas Study Session 6 deals with international trade and exchange rates.

The most important measure of economic activity is GDP, and you should be prepared to explain and calculate GDP using the alternative methods and adjustments. You must also understand how aggregate supply and aggregate demand interact with the business cycles and growth. Going beyond GDP, you need to understand the role of inflation and unemployment, and the relation between economic indicators and business cycles.

You need to understand the role of central banks and monetary policy and, specifically, the functions and tools of a central bank. Recognizing that there are limitations to what monetary policy can do, you should be prepared to describe fiscal policy, compare this with monetary policy, and understand the advantages and disadvantages of both monetary and fiscal policy.

You should be prepared to address why firms engage in international trade, what may happen when there are barriers to trade, and what the functions are of the World Bank, the IMF, and the WTO. The last topic in Economics is exchange rates and involves interpreting quotations and calculating changes in the relative value of currencies. Be prepared to tie the exchange rate calculations and interpretation to the economics of international trade.

The first reading in Economics contains a lot of basic material on supply and demand curves plus some calculations of elasticities.

LEARNING OUTCOME STATEMENTS

Application LOS	Knowledge LOS
13b **Explain** the principles of demand and supply	13a **Distinguish** among types of markets
13f **Calculate** and interpret individual and aggregate demand, inverse demand and supply functions, and interpret individual and aggregate demand and supply curves	13c **Describe** causes of shifts in and movements along demand and supply curves
13g **Calculate** and interpret the amount of excess demand or excess supply associated with a non-equilibrium price	13d **Describe** the process of aggregating demand and supply curves, the concept of equilibrium and mechanisms by which markets achieve equilibrium
13i **Calculate** and interpret consumer surplus, producer surplus, and total surplus	13e **Distinguish** between stable and unstable equilibria and identify instances of such equilibria
13k **Forecast** the effect of the introduction and removal of a market interference (e.g. a price floor or ceiling) on price and quantity	13h **Describe** the types of auctions and calculate the winning price(s) of an auction
13l **Calculate** and interpret price, income, and cross-price elasticities of demand, and describe factors that affect each measure	13j **Analyze** the effects of government regulation and intervention on demand and supply

APPLICATION LEARNING OUTCOME STATEMENTS

13b Explain the principles of demand and supply

Section 3.1 introduces the demand function and the demand curve. The key points to take away are that the demand curve is normally downward sloping due to the law of demand – as prices rise, people buy less of a good. An example is shown in Exhibit 1.

The supply function and supply curve are shown in Section 3.3 and Exhibit 3 shows a typical supply curve. The key point is that supply is normally upward sloping as producers are willing to sell more at higher prices.

Note that the readings usually refer to both supply and demand curves, but represent them as linear functions (straight lines).

13f Calculate and interpret individual and aggregate demand, inverse demand and supply functions, and interpret individual and aggregate demand and supply curves

Section 3.1 shows several examples of possible linear demand functions. Be prepared in the exam to put numbers into a demand function to predict demand. Rearranging the function so that it can be used to predict price is also shown. This version is known as the inverse demand function. Example 2 is a comprehensive demonstration of the use of a demand function.

As with demand, the section describes a linear supply function. The function that uses quantity supplied to predict price is the inverse supply function. Example 3 is a comprehensive demonstration of the use of a supply function.

13g Calculate and interpret the amount of excess demand or excess supply associated with a non-equilibrium price

This is just another straightforward application of the supply and demand functions. There is a simple illustration at the start of Section 3.7 showing the calculations which should be completed.

13i   Calculate and interpret consumer surplus, producer surplus, and total surplus

Consumer surplus is the difference between the price paid for the goods and the price the consumer is willing to pay. Producer surplus is the difference between the price received for the goods and the price the producer was willing to pay.

The LOS does specify **calculate**, so review Examples 9 and 10 to make sure you can calculate each surplus.

Another key point is that the total producer plus consumer surplus is maximized at the competitive equilibrium. Interference as discussed in LOS 13j and k, which causes a move away from the equilibrium, will mean that they are not maximized. The amount of surplus not realized is known as the deadweight loss. This is demonstrated on several diagrams throughout the readings (see, for example, Exhibits 16, 17 in LOS 13k). Remember, the diagrams are there to help explain these key points. Make sure you understand the conclusions rather than learning the diagrams for the sake of it. Obviously in an objective item question you will not be asked to draw a diagram.

13k Forecast the effect of the introduction and removal of a market interference (e.g. a price floor or ceiling) on price and quantity

You should know from earlier LOSs that markets that reach an equilibrium where demand and supply curves intersect and this will mazimize surplus. This LOS looks at the impact of governments imposing a price floor or ceiling. Section 3.13 covers the points you need, the key term to be comfortable with is deadweight loss – as mentioned in LOS 13i. This LOS is all about the fact that market interference can cause deadweight losses.

Price ceilings are illustrated in Exhibit 16 and price floors in Exhibit 17. There is also an example of the calculation of the deadweight loss in Example 11. This is worth undertaking as the LOS asks for a forecast of the effect of the introduction. It is possible you would therefore be asked to work these numbers.

Also note the impact of the introduction of a per-unit tax on sellers, as calculated in Example 12. Although price ceilings and floors are the two examples specifically mentioned in the LOS, the per-unit tax is also covered in detail in the readings.

13l   Calculate and interpret price, income, and cross-price elasticities of demand, and describe factors that affect each measure

Calculating elasticities is the main numerical LOS in this reading. The key aspect that often trips people up is the method used to calculate percentage movements. In order that the percentage movement calculated is the same whether prices/quantities are rising or falling, the average price or quantity is used rather than the starting price/quantity. For example, a movement in price from 100 to 120 would be calculated in these questions as a movement of 18.18%, i.e. 20/110 where 110 is the average of 100 and 120.

The elasticities that need to be calculated are:

Price elasticity of demand	Change in quantity sold given change in price
Income elasticity of demand	Change in quantity sold given change in consumer income
Cross-price elasticity of demand	Change in quantity sold given change in price of a complementary or substitute good

Make sure you work Example 13, which contains a numerical example on each, but equally importantly make sure you can interpret the results and identify the factors which affect elasticities.

For price elasticity, it is important to identify perfectly elastic (infinite elasticity), elastic (elasticity greater than one in absolute terms), unitary elastic (elasticity of one), inelastic (elasticity of less than one in absolute terms) and perfectly inelastic (elasticity of zero).

Income elasticity can be elastic (greater than one – luxury goods), positive but less than one (normal good), or negative (inferior good).

For cross-elasticity it is all about positive (substitutes) or negative (complements).

The factors which influence elasticity are also well covered in the reading. Make sure you are comfortable with the percentage of the budget spent on a good (more elastic), and length of time since last price change (less time, more elastic), and the fact that demand is always more elastic in the long run.

Finally, know the implication of elastic or inelastic demand on the revenue earned. People often trip up when presented with a linear demand curve. Elasticity is not unitary (one) at every point on a linear demand curve. At higher prices it is less than one – inelastic – and at higher prices greater than one – elastic (see Exhibit 20). Revenue is maximized in the middle when elasticity is unitary (one).

Knowledge learning outcome statements

13a Distinguish among types of markets

Section 2 is a very short section covering this LOS. It identifies factor markets, goods markets, and capital markets. Example 1 at the end of the section contains two good exam-style questions.

13c Describe causes of shifts in and movements along demand and supply curves

An important examinable point in this section is to identify that changing prices cause movements along the curve (a change in the quantity demanded/supplied), changing other variables shifts the curves (a change in demand/supply). Section 3.2 deals with demand and Section 3.4 looks at supply.

13d Describe the process of aggregating demand and supply curves, the concept of equilibrium and mechanisms by which markets achieve equilibrium

Section 3.5 covers the aggregation of the supply and demand functions. This simply involves adding together each individual consumer's demand function and each producer's supply function. This is a simple idea demonstrated in Example 4.

It is the concept of the equilibrium which is fundamental to this LOS. Section 3.6 defines market equilibrium and demonstrates the concept of the point where demand = supply in Exhibit 7. Section 3.8 describes the different types of auction which may be used to reach equilibrium, as discussed in LOS 13h.

13e Distinguish between stable and unstable equilibria and identify instances of such equilibria

Section 3.7 covers this LOS. The key is to compare Exhibit 9 with Exhibit 10. In Exhibit 9, the supply curve is downward sloping and leads to a stable equilibrium. Exhibit 10 shows downward-sloping supply curves which may lead to unstable equilibria. Also note Exhibit 11 which demonstrates a situation with a non-linear supply curve and multiple equilibria.

13h Describe the types of auctions and calculate the winning price(s) of an auction

There are five types of auction described in Section 3.8. Exam questions could give details of how the auction works and ask which type is being identified.

13j Analyze the effects of government regulation and intervention on demand and supply

Taxation, trade barriers, and price limits are all forms of government intervention. They are noted in LOS 13i so have already been covered.

Reading 13 sample question
(Answers on p. 301)

If the number of luxury items demanded decreases from 100 to 50 when the price increases from $500 to $800, the price elasticity of demand is closest to:

(A) −0.69
(B) −0.83
(C) −1.45

This reading concentrates mainly on the idea of utility and indifference curves.

Learning outcome statements

Application LOS	Knowledge LOS
14a **Describe** consumer choice theory and utility theory	14b **Distinguish** the use of indifference curves, opportunity sets, and budget constraints in decision-making
14c **Calculate** and interpret a budget constraint	14d **Determine** a consumer's equilibrium bundle of goods based on utility analysis
14e **Compare** substitution and income effects	
14f **Distinguish** between normal goods and inferior goods, and explain Giffen goods and Veblen goods in this context	

Application learning outcome statements

14a Describe consumer choice theory and utility theory

The first LOS introduces the opening assumptions which are used in the rest of the section. Read Section 3.1 quickly and attempt Example 1 and you will have the key ideas.

14c Calculate and interpret a budget constraint

Although this is a **calculate** LOS, it is a straightforward one. Given a total cash budget and the price of goods, the task is to identify the budget constraint and the slope of the constraint. If you are comfortable with the equation for a straight line, then jump straight to Example 4 in Section 4.1. If you can complete that then there is no need to go back to the whole reading.

14e Compare substitution and income effects

The substitution effect states that as its price declines, a good becomes more of a bargain relative to other goods, therefore more of the good is substituted in for other goods.

The income effect states that as price declines, the consumer's real income rises relative to the price of the good, and more of the good is purchased – if the good is normal. These key points are all covered in Section 6.2.

Economics

14f Distinguish between normal goods and inferior goods, and explain Giffen goods and Veblen goods in this context

Inferior goods are covered in Section 6.3. The key point to take away is that the income effect works in the opposite direction to the substitution effect.

Giffen goods are covered in Section 6.4. Here the income effect works in the opposite direction to the substitution effect and has a larger impact, leading to a positively sloped demand curve. Giffen goods are inferior goods.

Veblen goods are covered in Section 6.5. The key point here is that Veblen goods become more desirable as their price rises, the idea of conspicuous consumption. A consumer wants to be seen to consume goods with a higher status. Veblen goods have a positively sloped demand curve but are certainly not inferior goods.

KNOWLEDGE LEARNING OUTCOME STATEMENTS

14b Distinguish the use of indifference curves, opportunity sets, and budget constraints in decision making

Indifference curves are used to measure consumption choices which have the same level of utility. Section 3.4 outlines the key theory and Exhibits 3 and 4 show the indifference curves for typical investors. There is a huge overlap here with portfolio management, where the same indifference curve framework is used.

Example 3 should be completed to make sure you have a grasp of the key concepts used.

Opportunity sets describe the possible production for suppliers and consumption for consumers, given their respective budget constraints.

14d Determine a consumer's equilibrium bundle of goods based on utility analysis

Section 5.1 covers this LOS. The key is the marginal rate of substitution, which describes the rate at which the consumer is willing to give up one good in exchange for another. Example 5 demonstrates the use of the MRS to identify the equilibrium point where the budget is being optimized.

Reading 14 sample question
(Answers on p. 301)

Which of the following best describes the substitution effect?

(A) As the price of a good declines, one has more disposable income to substitute for more of the same good
(B) As the price of a good rises, other goods become cheaper relative to this good and consumers opt for the cheaper goods
(C) The effect on prices in a barter economy

This reading introduces the concepts that are used by the firm in making its production decision.

Learning Outcome Statements

Application LOS	Knowledge LOS
15a **Calculate**, interpret, and compare accounting profit, economic profit, normal profit, and economic rent	15c **Describe** the firm's factors of production
15b **Calculate** and interpret total, average, and marginal revenue	15e **Determine** and describe breakeven and shutdown points of production
15d **Calculate** and interpret total, average, marginal, fixed, and variable costs	15f **Explain** how economies of scale and diseconomies of scale affect costs
15j **Calculate** and interpret total, marginal, and average product of labor	15g **Describe** approaches to determining the profit-maximizing level of output
15k **Describe** the phenomenon of diminishing marginal returns and calculate and interpret the profit-maximizing utilization level of an input	15h **Distinguish** between short-run and long-run profit maximization
15l **Describe** the optimal combination of resources that minimizes cost	15i **Distinguish** among decreasing-cost, constant-cost, and increasing-cost industries and describe the long-run supply of each

Application Learning Outcome Statements

15a Calculate, interpret, and compare accounting profit, economic profit, normal profit, and economic rent

All four of the concepts required in this LOS are covered in Section 2.1. Accounting profit is the familiar figure reported in the income statement. The main point to remember is that it does not include implicit costs.

Economic profit includes a charge for the implicit costs, e.g. for traded companies the cost of equity, for entrepreneurs the salary forgone. Normal profits are the profits made by companies that make a zero economic profit, i.e. just enough accounting profit to cover implicit costs. In this case the company is returning exactly what the equity holder(s) require and there will be no impact on the value of the firm. As noted in the summary table in Exhibit 2, a profit greater than normal will have a positive impact, and less than normal a negative impact.

Calculations here should be straightforward. Given an accounting profit you need to deduct implicit costs to get to economic profit.

Economic rent is defined in Section 2.1.3. You should learn the definition, and the key circumstances in which it arises, i.e. for a resource with a fixed supply and a high level of demand.

15b Calculate and interpret total, average, and marginal revenue

This is a straightforward LOS. You need to learn the definition and calculation for all three measures. Exhibit 3 at the start of Section 3 summarizes all the terms that need learning for this LOS and LOS 15d. If this table makes sense then you can save time on the readings.

15d Calculate and interpret total, average, marginal, fixed, and variable costs

As noted above, Exhibit 2 summarizes the definitions you need. The idea of "marginal" revenues and costs is key to microeconomics. "Marginal" means one more. Section 3.1 walks through a long example that calculates all the terms required, so if the table in Exhibit 2 contains unfamiliar terms, it is worth walking through the example.

Exhibit 12 is a clear diagram which demonstrates the behavior of average and marginal cost. Note that marginal cost intersects with average cost at the minimum point of average cost. This will always be the case as when marginal cost is below average it reduces the average, and when it is above average it drags the average up.

15j Calculate and interpret total, marginal, and average product of labor

Section 3.2.1 covers this LOS. Each calculation is straightforward and Exhibit 36 gives a clear demonstration of each. Make sure you are clear with these basic calculations and then move on to the interpretation.

Total product generally increases until very high levels of labor, at which point adding workers may have a negative impact.

Average product will initially increase and then decrease. As with costs, the key relationships are best demonstrated in a diagram and Exhibit 39 shows the relationship between average product and marginal product (and compares it to average and marginal cost).

15k Describe the phenomenon of diminishing marginal returns and calculate and interpret the profit-maximizing utilization level of an input

Diminishing marginal returns are discussed in Section 3.2.2. This occurs when successive inputs have lower and lower marginal product – output will increase at a decreasing rate.

The interpretation involves using marginal product to determine the optimal input levels. At the profit-maximizing level, marginal product × price output (which is defined as marginal revenue product) is equal to the price of labor, i.e. MRP/Price labor = 1.

Example 12 walks through the type of calculation that may be required and should be completed.

15l Describe the optimal combination of resources that minimizes cost

Example 11 demonstrates the use of marginal product and input prices to calculate the combination of inputs which maximizes output per $ of input cost. The example demonstrates the point that given a choice between inputs, the one with the highest marginal product per price of input is chosen.

KNOWLEDGE LEARNING OUTCOME STATEMENTS

15c Describe the firm's factors of production

Section 3.1.2 lists the factors that need to be described. These are the factors that will be used to produce output. Note the term "production function," which describes the relationship between the factors of production and the output.

15e Determine and describe breakeven and shutdown points of production

A firm will break even when average total cost is equal to average revenue. A firm will continue to operate short term if average revenue is below average total cost, but only if it covers average variable cost.

At the point where average revenue dips below average variable cost the firm will shut down. Section 3.1.3 runs through this LOS but talks a lot about perfect competition. This is covered in detail in the next reading.

15f Explain how economies of scale and diseconomies of scale affect costs

Section 3.1.5 covers economies and diseconomies of scale. Exhibit 27 shows the effects and you should also note the factors which lead to both economies and diseconomies of scale.

15g Describe approaches to determining the profit-maximizing level of output

The key to the profit-maximizing level is marginal cost and marginal revenue. Profit is maximized where MR = MC. When marginal cost is below marginal revenue, the addition to total cost from making the unit is less than the addition to total revenue and hence the unit should be made. When MR is less than MC, the addition to total revenue is less than the addition to total cost and the unit should not be made.

15h Distinguish between short-run and long-run profit maximization

The short run in economics is defined as a period over which some inputs are fixed. The long run is when all inputs can be changed. For example, in the short run the amount of labor and raw materials used can be changed, but the rental on factory space cannot. The profit-maximizing decisions are noted in Section 3.1.6.

In the short run firms maximize profits by operating at the point where MR = MC, as noted in LOS 15g.

In the long run firms will maximize profits at the minimum efficient scale. This is the point at which the company experiences neither economies nor diseconomies of scale, as noted in Exhibit 31.

15i Distinguish among decreasing-cost, constant-cost, and increasing-cost industries and describe the long-run supply of each

Section 3.1.7 deals with this LOS. Your main focus should be on the long-run supply curve for each situation. You should note that for an increasing cost industry both prices and costs increase with output levels. For a decreasing cost industry prices and costs fall with output, and for a constant cost industry they are constant.

The resulting supply curve for each (upward, downward, and constant respectively) is shown in Exhibit 33.

Reading 15 sample question
(Answers on p. 301)

A firm could sell four units at $20 each, or five units at $18 each. The marginal revenue of the fifth unit is:

(A) $10
(B) $18
(C) $90

The different market structures are covered in this reading.

LEARNING OUTCOME STATEMENTS

Application LOS	Knowledge LOS
	16a **Describe** the characteristics of perfect competition, monopolistic competition, oligopoly, and pure monopoly
	16b **Explain** the relationships between price, marginal revenue, marginal cost, economic profit, and the elasticity of demand under each market structure
	16c **Describe** the firm's supply function under each market structure
	16d **Describe** and determine the optimal price and output for firms under each market structure
	16e **Explain** factors affecting long-run equilibrium under each market structure
	16f **Describe** pricing strategy under each market structure.
	16g **Describe** the use and limitations of concentration measures in identifying market structure
	16h **Identify** the type of market structure a firm is operating within

KNOWLEDGE LEARNING OUTCOME STATEMENTS

16a Describe the characteristics of perfect competition, monopolistic competition, oligopoly, and pure monopoly

The defining characteristics of each structure are covered in Section 2.2. There is a clear summary of everything required for this LOS in Exhibit 1, so you should commit this to memory. In addition, note the level of competition in each structure as below.

Monopoly

- No competition, sole supplier
- May result from patents, licenses or a natural monopoly where the producer faces a downwardsloping long-run average cost curve over the entire output schedule

Oligopoly

- Limited competition, several suppliers

Monopolistic competition

- Highly competitive

Perfect competition

- Highest level of competition

Although the LOS are arranged by topic for each type of market structure, the readings deal with each market structure in turn. It makes sense to organize your studies like this and hence this section will address the LOSs in turn for each market structure.

PERFECT COMPETITION

16b Explain the relationships between price, marginal revenue, marginal cost, economic profit, and the elasticity of demand under each market structure

Section 3.1 covers elasticity of demand in a lot of detail. The vast majority of this material has been covered in Reading 13. The key point you should note is that under perfect competition individual firms are price takers. They cannot dictate the price but they can sell as much as they want at the given market price. This means they have a horizontal, perfectly elastic demand curve.

Exhibit 6 demonstrates this curve and Example 2 shows an exam-style question based on it.

The second major point to note is that with the horizontal demand curve, price = demand = average revenue = marginal revenue.

16c Describe the firm's supply function under each market structure

Section 3.2 describes the supply function which is represented by the marginal cost curve. Note the shape of the supply curves for the individual firm and the industry in Exhibit 5.

16d Describe and determine the optimal price and output for firms under each market structure

Under perfect competition the profit-maximizing output is where marginal cost = marginal revenue. The major points you should note are that this output marginal cost is also equal to marginal benefit and the average cost is at a minimum. As a result this equilibrium is efficient. This is all covered in Section 3.3.

16e Explain the effects of demand changes, entry and exit of firms, and other factors on long-run equilibrium under each market structure

Section 3.4 covers this LOS. The key factors to focus on are that there are no barriers to entry or exit so long-run economic profits will be zero, as illustrated in Exhibit 10.

MONOPOLISTIC COMPETITION

16b Explain the relationships between price, marginal revenue, marginal cost, economic profit, and the elasticity of demand under each market structure

Section 4.1 covers this LOS. Focus on the key difference from perfect competition, which is the downward-sloping demand curve. This is illustrated in Exhibit 11. If you can understand and interpret this diagram, you have the main points.

16c Describe the firm's supply function under each market structure

Section 4.2 gives only a single paragraph on supply analysis for this structure, stating that the supply schedule is not well defined. The main point to remember, therefore, is that unlike perfect competition, it is not represented by the marginal cost schedule.

16d Describe and determine the profit-maximizing price and output for firms under each market structure

Section 4.3 covers profit-maximizing output. As with perfect competition, the firm chooses the output level where MR = MC. Unlike perfect competition, marginal cost is not equal to marginal benefit and the average cost is not minimized at this output level.

16e Explain factors affecting long-run equilibrium under each market structure

Section 4.4 addresses the long-run equilibrium, which is illustrated in Exhibit 12. Low barriers to entry mean zero economic profits. Note that the demand curve is downward sloping (this is true for all structures other than perfect competition).

OLIGOPOLY

16b Explain the relationships between price, marginal revenue, marginal cost, economic profit, and the elasticity of demand under each market structure

Section 5.1 addresses the key points. Due to the fact that there are only a small number of participants, there will be a degree of price interdependence. You need to be able to describe three situations – pricing interdependence (and the kinked demand curve), the Cournot assumption, and the Nash equilibrium.

16c Describe the firm's supply function under each market structure

As with monopolistic competition, the supply function is not well defined. The key point to take away here is the role of the dominant firm in setting output levels and prices.

16d Describe and determine the optimal price and output for firms under each market structure

Section 5.3 covers the profit-maximizing decision, making the point that the decision is not clear-cut as the level of interdependence and collusion is unclear. The only clear-cut conclusion to learn is that a dominant firm will choose an output level where MR = MC.

16e Explain factors affecting long-run equilibrium under each market structure

Section 5.4 contains the key message that long-term economic profits are possible for firms operating in an oligopoly market. The only other points covered here are that over time the dominant firm's market share and profits decline as firms are attracted to the industry, and that price wars should be avoided as they tend to reduce total revenue for participants.

MONOPOLY

16b Explain the relationships between price, marginal revenue, marginal cost, economic profit, and the elasticity of demand under each market structure

The key point for this LOS is that demand is downward sloping and marginal revenue is even steeper downward sloping. You should recall that this is a standard demand curve shape and so everything from Reading 13 on standard demand curves holds for a monopolist.

16c Describe the firm's supply function under each market structure

In Section 6.2, Exhibit 18 illustrates the monopolist's supply decision. Again, it is not well defined and there is no supply curve as the output decision is made to maximize profits where MR = MC, as outlined in LOS 16d.

16d Describe and determine the optimal price and output for firms under each market structure

The profit-maximizing output is where marginal cost is equal to marginal revenue. This point will result in a higher price and lower output equilibrium than under perfect competition. This should be an intuitive point to remember: a monopolist charges a higher price than a firm in a perfectly competitive market.

16e Explain factors affecting long-run equilibrium under each market structure

A monopolist is a single supplier in an industry with high barriers to entry. This means that economic profits can persist in the long run. Another key point which is discussed in Section 6.4 is the potential ability for price discrimination. This involves the monopolist charging consumers what they are willing to pay and thus capturing the whole consumer surplus. Make sure you pick up the definitions of first-degree, second-degree and third-degree price discrimination and work Example 3, which illustrates how each works.

Section 6.5 then addresses the regulation of the monopoly in the long run. You should note the different methods of regulating through setting price equal to marginal cost or long-run average cost and the implications of each.

16f Describe pricing strategy under each market structure

This LOS pulls together the pricing decision under each strategy. Note that the profit maximizing level where MR=MC applies in all cases except the oligopoly and monopolies that are subject to regulation.

Market structure	Section	Strategy
Perfect competition	3.3	Price = Average Revenue = Marginal Revenue = Marginal Cost
Monopolisitc competition	4.3	Price is set at the level where Marginal Revenue = Marginal Cost
Oligopoly	5.3	No single optimum price, depends on the circumstances and levels of interdependence and colusion
Monopoly	6.3	Price is set at the level where Marginal Revenue = Marginal Cost in the absence of regulation.

16g Describe the use and limitations of concentration measures in identifying market structure

Section 7 identifies the best theoretical measure as the elasticity of demand and supply in a market, but makes the point that it is difficult to measure and may change over time.

The section then focuses on two simpler measures, the concentration ratio and the Herfindahl–Hirschman index (HHI). Make sure you know the basic calculations for each and the advantages/disadvantages.

16h Identify the type of market structure a firm is operating within

This involves pulling together the information from the previous LOS in this reading and identifying the level of competition. The concentration measures from LOS 16f could be used in conjunction with a discussion of the level of competition, entry barriers, etc.

Reading 16 sample question
(Answers on p. 301)

In the short run, a company in perfect competition will continue to produce, although losses are being made, if:

(A) Fixed costs are covered
(B) Marginal costs are covered
(C) Average variable costs are covered

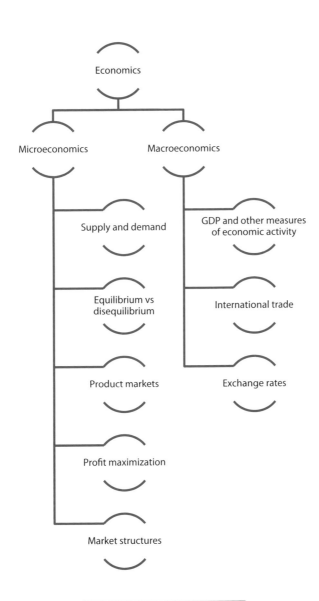

Topic:	Economics
Weight:	12%
Study sessions:	4–6
Readings:	13–21

The first reading in this study session introduces the idea of aggregate demand, aggregate supply, and GDP, along with the inputs required for growth.

LEARNING OUTCOME STATEMENTS

Application LOS	Knowledge LOS
17e **Explain** the fundamental relationship among saving, investment, the fiscal balance, and the trade balance	17a **Calculate** and explain gross domestic product (GDP) using expenditure and income approaches
17f **Explain** the IS and LM curves and how they combine to generate the aggregate demand curve	17b **Compare** the sum-of-value-added and value-of-final-output methods of calculating GDP
17g **Explain** the aggregate supply curve in the short run and long run	17c **Compare** nominal and real GDP and calculate and interpret the GDP deflator
17h **Explain** the causes of movements along and shifts in aggregate demand and supply curves	17d **Compare** GDP, national income, personal income, and personal disposable income
17i **Describe** how fluctuations in aggregate demand and aggregate supply cause short-run changes in the economy and the business cycle	17j **Explain** how a short run macroeconomic equilibrium may occur at a level above or below full employment
	17k **Analyze** the effect of combined changes in aggregate supply and demand on the economy
	17l **Describe** the sources, measurement, and sustainability of economic growth
	17m **Describe** the production function approach to analyzing the sources of economic growth
	17n **Distinguish** between input growth and growth of total factor productivity as components of economic growth

Economics

APPLICATION LEARNING OUTCOME STATEMENTS

17e Explain the fundamental relationship among saving, investment, the fiscal balance, and the trade balance

Section 2.2 breaks down GDP into the components listed in this LOS. Make sure you are comfortable with the basic formulas:

$$\text{Expenditure} = C + I + G + (X - M)$$

$$\text{Income } (Y) = C + S + T$$

as discussed in Section 3.1.1. In the economy as a whole, income is equal to expenditure, so:

$$C + I + G + (X - M) = C + S + T.$$

It is from this equation that the fundamental relationships required in this LOS can be discussed.

$(G - T)$ is the fiscal balance, $(X - M)$ is the trade balance, S is saving, and I is investment.

The key conclusions can be seen if the equation is rearranged to:

$$(G - T) = (S - I) - (X - M)$$

or

$$\text{Fiscal Balance} = (\text{Savings} - \text{Investment}) - \text{Trade Balance}$$

The use of this equation is demonstrated in Example 4.

17f Explain the IS and LM curves and how they combine to generate the aggregate demand curve

Section 3.1.1 uses the framework from LOS 17e to build the IS (investments savings) curve, and Section 3.1.2 the LM (liquidity/money supply) curve. It is useful to follow Example 5 through to help explain the construction of the IS curve. Exhibit 12 shows the slope of each curve and their intersection, demonstrating that with a higher real money supply, the intersection occurs at a higher real income level and lower real interest rate.

If the nominal money supply is held constant, a drop in prices increases the real money supply and increases real income. This leads to the downward-sloping aggregate demand curve shown in Exhibit 13.

17g Explain the aggregate supply curve in the short run and long run

The aggregate supply curve is covered in Section 3.2. Exhibit 14 illustrates the short-term and long-term curves. You should make sure you are able to identify the slopes of each and the factors which explain them – upward sloping for the short-term curve (SRAS) and vertical for the long-run curve (LRAS).

17h Explain the causes of movements along and shifts in aggregate demand and supply curves

Section 3.3.1 contains a list of seven key factors which will affect levels of aggregate expenditure and hence cause a shift in the aggregate demand curve. You should get comfortable with how each factor affects AD, and then attempt Example 8 to check your understanding.

Section 3.3.2 addresses shifts in the SRAS curve. There are five factors to learn here and an example (Example 9) which demonstrates the impact of one of the factors (unit labor cost).

Section 3.3.3 addresses shifts in the LRAS curve. There are only four factors here. The SRAS is a function of the potential output of the economy, so the four factors are those which would increase/decrease potential output.

There is a useful summary of factors and their impact on SRAS and LRAS in Exhibit 20. Work through Example 11 to check your understanding.

17i Describe how fluctuations in aggregate demand and aggregate supply cause short-run changes in the economy and the business cycle

Section 3.4 is a large part of the reading, covering four types of macroeconomic equilibrium. Focus first on the long-run equilibrium in Section 3.4.1 where the long-run equilibrium output is equal to potential GDP and the AD curve intersects both the SRAS and the LRAS at the same point, as illustrated in Exhibit 21.

Contrast this LR equilibrium with the three short-run situations in Sections 3.4.2–3.4.4. For each, note the price level, unemployment level, and output compared with the long-run equilibrium.

3.4.2   Recessionary gap   (Exhibit 22)
3.4.3   Inflationary gap   (Exhibit 24)
3.4.4   Stagflation   (Exhibit 25)

Exhibit 26 is a good summary. Work Example 13 to check your understanding.

KNOWLEDGE LEARNING OUTCOME STATEMENTS

17a Calculate and explain gross domestic product (GDP) using expenditure and income approaches

GDP is a measure of the aggregate output of an economy. Exhibit 1 illustrates the circular flow idea in an economy whereby total expenditure must equal total income. This leads to the idea that GDP can be measured using either expenditure or income, as discussed in Section 2.1.

Section 2.1.1 outlines some key issues regarding what is and what is not captured in GDP.

17b Compare the sum-of-value-added and value-of-final-output methods of calculating GDP

These two methods are covered with a simple numerical illustration in Exhibit 2 within Section 2.1.

17c Compare nominal and real GDP and calculate and interpret the GDP deflator

Section 2.1.2 covers this LOS. The effect of changing prices is removed to get to real GDP as economists are looking to measure movements in GDP caused by economic activity, not price changes. You should make sure you can follow the illustration of the calculation of the deflator and complete Example 2.

17d Compare GDP, national income, personal income, and personal disposable income

Section 2.3 defines all the terms required for this LOS. These should be committed to memory. The reading also gives example statistics to illustrate each term and a walk-through example (Example 3) to illustrate how they would be calculated (calculations are not directly asked for in the LOS but may be useful to help memorize the terms).

17j Explain how a short run macroeconomic equilibrium may occur at a level above or below full employment

This LOS is related to LOS 17e. It involves the use of the AD And AS curves model to identify equilibria above and below the long run full employment level output.

Section 3.4.2 covers a recessionary gap, where aggregate demand has weakened. Until wages and prices fall, the new equilibrium is below full employment. Once wages and prices fall, the short run aggregate supply curve will shift to the left. Keynes suggests that this mechanism will not work quickly, that unemployment does not cause wages to drop, and hence the equilibrium will persist.

If aggregate demand strengthens there will be an equilibrium above full employment until price levels rise and shift the short run supply curve back to the left. This is an inflationary gap and is covered in Section 3.4.3

17k Analyze the effect of combined changes in aggregate supply and demand on the economy

Once you have covered LOS 17j, move onto Section 3.4.4 and 3.4.5. These two sections show the effects of the supply curve moving, and summarize the impact of both curves moving. Essentially your task in the middle of this reading is to understand the AS and AD model and the summarize the possible outcomes when the AS and AD curves move.

17l Describe the sources, measurement, and sustainability of economic growth

Section 4.2 identifies and explains the five sources of economic growth. Make sure you can identify each of them. Section 4.3 then covers the measurement, taking into account growth in technology, labor, and capital.

17m Describe the production function approach to analyzing the sources of economic growth

Despite the LOS being **describe**, there are plenty of numerical examples that work through the calculation of growth as a function of technology, labor, and capital. You should work Example 17 to make sure you can track the numbers. Most of the detail that you need to learn, including the production function itself, is covered in Section 4.1.

17n Distinguish between input growth and growth of total factor productivity as components of economic growth

Section 4.2 contains the detail on productivity and specifically the importance of labor productivity growth to sustainable growth

Reading 17 sample question
(Answers on p. 302)

A decrease in aggregate demand could be caused by a:

(A) fall in prices
(B) fall in government expenditure
(C) fall in the number of unemployed

This is a relatively short reading covering several different theories that attempt to explain the business cycle.

LEARNING OUTCOME STATEMENTS

Application LOS	Knowledge LOS
18f **Explain** the construction of indices used to measure inflation	18a **Describe** the business cycle and its phases
	18b **Explain** the typical patterns of resource use fluctuation, housing sector activity, and external trade sector activity, as an economy moves through the business cycle
	18c **Describe** theories of the business cycle
	18d **Describe** types of unemployment and measures of unemployment
	18e **Explain** inflation, hyperinflation, disinflation, and deflation
	18g **Compare** inflation measures, including their uses and limitations
	18h **Distinguish** between cost-push and demand-pull inflation
	18i **Describe** economic indicators, including their uses and limitations
	18j **Identify** the past, current, or expected future business cycle phase of an economy based on economic indicators

APPLICATION LEARNING OUTCOME STATEMENTS

18f Explain the construction of indices used to measure inflation

This LOS involves memorizing several terms and several methods of calculating inflation. Although the LOS states only **explain**, the calculations and their differences are straightforward and there are several worked examples in the material, so it is worth being able to put the numbers through.

Section 4.2.2 covers the construction of the price indices needed for the LOS. Exhibit 5 contains consumption basket and price information that is then used to calculate the Laspeyres index, Paasche index, and Fisher index. Make sure you work through the numbers to identify the key similarities and differences.

Section 4.2.3 then covers the calculation of different types of consumer price indices, introducing the terms PCE, PPI, WPI, and TIPS, which you should familiarize yourself with.

KNOWLEDGE LEARNING OUTCOME STATEMENTS

18a Describe the business cycle and its phases

Section 2.1 gives an overview of the business cycle and Exhibit 1 summarizes the key facts to learn.

18b Explain the typical patterns of resource use fluctuation, housing sector activity, and external trade sector activity, as an economy moves through the business cycle

Section 2.1, titled "Resource use through the business cycle," covers this LOS. Panel B of exhibit 1 nicely summarizes the activity levels over the cycle. There is a specific section (2.2.1) on capital spending and another (2.2.2.) on inventory levels that cover the resource use part of the LOS. The key points to note are how the levels vary with the stages of the business cycle. Work Example 2 on capital spending and Example 3 on inventory fluctuation to make sure you are happy with the key points.

18c Describe theories of the business cycle

There are five different theories discussed in Section 3. Each theory identifies the factors that drive the cycle and you should make sure you can identify each one:

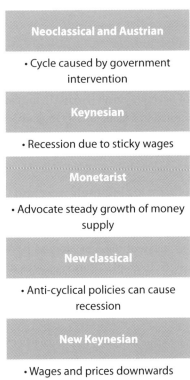

Neoclassical and Austrian
- Cycle caused by government intervention

Keynesian
- Recession due to sticky wages

Monetarist
- Advocate steady growth of money supply

New classical
- Anti-cyclical policies can cause recession

New Keynesian
- Wages and prices downwards sticky, government intervention useful

Economics

18d Describe types of unemployment and measures of unemployment

Section 4 covers this LOS and is again mostly about learning terminology. The types of unemployment are listed in Section 4.1 and should be committed to memory. Measures of unemployment are covered in Sections 4.1.1 and 4.1.2, which discuss the unemployment rate and productivity indicators.

18e Explain inflation, hyperinflation, disinflation, and deflation

Inflation should be a familiar term, but the key to this LOS is to identify the difference between disinflation (a decline in the inflation rate) and deflation (a sustained decrease in aggregate price level). Both are defined in Section 4.2.1 along with hyperinflation.

18g Compare inflation measures, including their uses and limitations

This LOS involves learning the biases that affect price index calculations. Each places an upward bias on the index, and you should be comfortable defining new products, quality, and substitution bias.

Link this LOS to LOS 18f on the construction of price indices. The Fisher index is an attempt to resolve the substitution bias.

18h Distinguish between cost-push and demand-pull inflation

The definitions of demand pull and cost push inflation are covered in Section 4.2.4. Also note the definitions of the non-accelerating inflation rate of unemployment (NAIRU), the natural rate of unemployment (NARU), and the velocity of money. They are tested in Examples 14, 15, and 16, and you should make sure you are comfortable with these questions.

18i Describe economic indicators, including their uses and limitations

Exhibit 7 in Section 5.1 contains an extensive list of key economic indicators. There is a large amount of information here – try to memorize as many of the indicators as possible, but the main point is to define leading, coincident, and lagging indicators. Example 28 also defines a diffusion index, which is then tested in Example 19.

18j Identify the past, current, or expected future business cycle phase of an economy based on economic indicators

This follows on directly from the previous LOS, and involves identifying whether each indicator is leading, coincident, or lagging.

Reading 18 sample question
(Answers on p. 302)

In which of the following phases of a business cycle is the inventory–sales ratio most likely the highest?

(A) Initial recovery
(B) Late expansion
(C) Beginning of a downturn

This is a comprehensive introduction to monetary and fiscal policy that sets the scene for later readings.

LEARNING OUTCOME STATEMENTS

Application LOS	Knowledge LOS
19a **Compare** monetary and fiscal policy	19b **Describe** functions and definitions of money
19c **Explain** the money creation process	19e **Describe** the Fisher effect
19d **Describe** theories of the demand for and supply of money	19f **Describe** the roles and objectives of central banks
19h **Describe** the implementation of monetary policy	19g **Contrast** the costs of expected and unexpected inflation
19k **Contrast** the use of inflation, interest rate, and exchange rate targeting by central banks	19i **Describe** the qualities of effective central banks
19l **Determine** whether a monetary policy is expansionary or contractionary	19j **Explain** the relationships between monetary policy and economic growth, inflation, interest, and exchange rates
19p **Describe** the arguments for and against being concerned with the size of a fiscal deficit (relative to GDP)	19m **Describe** the limitations of monetary policy
19q **Explain** the implementation of fiscal policy and the difficulties of implementation	19n **Describe** the roles and objectives of fiscal policy
19s **Explain** the interaction of monetary and fiscal policy	19o **Describe** the tools of fiscal policy, including their advantages and disadvantages
	19r **Determine** whether a fiscal policy is expansionary or contractionary

APPLICATION LEARNING OUTCOME STATEMENTS

19a Compare monetary and fiscal policy

This first LOS introduces the key definitions of monetary and fiscal policy. Example 1 in Section 2 tests your knowledge of the difference between the two. If you are comfortable with this example, you can move on to the detail in the LOS that follow.

19c Explain the money creation process

Section 2.1.2 covers the money creation process. Make sure you are happy with how a fractional reserve banking system works, reserve requirements, and the money multiplier. Example 2 contains an item set that uses the money multiplier to calculate how much money can be created from new deposits.

19d Describe theories of the demand for and supply of money

Three basic motives for holding money are listed at the start of Section 2.1.5 and then explained. Make sure you are comfortable with each by attempting Example 3.

Exhibit 4 then demonstrates the interaction of supply and demand, the supply being the fixed nominal amount of money circulating at any given time (hence a vertical supply curve). The intersection of supply and demand gives the nominal interest rate which equates the supply of, and demand for, money. Also note the term money neutrality, the idea that an increase in money supply in the long run simply leads to higher price levels.

19h Describe the implementation of monetary policy

The key to this LOS is to understand how the three main monetary policy tools are used. Section 2.3.2 covers the three main tools to become familiar with – open market operations, reserve requirements, and setting the central bank's policy rate.

Sections 2.3.4 and 2.3.5 then cover inflation targeting and exchange rate targeting as two frameworks that a central bank could use. Note the advantages and disadvantages of each.

19k Contrast the use of inflation, interest rate, and exchange rate targeting by central banks

KNOWLEDGE LEARNING OUTCOME STATEMENTS

19b Describe functions and definitions of money

This LOS is covered in Sections 2.1.1 through 2.1.4 and involves mostly memorizing facts. Section 2.1.1 covers the functions of money, finishing with a summary of the three basic functions of money, which should be memorized.

Section 2.1.3 covers the various definitions of money, which need committing to memory, along with some typical examples of measures used in Exhibit 3.

Section 2.1.4 covers the quantity theory of money, which involves a simple formula (the quantity equation of exchange) that explains the relationship between the quantity of money, velocity, price level, and real output.

The key conclusion to note is that given a constant velocity and real output, an increase in the quantity of money increases price levels.

19e Describe the Fisher effect

This is a simple equation that links nominal interest rates, inflation, and real rates. The main conclusion following on from money neutrality in the previous LOS is that real rates are stable in the long run, and variations in the nominal rate result from changes in inflation. Example 4 examines the key points from this LOS.

19f Describe the roles and objectives of central banks

Section 2.2 is a short section covering the roles that central banks might play. At the end of the section there is a summary of the roles normally taken on.

Section 2.3 is more extensive and looks at the objectives. There is a lot of information and examples given, but the key objectives to be comfortable with are price stability, maximum employment, and moderate long-term interest rates.

19g Contrast the costs of expected and unexpected inflation

19j Explain the relationships between monetary policy and economic growth, inflation, interest, and exchange rates

Monetary policy affects the growth, inflation, interest and exchange rates via the transmission mechanism shown in Exhibit 7 of Section 2.3.3. Use this diagram as the starting point for your study and make sure you can answer the questions in Example 8.

19i Describe the qualities of effective central banks

Within Section 2.3.4 on inflation targeting, three key concepts are outlined that are necessary for a central bank to be effective. They are independence, credibility, and transparency.

19l Determine whether a monetary policy is expansionary or contractionary

This LOS tests the basics of monetary policy and is effectively repeated in LOS 19f. Buying government bonds, lowering interest rates and reducing reserve requirements are all expansionary.

19m Describe the limitations of monetary policy

This LOS is covered in Section 2.5, which finishes off with a summary and illustrative example in Example 11. The key points to understand are the issues caused by bond market vigilantes, the cause and result of a liquidity trap, and the use of quantitative easing.

19n Describe the roles and objectives of fiscal polic

The roles and objectives are covered in Section 3.1. There are exhibits giving illustrations of historic data, but make sure you focus on the key points listed in Section 3.1.1 and the discussion of stabilizers and budget deficits and surpluses in Section 3.1.2.

The difficulties are listed in 3.3.2. Three lags are identified – recognition, action, and impact. A list of five wider issues are then given. At the end of this section, Example 18 contains a good set of seven questions testing your knowledge of fiscal policy.

19o Describe the tools of fiscal policy, including their advantages and disadvantages

Section 3.2 lists and explains the key tools. There is a detailed list of the different forms of government spending and government revenues (direct and indirect taxation), along with the desirable attributes of a tax policy.

Section 3.2.1 lists the advantages and disadvantages of each of the tools and these should be committed to memory.

19p Describe the arguments for and against being concerned with the size of a fiscal deficit (relative to GDP)

Section 3.1.3 deals directly with this LOS, clearly listing five arguments against and three in favor of being concerned with the national debt.

19q Explain the implementation of fiscal policy and the difficulties of implementation

Section 3.3.1 details the implementation of the policy, splitting fiscal policy into active and discretionary. This is a short section. Make sure you are familiar with the terms expansionary, contractionary, and automatic stabilizers.

19r Determine whether a fiscal policy is expansionary or contractionary

This LOS follows on from the definition of fiscal policy and is detailed in Section 3.1.1.

Economics

19s Explain the interaction of monetary and fiscal policy

This reading finishes with a discussion of the interaction in Section 4. The key point is to identify the implications of four possible policy scenarios.

Section 4.2 deals with quantitative easing, and Section 4.3 covers the importance of credibility of policy. Example 19 finishes the reading with three questions covering both monetary and fiscal policy.

Reading 19 sample question
(Answers on p. 302)

In the short run the impact of an unanticipated increase in the growth rate of the money supply for an economy at full-employment level is most likely to be:

(A) Increased real interest rates, reduced output, and decreased unemployment
(B) Reduced real interest rates, increased output, and increased unemployment
(C) Reduced real interest rates, increased output, and decreased unemployment

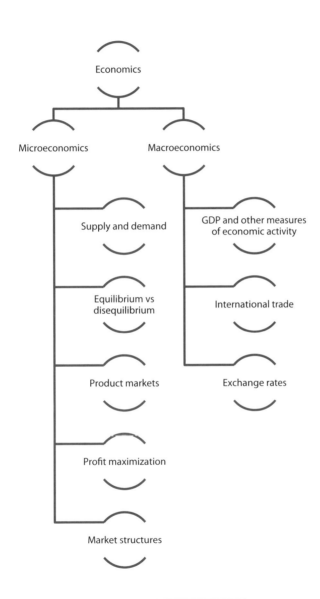

Topic:	Economics
Weight:	12%
Study sessions:	4–6
Readings:	13–21

Economics

This is a very factual reading that contains a lot of basic jargon regarding international trade.

LEARNING OUTCOME STATEMENTS

Application LOS	Knowledge LOS
20b **Describe** the benefits and costs of international trade	20a **Compare** gross domestic product and gross national product
20c **Distinguish** between comparative advantage and absolute advantage	20d **Explain** the Ricardian and Heckscher–Ohlin models of trade and the source(s) of comparative advantage in each model
20g **Describe** the balance of payments accounts including their components	20e **Compare** types of trade and capital restrictions and their economic implications
20h **Explain** how decisions by consumers, firms, and governments influence the balance of payments	20f **Explain** motivations for and advantages of trading blocs, common markets, and economic unions
	20i **Describe** functions and objectives of the international organizations that facilitate trade, including the World Bank, the International Monetary Fund, and the World Trade Organization

APPLICATION LEARNING OUTCOME STATEMENTS

20c Distinguish between comparative advantage and absolute advantage

This is covered in Section 2.4. Although the LOS states **distinguish**, in most examples this means picking out the comparative and absolute advantage from a set of numbers. Example 3 is adequate to get the understanding in a simple two-country, two-product example.

One of the key points to remember is that a country may have the absolute advantage in two goods, but it can by definition have the comparative advantage in only one good.

20d Explain the Ricardian and Heckscher–Ohlin models of trade and the source(s) of comparative advantage in each model

Section 2.4.2 covers both of these models. The Ricardian model considers labor as the only variable factor of production, whereas the Heckscher–Ohlin model considers both capital and labor as variable.

20h Explain how decisions by consumers, firms, and governments influence the balance of payments

This LOS involves using the national income identity formula which has already been seen in previous readings:

$$Y = C + I + G + X - M.$$

This is transformed in several steps to get the definition given as Equation 10:

$$CA = Sp + Sg - I.$$

where Sp is private sector spending and Sg is government saving. The key conclusions to note are what happens to the current account (CA) when private saving, private investment, and government investment levels vary.

KNOWLEDGE LEARNING OUTCOME STATEMENTS

20a Compare gross domestic product and gross national product

This is a straightforward pair of definitions to learn. They are covered at the start of section 2.1 under 'Basic Terminology'.

20b Describe the benefits and costs of international trade

Section 2.3 covers the costs and benefits of international trade. Example 2 contains five questions that address the key points. Although they are not exam style, they do bring out the key points from the section and are a good interactive way of learning the material.

20e Compare types of trade and capital restrictions and their economic implications

Sections 3.1–3.3 address this LOS under the following headings:

> **Tariffs**

> **Quotas**

> **Export subsidies**

20f Explain motivations for and advantages of trading blocs, common markets, and economic unions

Section 3.4 summarizes the content that needs to be learned for this LOS.

20g Describe the balance of payments accounts including their components

Section 4 of the reading addresses the balance of payments (BOP). This is a relatively long reading which contains a lot of real-world information to explain how the BOP system works. The key terms to learn are the current account, the capital account, and the financial account.

The BOP system is a basic dual-effect accounting system – every transaction will impact it twice.

20i Describe functions and objectives of the international organizations that facilitate trade, including the World Bank, the International Monetary Fund, and the World Trade Organization

Section 5 finishes the reading by covering the major international organizations in this LOS. The summary at the end of the reading is a good source for quickly noting down the key major facts surrounding each.

Reading 20 sample question
(Answers on p. 302)

In the context of the balance of payments (BOP) accounts, tourism, transportation, and business services are likely to be captured in which of the following components of the BOP?

(A) Capital account
(B) Current account
(C) Financial account

Economics

This reading has more calculations in it than most of the economics readings.

Learning outcome statements

Application LOS	Knowledge LOS
21a **Define** an exchange rate, and distinguish between nominal and real exchange rates and spot and forward exchange rates	21b **Describe** functions of and participants in the foreign exchange market
21c **Calculate** and interpret the percentage change in a currency relative to another currency	21h **Describe** exchange rate regimes
21d **Calculate** and interpret currency cross-rates	21i **Explain** the impact of exchange rates on countries' international trade and capital flows
21e **Convert** forward quotations expressed on a points basis or in percentage terms into outright forward quotations	
21f **Explain** the arbitrage relationship between spot rates, forward rates and interest rates	
21g **Calculate** and interpret a forward rate consistent with a spot rate and the interest rate in each currency	

Application learning outcome statements

21a Define an exchange rate, and distinguish between nominal and real exchange rates and spot and forward exchange rates

Although this LOS is only **define** and **distinguish**, there are several practice questions that require the manipulation of the rates. Example 1 is a comprehensive example of how to undertake the calculations. Make sure you are comfortable enough with this first section of the reading to be able to deal with all the calculations in Example 1 before you move on.

21c Calculate and interpret the percentage change in a currency relative to another currency

Section 3.1 walks through an example of the calculation required here which you should follow before attempting Example 4. A key skill for the exam is identifying not only the value of the movement but which currency is strengthening and which is weakening.

21d Calculate and interpret currency cross-rates

A cross-rate is calculated using two exchange rates and three currencies. For example, the GBPJPY cross-rate could be calculated using the GBPUSD and JPYUSD exchange rates with a bit of algebra:

$$\frac{GBP}{JPY} = \frac{GBP}{USD} \times \frac{USD}{JPY}$$

This is a very mechanical process which you should practice until you are comfortable with it. Section 3.2 walks through the whole calculation, before Example 5 tests both LOS 21d (percentage change) and 21e on cross-rates. Make sure you are happy with all seven questions in the example before you move on.

21e Convert forward quotations expressed on a points basis or in percentage terms into outright forward quotations

Forward rates are addressed in Section 3.3. The reading walks through all the calculations required for LOS 21f, g and h before testing them thoroughly in Example 6.

This first LOS on forwards simply requires you to calculate a forward given the spot and a spread, or vice versa.

21f Explain the arbitrage relationship between spot rates, forward rates and interest rates

As outlined in LOS 21g, the forward rate can be calculated using the spot rate and interest rate. If the formula given in section 3.3 does not work, then there is an arbitrage opportunity involving the spot rate and the forward rate. The section walks through examples of how to make an arbitrage profit when the relationships don't hold.

Although the LOS is to 'explain', the best way to understand the process is to work through the numerical examples.

21g Calculate and interpret the forward rate consistent with the spot rate and the interest rate in each currency

Forward rates can be calculated using the spot rate and interest rate for each currency. Section 3.3 finishes off by walking through how this calculation works. This is helpful to understand the calculation, but ultimately it is using the formula to calculate the forward rate that is key. This is demonstrated in Example 6, along with questions on LOS 21f and g.

Economics

Knowledge learning outcome statements

21b Describe functions of and participants in the foreign exchange market

Section 2.1 on functions and Section 2.2 on participants are both narrative sections that should review quickly and summarize the main points. Participants are broken down into buy side and sell side. The question at the end of Section 2.1 is more numerical and tests the application LOS rather than this one.

21h, i Describe exchange rate regimes, explain the impact of exchange rates on countries' international trade and capital flows

There are several different regimes outlined in Section 4 and these should be committed to memory. Start by trying to answer the six exam-style questions in Example 7. If you refer back to the readings to try and solve each of them you will pick up the main points needed for LOS 21i and j.

Reading 21 sample question
(Answers on p. 302)

A dealer provides the quotes in the table below. How much is GBP expected to appreciate against USD over the next year?

Ratio	Spot rate	Expected spot rate in 1 year
USD/GBP	1.5705	1.5752

(A) –0.3%
(B) 0.3%
(C) 3%

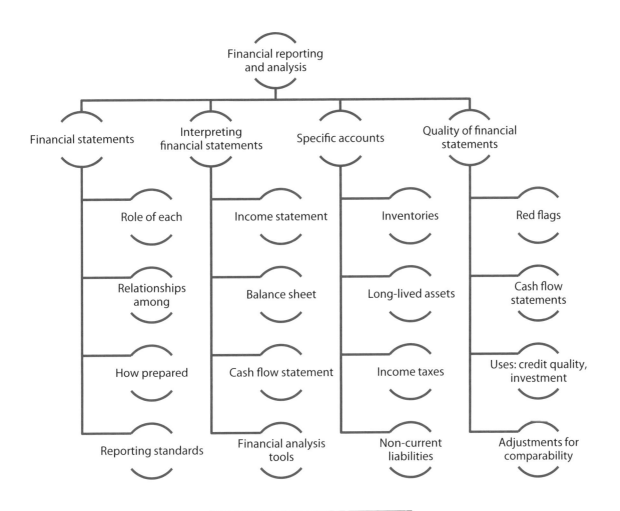

Topic:	Financial Reporting and Analysis
Weight:	20%
Study sessions:	7–10
Readings:	22–35

THE BIG PICTURE

Financial reporting and analysis has the largest weight of the ten topics on Level I and one of the largest weights on Level II, so it behoves you to devote some time brushing up on the principles of financial accounting, as well as the fundamentals of financial analysis.

The key to understanding this topic is to appreciate (1) the relationships among the statements, (2) the amount of flexibility that management has within accounting standards in terms of the choice of principles, and (3) how the statements, along with additional disclosures, can be used in the analysis of a business enterprise.

THE FINANCIAL STATEMENTS

Whereas there are four financial statements – income statement, balance sheet, cash flow statement, and statement of shareholders' equity – the focus is on the first three. You need to understand how these statements are created, and how they link together. You also need to appreciate that the objective of these statements is to provide useful information to investors, and that accounting standards are established to provide some uniformity and comparability of statements among firms.

One of the overhanging themes is the convergence of accounting standards globally, so you need to appreciate the differences between International Financial Reporting Standards (IFRS) and US Generally Accepted Accounting Standards (US GAAP). Even though the goal is convergence, they are not there yet. This means that analysts must be aware of the principles of accounting for the companies they analyze, and make appropriate adjustments for comparability.

With respect to the individual financial statements, the focus with respect to the income statements is the accrual method, including revenue and expense recognition, operating versus non-operating accounts, EPS, common-size analysis, and comprehensive income. With respect to the balance sheet, the focus is on the presentation and classification of accounts, common-size analysis, and liquidity and solvency ratios. The cash flow statement content focuses on (1) the substantive differences in classification for accounts in the cash flow statement when comparing IFRS with US GAAP, (2) the different approaches to creating the cash flow statement, and (3) the calculation of free cash flow from elements in the cash flow statement.

Further, you need to be prepared to calculate financial ratios, evaluate a company's financial condition or performance using financial ratios, and describe how an analyst would use financial statement information to forecast earnings.

SPECIFIC ACCOUNTING ISSUES

The accounting for specific accounts is singled out, which means that you need to focus on the accounting standards for these: inventories, long-lived assets, income taxes, and non-current liabilities. The laser focus on these accounts is a good lead in to the last component of this topic: quality. For example, by calculating profit under the different inventory accounting systems, you are getting a preview of (1) how the choices of inventory methods make it difficult to compare companies that use different methods, and (2) the potential for managing the bottom line by the judicious choice of inventory method.

Financial Reporting and Analysis

Making sense of deferred tax assets and liabilities is the more challenging aspect of understanding income taxes. Just remember that when the accounting for something for financial reporting purposes differs from the accounting for tax purposes, this gives rise to either a temporary or a permanent difference in income. If the difference is temporary, then a deferred asset (tax benefit to be received in the future) or liability (tax to be paid in the future) is created; if the difference is permanent, there is no deferred asset or liability.

The last of the accounting that you need to focus on is that for debt, including leases and pension benefits. Focus on how operating and financial leases differ in terms of the balance sheet and other disclosures, and the implication for the interpretation of these statements. With respect to pension accounting, compare how defined benefit and defined contribution plans affect financial statements. You need to be prepared to calculate leverage and coverage ratios, so give some thought as to how the accounting for leases and pension may affect these ratios.

QUALITY

The last content in this topic deals with the quality of financial statements, which relates to the earlier discussion of how statements are prepared and accounting standards. You need to understand why someone would want to manage earnings and cash flows, and how they can do this and still be consistent with accounting standards. Given the potential for the management of statements, you should be prepared to explain how the user of financial statements can adjust statements to make them comparable for purposes of evaluating a company's credit quality and as an investment.

Financial Reporting and Analysis

This reading introduces the financial statement analysis section of the curriculum. It is a high-level overview of financial statements, including the framework in which they are prepared and the ways that analysts use them. Do not spend too long reading this chapter because the key skills you need to learn are included in other chapters. This chapter contains some information to learn and retain, but very little applied knowledge.

For this reason, there are few calculations in this chapter. Rather, you will need to learn key lists of information, so put aside some time to make brief, bullet-pointed lists that you can refer back to as you return to study this chapter nearer the time of the exam.

LEARNING OUTCOME STATEMENTS

Application LOS	Knowledge LOS
22b **Describe** the roles of the key financial statements (statement of financial position, statement of comprehensive income, statement of changes in equity, and statement of cash flows) in evaluating a company's performance and financial position	22a **Describe** the roles of financial reporting and financial statement analysis
	22c **Describe** the importance of financial statement notes and supplementary information – including disclosures of accounting policies, methods, and estimates – and management's commentary
	22d **Describe** the objective of audits of financial statements, the types of audit reports, and the importance of effective internal controls
	22e **Identify** and explain information sources that analysts use in financial statement analysis besides annual financial statements and supplementary information
	22f **Describe** the steps in the financial statement analysis framework

APPLICATION LEARNING OUTCOME STATEMENTS

22b Describe the roles of the key financial statements (statement of financial position, statement of comprehensive income, statement of changes in equity, and statement of cash flows) in evaluating a company's performance and financial position

Keep your study time short on this section because the purpose of each financial statement will become clearer in subsequent chapters. The later readings drill down into the detail of each statement and explore account balances included on these statements in more depth.

For now, you need to know that the balance sheet shows the financial position of a company and review the account balances included on a balance sheet. Also, know that Assets = Liabilities + Owners' Equity. You will come back to this equation time and again. You also need to know that the income statement (P&L) shows Revenues – Expenses = Net Income. Again, you will come back to this in more depth later.

There is less information later on about the statement of changes in equity, so it is worth reading this carefully and looking at the example. Come back to this section after you have studied Readings 23, 25, and 26 when the context should be clearer.

The cash flow statement is covered again in Reading 27. For now, you need to know that the cash flow statement shows all cash flows in and out of the company for the period, classified by the nature of the cash flow.

The study manual includes an example of each of these statements that add some context. You should use these for reference as you study later chapters.

KNOWLEDGE LEARNING OUTCOME STATEMENTS

22a Describe the roles of financial reporting and financial statement analysis

Financial statements can be used in a wide range of analysis, a list of which is included in Section 2. The financial statements include information that helps analysts to assess the company's liquidity, solvency, and performance as well as evaluating how efficiently the management is controlling the company's assets.

Don't spend very long on this section – you should retain any information that you need to answer questions on this topic from one quick read-through. Make use of the exhibits provided in the manual, which will add context to this topic area, especially if you have not studied financial reporting and analysis before.

22c Describe the importance of financial statement notes and supplementary information – including disclosures of accounting policies, methods, and estimates – and management's commentary

There is a lot of useful information contained in the financial notes and supplementary schedules, and analysts find most of the information they need here. By understanding the accounting choices the company's management has made in presenting the information, an analyst can better make comparisons between entities. Where two companies have made different choices, the analyst should make adjustments to one company's accounts so that the results are directly comparable.

Typically, information on significant accounting policies, for example depreciation policies, revenue recognition, and information on the company's operating segments, can help the analyst to make these comparisons, as well as to better understand the nature of the risks to which the organization is exposed.

Financial Reporting
and Analysis

22d Describe the objective of audits of financial statements, the types of audit reports, and the importance of effective internal controls

An audit confirms whether the financial statements have been presented fairly in all material respects. If they have been, the auditor issues an unqualified (or "clean") opinion. Where they have not been presented fairly, the auditor includes a statement in the audit report that this is not the case, stating the reasons why.

This statement is usually a qualified opinion and could be either because there is information missing or unverifiable, or because of inaccuracies in the information presented. In more serious cases, the auditor could issue an adverse opinion when the financial statements are found to make no sense at all, or a disclaimer of opinion where the auditor can't give an opinion because there is no supporting evidence for anything included in the statements.

22e Identify and explain information sources that analysts use in financial statement analysis besides annual financial statements and supplementary information

Essentially, analysts use any and all financial information that might be relevant. Key pieces of information include the Management Discussion and Analysis section of the annual report or 10k, the auditor's report, proxy statements, interim reports, and any information on the Investor Relations section of the company's own website.

22f Describe the steps in the financial statement analysis framework

This is fairly straightforward. There are six stages to learn and you need to know two things: in what order an analyst performs these steps and what happens during each of them. There is a table in Section 4 that summarizes everything concisely. Learn this table and be prepared to recall the information in it.

Reading 22 sample question
(Answers on p. 303)

Which of the following is least likely to be a line in the statement of owner's equity?

(A) Common stock
(B) Deferred tax
(C) Retained earnings

This chapter provides the first piece of practical implementation of the dual effect. An understanding of the dual effect and how account balances are affected by different financial transactions is crucial for a good analyst. The CFA exam tests your ability to apply your knowledge to many different financial transactions and you need to be able to deal with a range of transactions quickly and accurately. In order to do this, you will need to gain a good grasp of the fundamental principles introduced in this chapter.

You should spend time making sure that you fully understand each of the sections in this chapter, as the investment of your time here will help you save time in later chapters. If you move on from this chapter without a full understanding of the topic area, you will undoubtedly have to return to this area at some point to try to work out the answers to future problems.

LEARNING OUTCOME STATEMENTS

Application LOS	Knowledge LOS
23a **Explain** the relationship of financial statement elements and accounts, and classify accounts into the financial statement elements	23c **Explain** the process of recording business transactions using an accounting system based on the accounting equation
23b **Explain** the accounting equation in its basic and expanded forms	23f **Describe** the flow of information in an accounting system
23d **Explain** the need for accruals and other adjustments in preparing financial statements	23g **Explain** the use of the results of the accounting process in security analysis
23e **Explain** the relationship among the income statement, balance sheet, statement of cash flows and statement of owners' equity	

APPLICATION LEARNING OUTCOME STATEMENTS

23a Explain the relationship of financial statement elements and accounts, and classify accounts into the financial statement elements

There are five different financial statement elements: assets, liabilities, equity, revenue, and expenses. Under the dual effect, all financial transactions that are recorded in the accounts will affect two of these elements. A transaction could affect just one of these elements, for instance two asset balances could change if management uses cash to buy a machine. In this case cash goes down, tangible assets increase. Alternatively, a transaction could affect two different elements, for example if management makes a sale for cash. In this case, the asset (cash) increases but the revenue element ("sales" or "revenues") also increases.

For any transaction that you are shown in the exam, you will need to first be able to identify which of the elements is affected by the transaction, e.g. "assets," then you will need to identify what type of account balance would specifically be affected, e.g. "cash" or "receivables." Finally you need to identify whether the balances that are affected will go down or up. A fundamental understanding of this process is vital to be able to undertake a variety of questions in the exam. Furthermore, the better your underlying understanding, the quicker you will be able to deal with the questions on this area.

To complete the requirements of this LOS it is also worth noting that you need to know that the balance sheet shows assets, liabilities, and equity, and that the income statement shows the revenue and expenses. The net income that is shown at the end of the income statement is added each year to the equity section of the balance sheet, which is how the dual entry system becomes complete and maintains its balance.

23b Explain the accounting equation in its basic and expanded forms

The basic accounting equation was covered in LOS 22b and is shown as:

$$\text{Assets} = \text{Liabilities} + \text{Owners' Equity}$$

Now that you have learned about the five financial statement elements, we can expand this to show how the dual effect works by saying:

$$\text{Assets} = \text{Liabilities} + \text{Contributed Capital} + \text{Beginning Retained Earnings}$$
$$+ \text{Revenue} - \text{Expenses} - \text{Dividends}$$

Example 1

Company A has the following balance sheet at the end of 2012:

	$m
Assets	150
Total assets	150
Liabilities	90
Owners' Equity	60
Total Liabilities and Owners' Equity	150

During 2013, the company makes profits as follows:

	$m
Revenue	70
Expenses	40
Net income	30

The profit, or net income, will add to the equity of the company as it is a profit that has been made which benefits the owners of the company. At the end of 2012, this account balance stood at $60m. It will increase by the $30m profit and by the end of 2013 it will stand at $90m ($60m + $30m).

If the company pays out a dividend of $5m, this will reduce the amount "owed" to the equity holders (the dividend is effectively a payout to them of what they are due). This will therefore reduce the value of owners' equity so that it will stand at $85m ($90m – $5m). Note that this dividend payout does not reduce the net income (as it is not shown in the income statement) but it does reduce owners' equity in the balance sheet. The reduction of equity because of the dividend payout will be shown in the statement of changes in equity as follows:

	$m
Equity at the end of 2012 as per the balance sheet	60
Plus net income generated in 2013 as per the income statement	30
Less dividends paid out to shareholders	(5)
Equity at the end of 2013 as per the balance sheet	85

Go back to the expanded formula and make sure that this now makes sense in the context of the numerical example shown here.

23d Explain the need for accruals and other adjustments in preparing financial statements

The financial statements are prepared on the accruals basis, which means that they show revenue recorded as it is earned, rather than when the cash is received, and expenses as they are incurred, rather than when the cash is paid out.

Due to the timing difference that exists between the recording of the revenue or expense and the cash movement, it is necessary to make an accrual adjustment in the financial statements.

Example 2
If a company receives cash in advance of a sale, for example if a customer pays in full for a vacation a month before that vacation, the company's cash will increase but revenue cannot be recorded as it has not yet been earned. A balancing adjustment is needed to ensure the accounts stay in balance; this is done by increasing a liability account called "unearned revenue." This liability stays on the balance sheet until the customer takes the vacation, at which point revenue is included in the income statement. Net income will increase as a result (and will ultimately flow through to increase equity). The opposing entry, which is to decrease unearned revenue, will reduce liabilities and will keep the balance sheet in check.

Exhibit 10 in the manual lists the adjusting entries that you need to be able to explain as being:

- Unearned revenue
- Prepaid expense
- Unbilled (accrued) revenue
- Accrued expenses

You should make sure that you fully understand why each of these account balances exists through use of similar examples to Example 2.

23e Explain the relationship among the income statement, balance sheet, statement of cash flows and statement of owners' equity

As you can see from Example 1, the income statement and balance sheets are linked by the annual addition of net income to equity.

The statement of owners' equity simply provides a breakdown of all the changes that have happened in all the equity balances from one balance sheet date to the next. In this sense it is purely a descriptive statement that is not part of the dual effect system.

The statement of cash flows is similar to the statement of owners' equity in that it is also not part of the dual effect system. It too is a descriptive statement which shows all the changes in the cash balance from one balance sheet date to the next. The statement of cash flows describes all cash in- and outflows classified by the nature of the cash flow. Reading 27 covers the statement of cash flows in more detail.

KNOWLEDGE LEARNING OUTCOME STATEMENTS

23c Explain the process of recording business transactions using an accounting system based on the accounting equation

The detailed process of recording transactions in the financial statements is beyond the scope of the CFA syllabus. For an analyst to be skilled at using financial information, it is not necessary to have a full understanding of how to use a T-account. For that reason, you will not have to do this in the exam, but should instead understand the process by which accountants put together the information. An appreciation of how this is done will help your understanding of how to adjust accounts to make sure that your financial statement analysis is more meaningful.

There are some illustrations of T-accounts and ledger entries in Section 4 of this chapter. Do not spend long trying to reproduce or remember any of the detail in here because it is unlikely to be practically useful in the exam. Rather, use it as a reference tool if you need context for any of the adjustments that you need to make in future.

The key information that you really need is included in LOS 23a and 23b. If you understand these points, then you are more likely to be able to deal with the later readings, and, more importantly, the questions in the exam.

The optional section at the back of this chapter relates very closely to this LOS. Again, don't spend too much time on this to begin with. Refer back to it only if you have difficulty answering questions on this section.

23f Describe the flow of information in an accounting system

Exhibit 11 offers a good summary of the information flow within an accounting system. In order to answer questions in the exam, you need to be able to identify the order in which this information is processed and also the basic characteristics of journal entries, the general ledger and T-accounts, the trial balance and adjusted trial balance, and the financial statements.

You should learn and be prepared to recall the information contained in Exhibit 11.

23g Explain the use of the results of the accounting process in security analysis

In the age of computerized accounting systems, it is much harder for accountants to commit fraud which involves misuse of the accounting systems. Analysts need to be aware that, although the accounting process is designed to standardize transactions as much as possible, there can be significant use of judgment within a set of accounts. This gives rise to the possibility that financial statements may be manipulated, for example in order for management to secure a higher valuation for the company's shares.

Reading 23 sample question
(Answers on p. 303)

Under US GAAP, which of the following is least likely to be included as part of investing cash flow?

(A) Tax payments
(B) Investments in affiliates
(C) Proceeds from sales of assets

The material in this chapter is reasonably theoretical in tone. There are some sections that could be applied to a mini-scenario in exam questions, but your study will mainly be committing the material to memory in order to draw on it at a later date.

You should aim to keep the time spent on this section to a minimum by studying as effectively as possible. Read the material actively; make notes as you go, underline key sentences, highlight listed items, etc. Ideally, you would create flashcards or lists that you will be able to refer to nearer to the exam as an aide-memoire.

This chapter's material does underpin a lot of the accounting treatments that you will see, but the exam questions are likely to be focused on recalling information from the lists and diagrams presented here.

LEARNING OUTCOME STATEMENTS

Application LOS	Knowledge LOS
	24a **Describe** the objective of financial statements and the importance of financial reporting standards in security analysis and valuation
	24b **Describe** the roles and desirable attributes of financial reporting standard-setting bodies and regulatory authorities in establishing and enforcing reporting standards, and describe the role of the International Organization of Securities Commissions
	24c **Describe** the status of global convergence of accounting standards and ongoing barriers to developing one universally accepted set of financial reporting standards
	24d **Describe** the International Accounting Standards Board's conceptual framework, including the objective and qualitative characteristics of financial statements, required reporting elements, and constraints and assumptions in preparing financial statements
	24e **Describe** general requirements for financial statements under IFRS
	24f **Compare** key concepts of financial reporting standards under IFRS and US GAAP reporting systems
	24g **Identify** the characteristics of a coherent financial reporting framework and the barriers to creating such a framework
	24h **Explain** the implications for financial analysis of differing financial reporting systems and the importance of monitoring developments in financial reporting standards
	24i **Analyze** company disclosures of significant accounting policies

KNOWLEDGE LEARNING OUTCOME STATEMENTS

24a Describe the objective of financial statements and the importance of financial reporting standards in security analysis and valuation

This LOS serves as an introduction to this section. Don't dwell too long on reading Section 2 and make sure that you pick out the key objectives of financial statements which are to provide:

- Useful information to the users of the accounts (learn the potential users of the accounts outlined in this section too)
- Standards that help the user to achieve a level of consistency regarding the judgments contained within the accounts

24b Describe the roles and desirable attributes of financial reporting standard-setting bodies and regulatory authorities in establishing and enforcing reporting standards, and describe the role of the International Organization of Securities Commissions

The simple rule is that standard-setters make the rules, regulatory authorities enforce the rules. The key accounting standard-setters that you need to be aware of are the International Accounting Standards Board (IASB) and the Financial Accounting Standards Board (FASB) in the US. The IASB sets IFRS, the FASB sets US GAAP. There is not much else to know in this section other than in order to be effective these bodies should be independent, professionally trained, and require input from a range of stakeholder groups.

24c Describe the status of global convergence of accounting standards and ongoing barriers to developing one universally accepted set of financial reporting standards

Read through this section very quickly and take some notes as you do so. The key points to note are few. Essentially, most of the world's major economies now require companies listed on their stock exchanges to report using either IFRS or standards so close to IFRS that they are practically the same. Only the US stands out as an exception to this rule, choosing to maintain the use of US GAAP.

The IASB and FASB had an agreement that their accounting standards should be harmonized by late 2011 and the SEC has issued guidance stating that it is desirable that US users of financial statements should be presented with IFRS-compliant information.

The main barrier to changing this is political pressure from lobbyists who lobby governments, policy makers, and standard-setters.

24d Describe the International Accounting Standards Board's conceptual framework, including the objective and qualitative characteristics of financial statements, required reporting elements, and constraints and assumptions in preparing financial statements

The IASB's framework for accounts is the key set of principles underpinning the preparation of financial statements. There is a diagram in Exhibit 2 which summarizes all the key points of the framework in one place. You should refer to this as you study for the exam and make sure that you can explain what each of the terms included on the diagram means and how they are relevant to providing an effective financial reporting framework.

There are various constraints of financial information. The key constraint is the cost incurred to prepare the information, although omitted information, the existence of non-quantifiable information, time delays from reporting to preparation, and the use of estimates also reduce the usefulness of financial information.

24e Describe general requirements for financial statements under IFRS

Exhibit 3 provides a key set of lists for this LOS. You need to know which financial statements are required for a complete set of financial reporting standards and also what general features these statements should include. You should be able to fully explain the terms relating to the structure and content of the statements.

Use the diagram in Exhibit 3 to test your knowledge. If there are any terms that you don't understand in that list, read on in the chapter until you understand them. If you are able to fully explain all terms in the diagram, you will be able to deal with questions on this LOS.

24f Compare key concepts of financial reporting standards under IFRS and US GAAP reporting systems

Exhibit 6 details the key conceptual differences between IFRS and US GAAP. These mainly refer to differences in the definitions of various terms associated with financial statement preparation.

Note that under the old rules, the SEC required companies presenting their results in the US under IFRS to provide a reconciliation note to US GAAP so that users could fully understand the differences in reporting system, but this is no longer the case.

24g Identify the characteristics of a coherent financial reporting framework and the barriers to creating such a framework

You need to learn the characteristics of an effective financial reporting framework which are that the framework should:

- Enhance transparency
- Include a comprehensive spectrum of financial transactions
- Ensure consistency between companies and time periods

Also learn the main barriers to producing this, which are:

- Different approaches to valuing assets
- Standard-setters alternating between rules-based, principles-based, or combination-based approaches to developing standards

- Conflicts between whether measurement at the balance sheet date or throughout the period of the income statement should have priority

LOS 24h Explain the implications for financial analysis of differing financial reporting systems and the importance of monitoring developments in financial reporting standards

There are three ways that analysts can keep up to date with developments. You should learn these and be able to recall them. These are:

1. Watching out for new products and services and understanding how they should be accounted for
2. Reading pronouncements by regulators, standard-setters, and others
3. Evaluating company disclosures for changes in accounting policies

LOS 24i Analyze company disclosures of significant accounting policies

Section 8.3 is a good warm-up for the later readings on financial reporting analysis and ratio analysis. The section highlights the key questions an analyst should ask as they are working through the accounting policies presented by management. The manual also contains sample disclosure from real-world companies, which can provide much-needed context on this topic. It is worth reading this section with reasonable attention to detail but quickly and actively.

Reading 24 sample question
(Answers on p. 303)

Which of the following entities currently develops the US Financial Accounting Standards?

(A) The Financial Services Authority
(B) The Financial Accounting Standards Board
(C) The Public Company Accounting Oversight Board

FINANCIAL REPORTING AND ANALYSIS: INCOME STATEMENTS, BALANCE SHEETS, AND CASH FLOW STATEMENTS

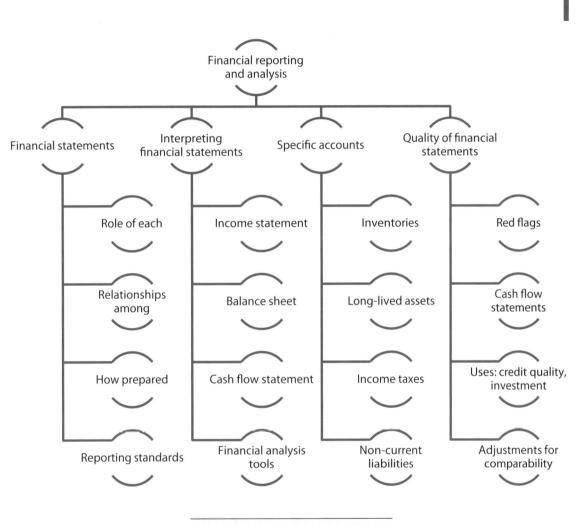

Topic:	Financial Reporting and Analysis
Weight:	20%
Study sessions:	7–10
Readings:	22–35

This reading introduces the income statement and other comprehensive income. It is a reasonably high-level introduction but does include some key calculations, such as the earnings per share calculation and revenue recognition calculations. Make sure that as you work through this section you spend proportionately longer on both revenue recognition and earnings per share.

As you work through the materials and see more examples, you will begin to understand the format and structure of the income statement. For this reason, don't spend too long at this stage reading and making notes on the remaining LOS in this reading. Work through them as quickly as possible as the other readings in this study session will also demand a lot of your time. You will also see some of these things again in later readings, which will help reinforce your learning.

LEARNING OUTCOME STATEMENTS

Application LOS	Knowledge LOS
25b **Describe** the general principles of revenue recognition and accrual accounting, specific revenue recognition applications (including accounting for long-term contracts, installment sales, barter transactions, and gross and net reporting of revenue), and the implications of revenue recognition principles for financial analysis	25a **Describe** the components of the income statement and alternative presentations of that statement
25c **Calculate** revenue given information that might influence the choice of revenue recognition method	25d **Describe** the general principles of expense recognition, specific expense recognition applications, and the implications of expense recognition choices for financial analysis
25g **Describe** how earnings per share is calculated and calculate and interpret a company's earnings per share (both basic and diluted earnings per share) for both simple and complex capital structures	25e **Describe** the financial reporting treatment and analysis of non-recurring items (including discontinued operations, extraordinary items, and unusual or infrequent items) and changes in accounting standards
25h **Distinguish** between dilutive and anti-dilutive securities, and describe the implications of each for the earnings per share calculation	25f **Distinguish** between the operating and non-operating components of the income statement
25i **Convert** the income statements to common-size income statements	25k **Describe**, **calculate** and **interpret** comprehensive income
25j **Evaluate** a company's financial performance using common-size income statements and financial ratios based on the income statement	25l **Describe** other comprehensive income, and identify the major types of items included in it

APPLICATION LEARNING OUTCOME STATEMENTS

25b Describe the general principles of revenue recognition and accrual accounting, specific revenue recognition applications (including accounting for long-term contracts, installment sales, barter transactions, and gross and net reporting of revenue), and the implications of revenue recognition principles for financial analysis

The readings lay out the criteria for revenue recognition. You should learn these in case you get a direct knowledge question asking you to recall them. However, it is likely to be more important to focus on the special instances of revenue recognition and to be able to deal with these.

The special cases of revenue recognition are:

- Long-term contracts
- Installment sales
- Barter transactions
- Gross versus net reporting

There are examples of each of these (apart from barter transactions) in the CFA Institute readings. You should work these examples and make sure that you fully understand how to calculate the revenue shown in the solutions.

25c Calculate revenue given information that might influence the choice of revenue recognition method

Having worked the revenue examples in the readings, you should now be able to calculate the revenue to be recognized under each of the transactions shown. However, it is unlikely that the exam questions will follow the exact format of the examples in the book. It is likely that you will have to deal with a different scenario and that you will have to apply your knowledge.

Work through the practice problems in the readings, which contain further examples of revenue recognition calculations.

25g Describe how earnings per share is calculated and calculate and interpret a company's earnings per share (both basic and diluted earnings per share) for both simple and complex capital structures

EPS is an important performance indicator and as such it is imperative for a good analyst to completely understand how this metric is calculated. In order to compare companies which have different operating strategies and also different capital structures, an analyst may have to understand the effects that the differences have on the EPS calculation.

EPS calculations are not as simple as merely dividing the company's annual earnings by the number of shares outstanding. For this reason, you need to spend a relatively large amount of time on the EPS calculations.

There are ten examples for the EPS calculation included in the CFA Institute readings. It is vital that you work through all of these examples and that you fully understand how to calculate the various components of EPS and diluted EPS.

25h Distinguish between dilutive and anti-dilutive securities, and describe the implications of each for the earnings per share calculation

This LOS is very simple if you have worked through the examples referred to in LOS 25g. If you understand the calculations, you will know that if the securities convert and make EPS lower, they dilute EPS. If the EPS is not lower as a result of conversion, then the securities are called anti-dilutive securities and they should be excluded from the EPS calculation.

25i Convert the income statements to common-size income statements

A common-size income statement is one which shows all components of the income statement as a percentage of revenue. There are several examples of this in Section 7 of this reading – go directly to these and ensure they make sense to you.

Make sure you understand and can explain how and why it might be useful to compare the common-size income statements of two companies.

25j Evaluate a company's financial performance using common-size income statements and financial ratios based on the income statement

Be able to calculate gross and net profit margins at this stage. You will learn more in later readings about other ratios that you can use for more in-depth analysis.

You should also be able to draw conclusions about a company's performance relative to one of its competitors from common-size income statement information that you are given. This is relatively simple to do, so don't spend too long on this section.

KNOWLEDGE LEARNING OUTCOME STATEMENTS

25a Describe the components of the income statement and alternative presentations of that statement

The readings provide two extracts of income statements and highlight the differences in presentation between companies reporting under US GAAP and under IFRS. If you are not familiar with the income statement, try to download and read the income statements of real-life companies so that you become used to the peculiarities of different reporting conventions.

Another thing to become comfortable with at this point is the differing terms for profit metrics, for example operating profit can also be called EBIT, but they are not necessarily the same. This can be confusing and the more you understand the components of the income statement, the easier it will be to perform analysis on the financial statements later on.

25d Describe the general principles of expense recognition, specific expense recognition applications, and the implications of expense recognition choices for financial analysis

This LOS addresses the idea of the matching principle, which is matching the costs to the same period as the income they generate. The readings provide some information about costing of inventories, which is covered again in Reading 29.

At this point, focus on understanding how the accounting for doubtful accounts, warranties, and depreciation affects financial analysis. There is a comprehensive example about depreciation methods. Work though this slowly to understand the calculation of depreciation, noting that you will see more information on this again in Reading 30. The key thing at the end of this reading is to be able to explain why an analyst needs to consider these items carefully.

In summary, the reason the analyst needs to examine these areas thoroughly is that they tend to be ones where judgment is applied to the accounting policy choices. Where there is room to apply judgment, there is often a lack of direct comparability between different companies. This makes it important for an analyst to check whether they are comparing "apples to apples" when reading a set of financial statements. Be able to use examples from this section to illustrate this point. Although the exam is multi-choice, if you can do this, you will be able to tackle any exam question.

25e Describe the financial reporting treatment and analysis of non-recurring items (including discontinued operations, extraordinary items, and unusual or infrequent items) and changes in accounting standards

In order for an analyst to value a company's equity accurately, they will often have to start by considering what a normal profit or cash flow level is. From here, the analyst can forecast a more accurate future position. Bear this in mind when you read this section – the point of the rules regarding non-recurring items is that the analyst has a better picture about the "normal" level of profits.

25f Distinguish between the operating and non-operating components of the income statement

This LOS is very straightforward. The operating section of the income statement relates to income and expenses from the company's operations, whereas non-operating includes mainly expenses but also income from any other sources (this is usually finance income or expenses and taxation, but there could be others).

25k Describe, calculate and interpret comprehensive income

Net income shows mainly realized gains and losses during the period. There are some other types of gains and losses (for example, revaluation gains on PPE or gains on financial assets that are Available for Sale), which are not included within net income but which are added to equity through other comprehensive income.

The general formula for calculations on this area is therefore:

Starting shareholder's equity	X
Net income/loss for the period	X/(X)
Other gains and losses not included in net income	X/(X)
Closing shareholder's equity	X

25l Describe other comprehensive income, and identify the major types of items included in it

There are a few types of gains and losses which are not included within net income. These tend to relate to complex accounting treatments of foreign exchange, financial instruments, and employment benefits. The actual accounting rules for these areas is outside of the scope of the Level I syllabus, but you should know that these gains and losses do affect equity (gains increase equity, losses decrease equity) without being shown in net income.

Reading 25 sample question
(Answers on p. 303)

P Limited has net income of $300,000 for the present financial year. The company has weighted average number of shares outstanding of 100,000. P Limited has issued a 10% convertible debenture bond issue amounting to $500,000 convertible into 5,000 common shares. Tax rate is 40%. Compute the diluted EPS.

(A) 3.00
(B) 3.14
(C) 3.24

This reading provides an introduction to the balance sheet and is an overview of a number of asset, liability, and equity classes. The reading breaks down the different elements you might expect to see on a balance sheet and includes high-level information about the accounting rules that govern these elements.

Be aware that most of the important balance sheet elements will be covered in a lot more depth in later readings. For example, you will be introduced to inventories in this section, but Reading 29 covers inventories in great depth. You can save a lot of time by making sure that you work through this reading quickly.

If you have some accounting knowledge already, then a good tip might be to start with the practice problems included at the end of this reading. If you get all these practice problems correct, go on to Reading 27. Don't move on until you can answer all the practice problems though, because if your basic knowledge is weak, the later sections will take longer to work through and your understanding will not be as robust.

LEARNING OUTCOME STATEMENTS

Application LOS	Knowledge LOS
26h **Convert** balance sheets to common-size balance sheets and interpret the common-size balance sheets	26a **Describe** the elements of the balance sheet: assets, liabilities, and equity
26i **Calculate** and interpret liquidity and solvency ratios	26b **Describe** the uses and limitations of the balance sheet in financial analysis
	26c **Describe** alternative formats of balance sheet presentation
	26d **Distinguish** between current and non-current assets, and current and non-current liabilities
	26e **Describe** different types of assets and liabilities and the measurement bases of each
	26f **Describe** the components of shareholders' equity
	26g **Analyze** balance sheets and statements of changes in equity

APPLICATION LEARNING OUTCOME STATEMENTS

26h Convert balance sheets to common-size balance sheets and interpret the common-size balance sheets

Just as you saw with the income statement in Reading 25, common-size analysis involves benchmarking every line item on the balance sheet as a percentage of another. Typically balance sheets are converted by showing each line item as a percentage of total assets. There is an example in Exhibit 17. Review this closely. You should be able to make inferences about the relative asset levels of Companies A, B, and C from this analysis.

This analysis will become easier as you work through subsequent readings and build up your knowledge of each line item in more depth, so you may want to return to it when you conclude your studies on Financial Reporting and Analysis.

26i Calculate and interpret liquidity and solvency ratios

Exhibit 19 provides an excellent summary of the ratios that you need to learn and understand in this section. Go straight to this summary and make sure you can see how these ratios would be useful to an analyst. The key message you should take from this summary is that by comparing asset levels to liability levels, an analyst can judge whether the company has cash to pay off debts in the short term. Also by comparing the level of debt to the level of equity, an analyst can judge whether the company has a stable and solvent capital structure to ensure that it is able to meet its obligations over a longer term.

KNOWLEDGE LEARNING OUTCOME STATEMENTS

26a Describe the elements of the balance sheet: assets, liabilities, and equity

Learn the definitions of each of the balance sheet elements in case this is tested through a factual question. Most of the application of this LOS involves you being familiar with items on the balance sheet and knowing how they are presented. This is covered in the rest of this reading and also in most of the subsequent Financial Reporting and Analysis readings, so once you are comfortable with the definitions, move on.

26b Describe the uses and limitations of the balance sheet in financial analysis

The balance sheet is useful to calculate ratios which help determine liquidity, solvency, and hence creditworthiness. This is because it provides lots of information about the cash position of a company and also the company's obligations split out into current and non-current portions.

There are several weaknesses of the balance sheet. The first is that the valuation of non-current assets is done on an historic basis, so the values don't correspond to market values. This makes the balance sheet a terrible indicator of a company's fair market value. Second, the information is typically out of date by the time it is published. Lastly, many components of a company's value, for example customer goodwill and employee loyalty, are not included on the balance sheet.

26c Describe alternative formats of balance sheet presentation

Most balance sheets are presented by showing the following sub-headings:

- Current assets
- Non-current assets
- Current liabilities
- Non-current liabilities
- Equity

Depending on where you are in the world, these headings may be in a different order.

There is an alternative method of presenting the information, which is to break down the asset classes by their relative liquidity. An example of this is shown in Exhibit 3. Take a look at this for reference, but note that this is rare and not at all the norm.

26d Distinguish between current and non-current assets, and current and non-current liabilities

This LOS is relatively simple. The general rule is that non-current refers to assets that are going to be used in the business for more than 12 months; current assets will be used up in fewer than 12 months. Liabilities are non-current if they fall due after 12 months, current if they fall due within 12 months.

26e Describe different types of assets and liabilities and the measurement bases of each

As you work through this section, keep a list of the different types of asset and liability classes that you see and make quick notes on the measurement basis for each one. Bear in mind that you will see more rules on all of these areas later in Readings 29–32, so you don't need to get too caught up with these rules now.

Your list should look something like this:

Balance sheet item	Measurement basis
Property, Plant and Equipment	Historic cost less accumulated depreciation IFRS allows revaluation model Must impair if recoverable amount is lower than the balance sheet value

26f Describe the components of shareholders' equity

Learn the six different components that are listed in the CFA Institute readings and be able to give examples of what would be included in each line item. You could be required to classify an equity item as one of these six types of equity in an exam question. The six components are:

- Capital contributed by owners
- Preferred shares
- Treasury shares
- Retained earnings
- Accumulated other comprehensive income
- Non-controlling interest

26g Analyze balance sheets and statements of changes in equity

You will learn a lot more about the balance sheet as you work through Readings 29–32, so you should put this LOS on hold until you have more experience of each area.

Study Session 10 focuses entirely on analysis techniques and you will learn a lot in that session that will cover this LOS.

Reading 26 sample question
(Answers on p. 304)

For financial assets classified as available for sale, which of the following best describes how it is measured on the balance sheet?

(A) Measured at fair value
(B) Measured at historic cost
(C) Measured at amortized cost

This is a key reading in Study Session 8 because it is crucial to get an understanding of the difference between net income and cash flows as early as possible. Net income is from the income statement and part of the accruals system, cash flow is not. It is deceptively simple – the cash flow statement just lists actual cash flows whereas net income is distorted by accrual-based income and expense figures.

The application LOS focus on manipulating net income to get to cash flow figures and vice versa. The knowledge LOS are more straightforward and involve learning the differences in disclosures and accounting treatments under IFRS and US GAAP.

Focus your time initially on the key techniques and rules for calculating cash flows, but make sure you also put aside some time to learn the different disclosures that are required.

LEARNING OUTCOME STATEMENTS

Application LOS	Knowledge LOS
27a **Compare** cash flows from operating, investing, and financing activities and classify cash flow items as relating to one of those three categories given a description of the items	27b **Describe** how non-cash investing and financing activities are reported
27d **Distinguish** between the direct and indirect methods of presenting cash from operating activities and describe the arguments in favor of each method	27c **Contrast** cash flow statements prepared under International Financial Reporting Standards (IFRS) and US Generally Accepted Accounting Principles (US GAAP)
27e **Describe** how the cash flow statement is linked to the income statement and the balance sheet	27h **Analyze** and interpret both reported and common-size cash flow statements
27f **Describe** the steps in the preparation of direct and indirect cash flow statements, including how cash flows can be computed using income statement and balance sheet data	27i **Calculate** and interpret free cash flow to the firm, free cash flow to equity, and performance and coverage cash flow ratios
27g **Convert** cash flows from the indirect to the direct method	

APPLICATION LEARNING OUTCOME STATEMENTS

27a Compare cash flows from operating, investing, and financing activities and classify cash flow items as relating to one of those three categories given a description of the items

The cash flow statement shows the total cash flow for the year. It is broken down into cash flow from operations (CFO), investing (CFI), and financing (CFF). Section 2.1 covers the LOS.

- CFO shows cash flows from day-to-day activities – cash from customers, paid to suppliers, salaries, etc.
- CFI shows inflows from investing in assets, notably PPE and proceeds from their sale
- CFF shows cash received from issuing debt or equity or proceeds from redeeming debt or equity

This is a straightforward LOS. Given a cash flow in a question, the task is to correctly classify it as CFO, CFI, or CFF.

27d, e, f, g Describe the steps in converting direct to indirect, distinguish between the methods, convert cash flows from direct to indirect

There are several LOS on the calculation and interpretation of the direct and indirect methods. These are two methods which can be used to get to CFO. Both give the same result for CFO – the direct method adds together cash flows and disregards non-cash flows (such as depreciation). The indirect method starts with net income, which must then be adjusted to remove non-cash flows.

This is because the income statement (and net income) is prepared on the accruals basis, whereas the cash flow statement shows only cash flows.

Questions in the exam can be either written or calculation style focusing on calculating CFO, CFI, or CFF, or identifying which category individual cash flows should be in. Work through all the examples in Section 2.3 and Section 3 of Reading 27 until you are comfortable manipulating the cash flows.

The following examples show the basic calculations that need to be mastered.

Example 1 – Direct method

	$
Cash received from customers	85,000
Cash paid to suppliers	42,000
Taxes paid	12,000
Depreciation expense	14,000
Profit on sale of PPE	1,000

Calculate CFO for the year given the information above.

Answer

	$
Cash received from customers	85,000
Cash paid to suppliers	(42,000)
Taxes paid	(12,000)
CFO	31,000

Depreciation expense is ignored as it is not a cash flow. The easiest way to remember this is to think about its dual effect from Study Session 7. It decreases NBV of assets on the balance sheet, and is charged as an expense. Neither side of that dual effect hits cash, therefore it does not impact the cash flow.

Similarly, profit on sale of PPE is not a cash flow, it is the difference between the NBV of assets disposed of and the cash flow received. What's needed for the cash flow statement is the proceeds received, but they will be part of CFI not CFO.

Example 2 – Indirect method

	$
Net income	44,000
Depreciation expense	14,000
Profit on sale of PPE	1,000
Increase in accounts receivable	4,000
Increase in accounts payable	3,500
Decrease in inventory	2,000

Answer

	$
Net income	44,000
ADD: depreciation expense	14,000
DEDUCT: profit on sale of PPE	(1,000)
DEDUCT: increase in accounts receivable	(4,000)
ADD: increase in accounts payable	3,500
ADD: decrease in inventory	2,000
CFO	58,500

This example highlights the key skills you need to deal quickly with cash flow calculation questions on the day. We are not given the individual cash flows that make up CFO so we need to calculate from net income.

The depreciation of $14,000 has been charged as an expense, which has reduced net income, but it is not a cash outflow so hasn't reduced cash flows. We therefore need to add it back to net income to get to CFO. This is true for all non-cash expenses.

The profit on sale of PPE has been included in net income but is not a cash inflow, so it must be deducted to get to CFO. The sale of PPE will generate cash proceeds, but they will be recognized in CFI, and would be calculated as the profit on sale plus the net book value of the asset disposed of. A loss on sale would have been added back.

An increase in accounts receivable means revenue has been recognized in the income statement (and hence the $4,000 is part of the $44,000 net income) but the cash has not yet been received. Net income is therefore $4,000 higher than the cash flow. The increase is therefore deducted from net income to get to CFO. This is true for accounts receivable and inventory on the balance sheet. If they increase, then the increase must be deducted from net income to get to CFO. If they decrease, they must be added back.

An increase in accounts payable means goods have been purchased and the expense recognized in the income statement (and hence the $3,500 has been deducted to get to net income) but the cash has not yet been paid out. Net income is therefore $3,500 lower than cash flow. The increase is therefore added to net income to get to CFO. If accounts payable decrease, the decrease must be deducted from net income.

The decrease in inventory represents $2,000 of inventory which has been charged as an expense but has been paid for in previous years. It is not therefore a cash outflow this year, so will be added back to get to CFO.

These are key concepts that will be applied consistently to calculation questions. Putting these rules into practice on as many questions as possible is the best way to master these concepts.

Key summary

Increase in assets on balance sheet (AR, inventory): Deduct from net income to get CFO	Decrease in assets on balance sheet (AR, inventory): Add back to net income to get CFO
Increase in liabilities on balance sheet (AP, tax payable): Add back to net income to get CFO	Decrease in liabilities on balance sheet (AP, tax payable): Add back to net income to get CFO

KNOWLEDGE LEARNING OUTCOME STATEMENTS

27i Calculate and interpret free cash flow to firm, equity and performance ratios

This is a straightforward LOS which requires the formula for free cash flow to the firm and to equity to be memorized. Section 4.3 covers how to use the formula and is only two pages long.

The free cash flow to the firm (FCFF) is the cash available to pay to all providers of capital. This means everyone who provides debt and equity, so it's before interest. Free cash flow to equity (FCFE) is what's left for equity holders, so it's after interest and the cash flow from raising or paying down debt.

The formula is easiest to remember in two stages. The first stage is to get CFO, which we already know how to get from the earlier LOS.

$$CFO = \text{Net income} + \text{Non-cash charges} - \text{Working capital investment}$$

Then:

$$FCFF = CFO + \text{Interest }(1 - t) - \text{Fixed capital investment}$$

$$FCFE = CFO +/- \text{Net debt repayment} - \text{Fixed capital investment}$$

27b Describe how non-cash investing and financing activities are reported

Transactions which affect capital or investments cannot be part of the cash flow statement as they are not cash. They are, however, separately disclosed. Examples would be the conversion of a convertible bond, or the swapping an item of PPE for another one.

27h Analyze and interpret reported and common-size cash flow statements

This is one of three common-size statement LOS in the syllabus. This is covered with the balance sheet and income statement LOS in the ratio interpretation section.

27c Contrast IFRS and US GAAP

There is a straightforward list of differences to learn – the summary table in Section 2.2 covers it all. Remember there is also a LOS in Study Session 10 which requires all the differences between IFRS and US GAAP so this is repeated there.

Notice that under US GAAP interest paid is classified as CFO in the cash flow statement, but it is classified as a non-operating item on the income statement.

Reading 27 sample questions
(Answers on p. 304)

1   In a US GAAP cash flow statement, dividends paid should be classified as:

(A) Cash flow from operations and dividends received as cash flow from operations
(B) Cash flow from financing and dividends received as cash flow from operations
(C) Cash flow from investing and dividends received as cash flow from operations

2   Assume US GAAP, determine the cash flow from operations given the following table:

Cash payment of dividends	$60
Sale of equipment	$20
Net income	$50
Purchase of land	$30
Increase in accounts payable	$40
Sale of preferred stock	$50
Increase in deferred tax liability	$10
Profit on sale of equipment	$30

(A) $30
(B) $40
(C) $70

This reading includes a lot of LOS that are highly applied. This means that you will likely be tested on higher-level learning. It is likely that the questions on this section will not simply be learning and regurgitating but will be applied.

Watch out for the examiner calculating ratios for you, then you having to interpret, not just testing that you can divide one number by another.

You should spend a lot of time on this reading.

LEARNING OUTCOME STATEMENTS

Application LOS	Knowledge LOS
28b **Classify**, **calculate** and **interpret** activity, liquidity, solvency, profitability, and valuation ratios	28a **Describe** the tools and techniques used in financial analysis, including their uses and limitations
28c **Describe** the relationship among ratios and evaluate a company using financial analysis	28f **Describe** how ratio analysis and other techniques can be used to model and forecast earnings
28d **Demonstrate** the application of the DuPont analysis of return on equity, and calculate and interpret the effects of changes in its components	
28e **Calculate** and interpret ratios used in equity analysis, credit analysis, and segment analysis	

APPLICATION LEARNING OUTCOME STATEMENTS

28b Classify, calculate and interpret activity, liquidity, solvency, profitability, and valuation ratios

You should spend a lot of time on this LOS because there are a lot of things to learn but also a lot of applications to understand.

There are three things that you should try to do as you work through this section:

1. Learn the ratios and how they are calculated (what goes on the top of the fraction, what goes on the bottom of the fraction)
2. Be able to explain to someone else why this ratio is useful to an analyst – what does it show and what do analysts look for?
3. Keep in mind the big picture – how does this ratio relate to other ratios?

Remember that if the examiner wants to write a difficult question on this area, they will present you with the ratio that has already been calculated and then will ask you to interpret the ratio and "tell a story" about what it shows. For example, presented with current and quick ratios for two companies, you should be able to deduce which company is more liquid. This would be a relatively simple question, but be aware that they could be more complicated.

There are a number of summaries in the readings which you should aim to bring together in your study notes:

- Activity ratios are summarized in Exhibit 10
- Liquidity ratios are summarized in Exhibit 12
- Solvency ratios are summarized in Exhibit 14
- Profitability ratios are summarized in Exhibit 15
- Valuation ratios are summarized in Exhibit 18

28c Describe the relationship among ratios and evaluate a company using financial analysis

In simple terms, you cannot perform analysis using only one ratio. For financial analysis to be meaningful, a good analyst will aim to build a picture using a range of ratios and trends therein.

Examples 13 and 14 in the CFA Institute manual bring this idea to life using some numerical mini-scenarios. Work through these examples so that you can see how different ratios should interact and to learn what conclusions analysts would make.

28d Demonstrate the application of the DuPont analysis of return on equity, and calculate and interpret the effects of changes in its components

The DuPont formula is a great way for analysts to break down the different components of a company's financial performance, specifically the constituent parts of return on equity.

You need to learn the formula, but also, more importantly, you need to understand each of the separate elements of the formula.

Work through this section very slowly and make sure that you attempt Examples 15 and 16, which will test your understanding of the formula, not just your ability to calculate it.

28e Calculate and interpret ratios used in equity analysis, credit analysis, and segment analysis

Now that you have learned all the different types of ratios, it is time to classify them to identify which ones are most useful for a wide range of analysis.

To summarize:

Equity analysis uses:	Credit analysis is based on:	Segment analysis uses:
Valuation ratios	The work of the ratings agencies	Segment ratios (see Exhibit 21)
EPS analysis	Ratios selected by the ratings	A wide variety of ratios but
Dividend information	agencies (see Exhibit 20)	generally calculated from limited
Payout		segmental disclosures
Retention rate		
Sustainable growth rate		
Industry-specific ratios (see Exhibit 19)		

You should make sure that you understand all the terms used in the box above after you have finished reading this section of the CFA Institute manual.

KNOWLEDGE LEARNING OUTCOME STATEMENTS

28a Describe the tools and techniques used in financial analysis, including their uses and limitations

There is some repetition in this LOS from Reading 22, which covers the financial analysis process. Make sure that you can recall all the stages of this process in the correct order.

The main techniques used by analysts are as follows:

- Ratio analysis
- Common-size analysis
- Graphs
- Regression analysis

You should spend most time on ratio analysis and common-size analysis, less on graphs and regression analysis.

Ratio analysis will likely form the basis of most of the financial analysis questions on the Level I exam as it is a broad topic with many applications. You should learn the list of limitations of ratio analysis included in the CFA Institute manual in Section 3.1.2 of this reading.

You will have seen some of the common-size information before in Readings 25 and 26. Take care to read the information on trend analysis in Section 3.2.4 and that on the relationships between financial statements in Section 3.2.5 as this brings some color to the analysis and gives some context to how this analysis is performed in practice.

28f Describe how ratio analysis and other techniques can be used to model and forecast earnings

You need to be able to recall that there are three main techniques that you are expected to know:

1. Sensitivity analysis
2. Scenario analysis
3. Simulation

Be able to explain how each of these is used. Questions on this area could set out some information about analysis that a person is doing and then ask you to identify what kind of analysis this would be.

Reading 28 sample question
(Answers on p. 304)

A company's current ratio is 0.8. If the company then uses cash to pay back a loan that is repayable within one year, which of the following is most accurate?

(A) Current ratio would decrease and the asset turnover ratio would increase
(B) Current ratio would decrease and the asset turnover ratio would decrease
(C) Current ratio would increase and the asset turnover ratio would decrease

FINANCIAL REPORTING AND ANALYSIS: INVENTORIES, LONG-LIVED ASSETS, INCOME TAXES, AND NON-CURRENT LIABILITIES

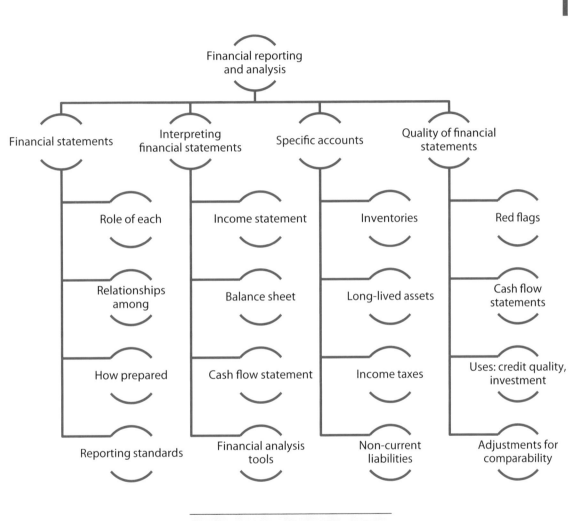

Topic:	Financial Reporting and Analysis
Weight:	20%
Study sessions:	7–10
Readings:	22–35

This reading focuses on the accounting treatments for inventories. There are three main things to check off as you study:

1. Can you identify whether a cost should be an expense in the period, or included in the cost of inventories?
2. Are you able to calculate the value of cost of sales and closing inventories using FIFO, LIFO, and weighted average cost?
3. When presented with information about costs and selling prices, can you work out whether there is any impairment to the inventory?

If the answer to all three of these questions is yes, then you will be able to deal with most of the applied questions in this reading. Most of the remaining information is fairly straightforward learning.

LEARNING OUTCOME STATEMENTS

Application LOS	Knowledge LOS
29a **Distinguish** between costs included in inventories and costs recognized as expenses in the period in which they are incurred	29b **Describe** different inventory valuation methods (cost formulas)
29c **Calculate** cost of sales and ending inventory using different inventory valuation methods and explain the impact of inventory valuation method choice on gross profit	29g **Describe** the financial statement presentation and disclosures relating to inventories
29d **Calculate** and **compare** costs of sales, gross profit, and ending inventory using perpetual and periodic inventory systems	
29e **Compare** cost of sales, ending inventory, and gross profit using different inventory valuation methods	
29f **Describe** the measurement of inventory at the lower of cost and net realizable value	
29h **Calculate** and **interpret** ratios used to evaluate inventory management	

APPLICATION LEARNING OUTCOME STATEMENTS

29a Distinguish between costs included in inventories and costs recognized as expenses in the period in which they are incurred

Example 1 in the CFA Institute readings provides some excellent examples of costs which you might have to identify as either an expense for the period or items that would be included in the cost of inventories.

Work through the example and keep a list of the different types of cost. Add to this list each time you complete more questions on this topic area until you have a comprehensive list of costs for reference as you study.

29c Calculate cost of sales and ending inventory using different inventory valuation methods and explain the impact of inventory valuation method choice on gross profit

This LOS requires you to calculate both cost of sales and closing inventories using all three methods:

1. FIFO
2. LIFO
3. Weighted average cost

Spend a lot of time learning how to do these calculations by working through Example 2. This calculation will provide you with insight as to how the cost of sales balance and closing inventory balance will be affected if prices are rising, and also if prices are falling.

Questions could ask you to calculate the value of cost of sales or inventory given purchase levels, usage numbers, and prices. You could also be asked to calculate the effect on gross profit, so be prepared for that and read the question carefully.

You could also be asked what the impact would be on cost of sales or closing inventories given price increases/decreases in the period and using the different methods. You might not necessarily be given numbers to calculate this, so you need to know how to figure this out quickly. The alternative approach is to learn it.

29d Calculate and compare costs of sales, gross profit, and ending inventory using perpetual and periodic inventory systems

This LOS is best illustrated through an example. Example 3 in the CFA Institute readings provides a comprehensive example to illustrate the comparison. Work through this example.

You are unlikely to have to work through this much information in the CFA exam questions, which tend to be a lot shorter. You might have to calculate similar information from a much lower number of purchases and prices.

29e Compare cost of sales, ending inventory, and gross profit using different inventory valuation methods

Use the calculations you worked through in LOS 29c and test yourself to see whether you can produce a tabular summary of the effect on cost of sales, ending inventory, and gross profit using the different inventory valuation methods.

Your table should look like this in a period of rising prices, with constant or increasing levels of inventory:

	Cost of sales	Ending inventory	Gross profit
FIFO	Higher	Lower	Lower
LIFO	Lower	Higher	Higher

The table would look like this in a period of falling prices, with constant or increasing levels of inventory:

	Cost of sales	Ending inventory	Gross profit
FIFO	Lower	Higher	Higher
LIFO	Higher	Lower	Lower

29f Describe the measurement of inventory at the lower of cost and net realizable value

In summary, if the net realizable value of a company's inventory falls below the value at which it is being held on the balance sheet then the inventory is impaired. The essential points to learn are the differences between the amount of the impairment as calculated under IFRS and also the amount of the impairment as calculated under US GAAP.

Under IFRS, the impairment is calculated as being the difference between the cost of inventory and the net realizable value (selling price – net selling costs).

Under US GAAP the impairment is calculated as being the difference between the cost of the inventory and the market price. Market price is calculated as current replacement cost subject to upper and lower limits. The upper limit is net realizable value. The lower limit is net realizable value less a normal profit margin.

Work through Example 4 to make sure you can apply these rules to a mini-scenario such as that which you might face in the exam.

29h Calculate and interpret ratios used to evaluate inventory management

The key inventory ratios are:

- Inventory turnover
- Days inventory on hand
- Gross profit margin

You will have seen these ratios before in earlier readings. There is an illustration in Exhibit 1 which provides some excellent context on these ratios. Once you are sure that you can calculate each of the ratios, read through this illustration and apply the learning you have done to the numbers that have been provided. Answer the questions in Example 5 to confirm that you have understood all the material correctly.

Financial Reporting and Analysis

KNOWLEDGE LEARNING OUTCOME STATEMENTS

29b Describe different inventory valuation methods (cost formulas)

There are three valuation methods to learn:

1. FIFO
2. LIFO
3. Weighted average cost

The calculations that you have to do to meet LOS 29c will provide more color to the implications of selecting any one of these methods relative to the other options. Through doing the calculations of inventory values under each method, you will be able to see exactly how the valuation methods work.

29g Describe the financial statement presentation and disclosures relating to inventories

There is no applied knowledge in this LOS. You are required to learn the list of disclosures provided in the CFA Institute's reading, under Section 5.

Note that US GAAP and IFRS requirements are different. You need to learn both.

Reading 29 sample questions
(Answers on p. 305)

1. A firm has beginning inventory of 1,418 units (cost $4 per unit), purchases 1,112 units at $12 per unit, and sells 1,918 units for $26 per unit. Assuming SGA expenses of $5,298 per annum, the earnings before taxes using the FIFO method is closest to:

    (A) $11,672
    (B) $27,600
    (C) $32,898

2. A switch from first in first out (FIFO) to last in first out (LIFO) will most likely lead to a:

    (A) decreased cost of sales
    (B) lower quick ratio during periods of rising prices
    (C) lower current ratio during periods of rising prices

This reading is a comprehensive look at the non-current assets you might expect to find on most companies' balance sheets. The reading covers property, plant, and equipment (PPE), intangible assets including goodwill, and investment property. Despite the range of topic areas covered, some of the principles that apply to PPE also apply to intangibles, for example amortization. This means that you should get some benefit from the repetition of content. Be careful, though, to note the differences between accounting for tangible assets compared with intangibles.

Spend proportionately longer on two key areas: the calculations to make sure that you are accurate and the financial analysis to make sure that you understand the implications of capitalizing assets compared with expensing them.

LEARNING OUTCOME STATEMENTS

Application LOS	Knowledge LOS
30a **Distinguish** between costs that are capitalized and costs that are expensed in the period in which they are incurred	30g **Describe** the revaluation model
30b **Compare** the financial reporting of the following classifications of intangible assets: purchased, internally developed, acquired in a business combination	30h **Explain** the impairment of property, plant, and equipment, and intangible assets
30c **Describe** the different depreciation methods for property, plant, and equipment, the effect of the choice of depreciation method on the financial statements, and the effects of assumptions concerning useful life and residual value on depreciation expense	30i **Explain** the de-recognition of property, plant, and equipment, and intangible assets
30d **Calculate** depreciation expense	30j **Describe** financial statement presentation of and disclosures relating to property, plant, and equipment, and intangible assets
30e **Describe** the different amortization methods for intangible assets with finite lives, the effect of the choice of amortization method on the financial statements, and the effects of assumptions concerning useful life and residual value on amortization expense	30k **Compare** the financial reporting of investment property with that of property, plant, and equipment
30f **Calculate** amortization expense	

APPLICATION LEARNING OUTCOME STATEMENTS

30a Distinguish between costs that are capitalized and costs that are expensed in the period in which they are incurred

There are two things to learn to satisfy this LOS. First, you need to know which costs can be capitalized when acquiring PPE. This is the same idea as you saw in the earlier reading on inventory. Work through Example 1 to help you understand this.

The second thing that you need to know is how to calculate the amount of borrowing costs that can be capitalized if a company has taken out a loan to fund the construction of an asset. Example 2 shows this clearly.

30b Compare the financial reporting of the following classifications of intangible assets: purchased, internally developed, acquired in a business combination

For purchased intangible assets, the same rules apply as those for PPE.

For internally generated intangible assets, the general rule is to expense any costs but read the text carefully because research and development costs are treated differently. Work Example 3, which should help you to see how these are treated under both IFRS and US GAAP.

When a company pays more than the book value for assets in a business combination, goodwill will arise. The dual effect is:

- Cash (for simplicity) goes down by the amount paid
- Assets go up by the book value of assets received
- The balancing amount is goodwill (an intangible non-current asset)

Goodwill is treated like any other intangible, but the useful life is more difficult to determine.

30c Describe the different depreciation methods for property, plant, and equipment, the effect of the choice of depreciation method on the financial statements, and the effects of assumptions concerning useful life and residual value on depreciation expense

Example 4, as you will see in the next LOS, provides a comprehensive example of how to calculate depreciation. Although this is an important skill, even more important to the analyst is the ability to read into the footnotes and determine what effects changes in depreciation policies have on a company's metrics.

It is also important for an analyst to understand what effects there are on the key metrics resulting from two companies applying different depreciation policies, and different estimates of useful life and residual value. Example 4 follows on from the calculations by illustrating what would happen to key metrics. You should read the narrative that accompanies these calculations. Do not focus on the numbers alone – the implications are just as important and exam questions may focus solely on testing your understanding of the implications.

30d Calculate depreciation expense

You need to be able to calculate depreciation using any one of three methods:

- Straight line
- Double-declining balance
- Units-of-production

Example 4 demonstrates how to do this. Work through it and learn each method so that you can apply the formula to different situations.

30e Describe the different amortization methods for intangible assets with finite lives, the effect of the choice of amortization method on the financial statements, and the effects of assumptions concerning useful life and residual value on amortization expense

Amortization is simply depreciation on intangible assets. All the principles that you learned from the LOS above apply to this one.

The key difference between tangible and intangible assets is that intangible assets tend to be classified as having indefinite lives more often than tangible assets do, in which case they would not be amortized and would instead have an annual impairment review.

30f Calculate amortization expense

Amortization is simply depreciation on intangible assets. The same methods used to calculate depreciation for tangible assets are allowed for intangible assets. The one difficulty companies might face is working out the useful life of the asset. Intangible assets can be classified as having indefinite lives, in which case they would not be amortized and would instead have an annual impairment review.

KNOWLEDGE LEARNING OUTCOME STATEMENTS

30g Describe the revaluation model

Note that the revaluation model is applicable only for companies following IFRS, so take care in the exam questions to establish whether this is the case. If it is not, US GAAP does not allow the revaluation model.

The revaluation model brings any assets revalued to current market value (or fair value) and hence is similar in principle to the "mark to market" accounting applied to some financial instruments.

You are not required to provide any calculations for this LOS, but be aware that any increase in value is not shown through the income statement; rather it goes straight to equity through the revaluation surplus. Questions on financial analysis may require you to make appropriate adjustments for revaluations and so you need to know which balances will be affected (PPE and the revaluation surplus).

30h Explain the impairment of property, plant, and equipment, and intangible assets

When an asset is no longer expected to generate the same level of economic benefits as before, the value of the asset is likely to decline. If the value declines to one that is below the balance sheet value, the asset is impaired and should be "written down."

Financial Reporting and Analysis

The dual effect for this is:

- Assets decrease
- Impairment expense increases

There are some detailed rules about how you calculate asset values under IFRS and also under US GAAP. To understand these fully it is best to take a numeric example. Example 9 in the reading provides one such example, so work through it and make sure you know the difference in treatment between IFRS and US GAAP. Read the question carefully in the exam to make sure that you are applying the correct rules.

30i Explain the de-recognition of property, plant, and equipment, and intangible assets

If assets are sold, whether they are PPE or intangible assets, the dual effect that is recorded in the accounts would be:

- Assets decrease by the carrying value
- Cash increases by the sales proceeds
- Any balancing item is either a profit (gain) or loss (expense) on disposal in the income statement

If the assets are abandoned, there will not be any sales proceeds – this will be zero and the balancing item is sure to be a loss on disposal in the income statement.

Where the sale hasn't happened by year end, but where the managers have decided to sell the asset, you will see a "held for sale asset" on the balance sheet. This classification tells an analyst that the assets will not be there in the next period to generate economic benefits.

30j Describe financial statement presentation of and disclosures relating to property, plant, and equipment, and intangible assets

The disclosure requirements for PPE and intangible assets are very detailed under IFRS. The US GAAP requirements are less onerous. Example 11 contains two exhibits (5 and 6) which show the IFRS disclosures. As you read through these, make a list of line items that are included in these footnotes.

As you read through the text in this section, also make notes about the things which would not be included for a US company. Your list should serve as a study aid when you review this section closer to the exam.

30k Compare the financial reporting of investment property with that of property, plant, and equipment

Investment property companies are ones which own property for the purpose of renting out space, or which buy and sell properties for capital gains. To this end, under IFRS, companies are allowed to mark their property values to market using a fair value option. This is a choice, so companies don't have to do this, they can also follow the standard cost model for PPE. Under the fair value option, gains and losses will affect net income because the aim of the company's trading activity is to make a profit from changes in property values.

US GAAP does not have an equivalent set of rules.

There is an illustrative set of disclosures from an IFRS company included in the readings within Example 12 if you would like to see how this looks in practice.

Reading 30 sample questions
(Answers on p. 305)

1. An asset was bought costing $25,000 with an estimated life of five years. The asset was depreciated straight line over the estimated life. Three years later the asset was sold for $15,000. What was the profit or loss on disposal?

    (A) $10,000 loss
    (B) $5,000 loss
    (C) $5,000 profit

2. Northwood Company chooses to capitalize an item of expenditure as a long-term asset that Westford Company chooses to expense. If all other things were equal, in the year of the expense Westford would most likely have a:

    (A) Higher net income and higher shareholder's equity than Northwood
    (B) Higher net income but lower shareholder's equity than Northwood
    (C) Lower net income and lower shareholder's equity than Northwood

Income taxes and the accounting thereof are complex. Vital to understanding of the accounting treatments in this area are two key facts:

1. The tax expense shown in the financial statements comprises current tax, as calculated in accordance with the tax legislation in a given jurisdiction, and also deferred taxes
2. Deferred tax calculations are the application of the matching principle which has been explained in previous readings

The fundamental concept of matching leads to the conclusion that the income tax expense shown in the income statement should be compiled on the same basis as other elements in the accounts. So, if the tax regime in a given country deviates from the accounting regime for any transaction, it may be necessary to adjust the accounts.

The LOS on this area focus on the description of the elements of and terminology involved in the calculation of deferred tax, so make sure as you go through this reading that you understand the principles involved. That said, there is also a LOS which requires calculations, so you must also spend some time on the examples provided so that you will be able to tackle numeric questions in the exam.

LEARNING OUTCOME STATEMENTS

Application LOS	Knowledge LOS
31b **Explain** how different deferred tax liabilities and assets are created and the factors that determine how a company's deferred tax liabilities and assets should be treated for the purposes of financial analysis	31a **Describe** the differences between accounting profit and taxable income, and define key terms, including deferred tax assets, deferred tax liabilities, valuation allowance, taxes payable, and income tax expense
31c **Determine** the tax base of a company's assets and liabilities	31g **Describe** the valuation allowance for deferred tax assets – when it is required and what impact it has on financial statements
31d **Calculate** income tax expense, income taxes payable, deferred tax assets, and deferred tax liabilities, and calculate and interpret the adjustment to the financial statements related to a change in the income tax rate	31i **Analyze** disclosures relating to deferred tax items and the effective tax rate reconciliation, and explain how information included in these disclosures affects a company's financial statements and financial ratios
31e **Evaluate** the impact of tax rate changes on a company's financial statements and ratios	31j **Identify** the key provisions of and differences between income tax accounting under IFRS and US GAAP
31f **Distinguish** between temporary and permanent differences in pre-tax accounting income and taxable income	
31h **Compare** a company's deferred tax items	

APPLICATION LEARNING OUTCOME STATEMENTS

31b Explain how different deferred tax liabilities and assets are created and the factors that determine how a company's deferred tax liabilities and assets should be treated for the purposes of financial analysis

Example 1 in the readings provides a comprehensive example to illustrate exactly how deferred tax assets and liabilities are created.

This LOS requires that you can show understanding of the principles of deferred tax, rather than any associated calculations. Make sure that you focus on understanding deferred tax because the exam questions could easily be weighted towards narrative and away from calculations on this area.

31c Determine the tax base of a company's assets and liabilities

Tax bases of assets and liabilities are the amounts ascribed to them for tax purposes. This helps to work out the temporary differences.

Examples 2 and 3 provide some good examples of assets and liabilities for which you might have to determine the tax base. If you learn these, you are likely to see the same things come up in any exam questions on this area.

31d Calculate income tax expense, income taxes payable, deferred tax assets, and deferred tax liabilities, and calculate and interpret the adjustment to the financial statements related to a change in the income tax rate

Example 4 checks that you can calculate the temporary differences that arise on the treatment of assets and liabilities. If you can understand the principles at play here, then you should be able to deal with most questions on the calculation of deferred tax.

The key steps are:

1. Determine whether there is a temporary difference
2. If there is, determine the amount of this difference
3. Multiply the difference by the tax rate
4. Decide whether this represents a liability (more tax in future, less tax now) or an asset (more tax now, less in the future)
5. Make the appropriate adjustments in the accounts

31e Evaluate the impact of tax rate changes on a company's financial statements and ratios

If tax rates change, you will need to apply the new rates to the temporary differences. This will change the value of the deferred tax assets and liabilities. Section 3.3 in the reading provides a numeric example which illustrates the point, but bear in mind, you are not being asked to perform calculations in this LOS.

31f Distinguish between temporary and permanent differences in pre-tax accounting income and taxable income

If you have worked Example 4 already, as advised for LOS 31d, you will have satisfied already the requirements of this section.

31h Compare a company's deferred tax items

Focus on how all of the following things affect deferred tax:

- Capital allowances for tax purposes versus depreciation
- Tax losses
- Revaluations of PPE

If you can explain how each of these things gives rise to deferred tax then you should be able to deal with the exam questions on this area. The readings give you more information on this, so read up on any of the above that you still don't fully understand.

KNOWLEDGE LEARNING OUTCOME STATEMENTS

31a Describe the differences between accounting profit and taxable income, and define key terms, including deferred tax assets, deferred tax liabilities, valuation allowance, taxes payable, and income tax expense

Make use of the glossary at the back of the CFA Institute readings to summarize the definitions of each of the terms in this LOS. As you work through the examples, you will be introduced to each of the above terms. The numeric examples will bring to life the concepts, so you should make sure that where you see these terms in the solutions to the examples, you are able to explain each one in your own words.

Before moving on to the next LOS, understand that the profit before tax shown in the financial statements is prepared on a different basis to the taxable income that companies have to calculate to determine how much income tax they pay.

31g Describe the valuation allowance for deferred tax assets – when it is required and what impact it has on financial statements

A valuation allowance exists if a company cannot utilize all of its losses against future profits. If this is increasing, it means that the company anticipates that less of the loss will be used against future profits. This is because it anticipates that future profits will fall or be non-existent.

A decreasing valuation allowance is a good sign – it means that the company is likely to be able to use the losses against future profits. This reduces the future tax bill, hence there is a deferred tax asset associated with this.

31i Analyze disclosures relating to deferred tax items and the effective tax rate reconciliation, and explain how information included in these disclosures affects a company's financial statements and financial ratios

The disclosure requirements for this area are comprehensive. The questions in the CFA Level I exam focus on trying to establish that you understand how the information included affects financial ratios, so as you read the disclosures, make sure you focus on thinking about the ratios that you have learned and how the items you see might affect them.

Bear in mind, though, that illustrative disclosures have been provided and try to make a list and remember as many of the points included in Exhibits 2, 3 and 4 as you can.

31j Identify the key provisions of and differences between income tax accounting under IFRS and US GAAP

Exhibit 5 provides a helpful summary table of all the differences between IFRS and US GAAP in this area of accounting. This table is very detailed and provides a comprehensive list of every single difference. As the differences have been included in the readings, you could be asked questions on this, but any question on this area is likely to be quite obscure. These questions are something of a lottery.

Reading 31 sample question
(Answers on p. 305)

A company has revenues that are recognized in the income statement before the income is taxed by the local tax authorities. This will create:

(A) A deferred tax asset
(B) A deferred tax liability
(C) Both a deferred tax asset and a liability

This reading covers a number of accounting topics: bonds, leases, and pensions. You will need to draw on your knowledge from the Quantitative Methods section as you work through this reading.

If you have not yet studied the readings on time value of money and calculating effective interest rates, it is advisable that you study these first. You should also focus on making sure that you learn how your calculator works so that you can save time on the calculations in the exam.

Once you are comfortable with the calculations you should focus on the accounting treatments for each area in turn. This is likely to take some time, so you may find that you spend relatively longer on this reading.

LEARNING OUTCOME STATEMENTS

Application LOS	Knowledge LOS
32a **Determine** the initial recognition, initial measurement, and subsequent measurement of bonds	32c **Discuss** the de-recognition of debt
32b **Discuss** the effective interest method and calculate interest expense amortization of bond discounts/ premiums, and interest payments	32d **Explain** the role of debt covenants in protecting creditors
32h **Determine** the initial recognition, initial measurement and subsequent measurement of finance leases	32e **Discuss** the financial statement presentation of and disclosures relating to debt
32l **Calculate** and interpret leverage and coverage ratios	32f **Discuss** the motivations for leasing assets instead of purchasing them
	32g **Distinguish** between a finance lease and an operating lease from the perspectives of the lessor and lessee
	32i **Compare** the disclosures relating to finance and operating leases
	32j **Describe** defined contribution and defined benefit pension plans
	32k **Compare** the presentation and disclosure of defined contribution and defined benefit pension plans

APPLICATION LEARNING OUTCOME STATEMENTS

32a Determine the initial recognition, initial measurement, and subsequent measurement of bonds

If you have not yet studied the Fixed Income readings, you may not be familiar with bonds. If this is the case, the first thing you should do in this section is make sure that you understand what a bond is and how bonds work.

The key things to know are:

- Bonds are a promise from one party (the borrower) to pay another party (the lender) a series of cash flows
- The borrower loans some money from the lender, which will be repaid in future at a set date (maturity date)
- In the interim, the borrower pays a series of coupon payments in cash to the lender, usually every six months or, less commonly, annually. The coupon payments are determined by applying a coupon rate to the face value of the bond
- Some bonds do not pay coupons (zero coupon bonds)
- The bond can be issued at a discount, in which case the borrower receives less than the face value in cash, or at a premium, in which case the borrower receives more than the face value in cash

You need to be comfortable with all the terminology used in the key points above and be able to apply them to practical examples. The CFA Institute reading includes two examples, Examples 1 and 2, to show how the initial accounting works. As you work through the examples, consider what the dual effects would be in the financial statements. This should help you to put the information in context and will help your financial analysis.

When the borrower receives the cash from the lender, two things will happen:

- Cash will increase by the amount received
- The borrower has an obligation to repay the cash in future and so a liability is created

Example 1 shows how to calculate the cash received. This involves doing calculations that you will have seen before as you studied Quantitative Methods. Remember to use your calculator effectively to speed up these calculations.

32b Discuss the effective interest method and calculate interest expense amortization of bond discounts/premiums, and interest payments

The effective interest rate of the bonds (or the yield to maturity) is the rate that discounts the future cash flows exactly to the selling price of the bond.

It is important to note that the effective interest rate is used to calculate the interest expense that is included in the income statement for the period. The coupon payments, although commonly referred to as the "interest" on the bond, are not reflected in the income statement. The coupon payments are the cash flows associated with the bond.

It is again useful, as you work though Examples 3 and 4 in the CFA Institute reading, to think about the dual effects of each of the different stages of accounting for bonds. These are as shown in the table below:

	Dual effect	Calculating the amount
Account for initial recognition of the bond	Cash increases Liabilities increase	Use the proceeds at issue, calculated using the time value of money function on the calculator
Account for the interest on the bond in the income statement	Liabilities increase Interest expense increases	Calculated as the opening liability owed multiplied by the effective interest rate
Reflect the coupon payments on the bond	Cash decreases Liabilities decrease	Calculated by multiplying the coupon rate by the face value of the bond

32h Determine the initial recognition, initial measurement and subsequent measurement of finance leases

There are four accounting entries for a finance (or capital) lease, shown in the table below.

	Dual effect	Calculating the amount
Capitalize the asset on the balance sheet	PPE increases Finance lease liability increases	Included at the lower of the fair value of the asset and the present value of the minimum lease payments
Depreciate the asset	PPE decreases Depreciation expense increases	Straight line depreciation over the shorter of useful life or lease term
Account for interest on the financing	Finance lease liability increases Interest expense increases	Multiply the opening finance lease liability by the effective interest rate on the lease
Account for the lease repayments	Cash decreases Finance lease liability decreases	Include the periodic lease repayment

Complete Examples 10 through 14 in the reading to test that you can apply your knowledge to numerical examples.

32l Calculate and interpret leverage and coverage ratios

At this stage in your studies you should already be able to calculate the ratios included in this section. Go straight to Exhibit 3 and review the ratios in the table; these should be familiar to you. Test whether you can put your knowledge into action by attempting Example 16.

Do not focus on the calculations; rather, concentrate on being able to provide the commentary. If you cannot comment on the ratios, it is likely that your underlying understanding is not strong enough.

KNOWLEDGE LEARNING OUTCOME STATEMENTS

32c Discuss the de-recognition of debt

At maturity, the liability on the bond will be equal to the amount to be repaid. The dual effect is to lower cash by the amount of the repayment and to extinguish the liability.

If the bond is repaid, or bought back at any period before maturity, it is likely that the liability will not be equal to the amount to be repaid and hence the dual effect will not balance. If the amount repaid is lower than the liability held on the balance sheet, an expense is recognized for the difference.

If the amount to be repaid is higher than the liability on the balance sheet, a gain is recognized for the difference.

32d Explain the role of debt covenants in protecting creditors

You will see more about debt covenants in the Fixed Income readings. In order to complete this LOS, look at Example 7 in the CFA Institute readings, which is taken from a real company's filing. It includes examples of both affirmative and negative covenants. You should be able to distinguish between these in order to satisfy this LOS.

32e Discuss the financial statement presentation of and disclosures relating to debt

Most of the information about non-current liabilities that is useful to analysts is included in the footnotes to the accounts. The disclosure requirements are detailed and so the illustration provided in the CFA Institute readings is helpful in bringing this to life. Examine Exhibit 1 and make a bullet point list of things that are disclosed to aid your review of this section.

32f Discuss the motivations for leasing assets instead of purchasing them

Learn the key advantages of leasing, which are that:

- Leases generally provide cheaper financing – lower down payments are required and interest rates tend to be lower
- There may be tax advantages
- Lessees avoid the costs of obsolescence, maintenance, and disposal
- Lease contracts may be less restrictive than loan agreements
- Certain types of lease provide off-balance sheet financing

32g Distinguish between a finance lease and an operating lease from the perspectives of the lessor and lessee

There are several "clues" that a lease should be classified as a finance (or capital) lease under IFRS. These are included in a bullet point list in Section 3.2 of the reading. Learn this list.

There is also a list of criteria under US GAAP – you must also learn these. Notice that the US treatment is more prescriptive and leaves less room for subjectivity.

32i Compare the disclosures relating to finance and operating leases

Review the table in Exhibit 2 of the readings. This table summarizes the key accounting treatments for both finance and operating leases. You should learn the contents of this table.

Pay extra attention to the entries on the statement of cash flows. Although the cash payments are simple, the classification of finance lease cash flows is not straightforward. Cash flows have to be classified between the interest element of the payment (which is then treated in the same way as regular interest) and the capital repayment element of the payment (which is treated in the same way as regular repayments of capital within CFF).

32j Describe defined contribution and defined benefit pension plans

The good news is that, at Level I, you do not need to perform any calculations on either defined contribution or defined benefit pension plans.

The key things you need to know are as follows:

- Employers who offer defined contribution plans guarantee employees that they will pay set contributions into retirement savings plans. The employees bear all the risk about the future value of these investments.
- In a defined benefit plan, the company offers employees a set retirement package and the company must invest in order to meet this obligation when the employees retire
- The company has an obligation to pay employees when they retire and so must show the liability, net of any assets set aside to meet the obligation, on the balance sheet

You should also be able to explain some of the key terminology associated with the accounting for defined benefit plans. Make sure that you can define the following terms:

- Employee's service cost for the period
- Interest expense
- Actuarial gains or losses
- Past service cost
- Expected return on plan assets

32k Compare the presentation and disclosure of defined contribution and defined benefit pension plans

Read through Example 15, noting two things:

- The amounts included for the defined contribution plans have been included in the "Employee costs" note. This is a one-line entry and has simple disclosure
- The disclosures for the defined benefit plans are more comprehensive and include explanations of both the balance sheet and income statement notes

Reading 32 sample questions
(Answers on pp. 305 and 306)

1. A company enters into a five-year lease that requires payments of $5,000/yr. If it is a capital lease, which of the following is closest to the amount recorded as debt for the lease at the end of the first year (assume interest rates of 10% p.a.)?

    (A) $15,850
    (B) $17,058
    (C) $18,954

2. A defined benefit pension scheme is underfunded. Assuming US GAAP applied, this will be shown on the balance sheet as:

    (A) An asset
    (B) A liability
    (C) Shareholder's equity

STUDY SESSION 10
FINANCIAL REPORTING AND ANALYSIS:
EVALUATING FINANCIAL REPORTING QUALITY
AND OTHER APPLICATIONS

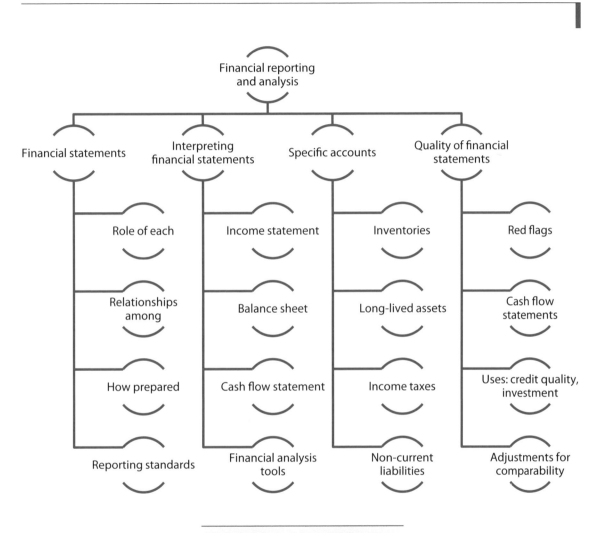

Financial reporting and analysis

Financial statements
- Role of each
- Relationships among
- How prepared
- Reporting standards

Interpreting financial statements
- Income statement
- Balance sheet
- Cash flow statement
- Financial analysis tools

Specific accounts
- Inventories
- Long-lived assets
- Income taxes
- Non-current liabilities

Quality of financial statements
- Red flags
- Cash flow statements
- Uses: credit quality, investment
- Adjustments for comparability

Topic:	Financial Reporting and Analysis
Weight:	20%
Study sessions:	7–10
Readings:	22–35

Financial Reporting and Analysis

This brief reading provides some information that analysts might find useful about the warning signs that should alert them to a higher level of risk that the financial statements might be mis-stated. There are a number of different things that an analyst can look out for, both quantitative and qualitative.

The Level I examination questions are usually very short and so you should expect that the method of testing this topic area is likely to be through questions that test your recall of the key points of each LOS. It is unlikely that you will be faced with lengthy scenarios where you have to identify warning signs.

The reading also includes examples from famous accounting frauds, which you should read if you don't have an accounting background, or if you are not familiar with these accounting frauds.

LEARNING OUTCOME STATEMENTS

Application LOS	Knowledge LOS
	33a **Describe** incentives that might induce a company's management to over report or under report earnings
	33b **Describe** activities that will result in low quality of earnings
	33c **Describe** the three conditions that are generally present when fraud occurs, including the risk factors related to these conditions
	33d **Describe** common accounting warning signs and methods for detecting each

KNOWLEDGE LEARNING OUTCOME STATEMENTS

33a Describe incentives that might induce a company's management to over report or under report earnings

Exhibits 1, 2, and 3 provide some excellent indicators that fraud or manipulation of the accounts might be present. The list is drawn from source materials that auditors use and so it is fairly comprehensive. Note that much of the list is common sense and so few of these points need to be "learned." That said, you need to read the list and satisfy yourself that you understand why each of these factors increases the risk of fraud.

33b Describe activities that will result in low quality of earnings

Learn the list of activities:

1. Selecting accounting treatments that give the "right" results, regardless of suitability
2. Using loopholes in accounting treatments to structure transactions so that the accounting fits the desired results

3. Using unrealistic estimates and assumptions
4. Stretching the definitions within accounting standards to justify dubious accounting treatment

33c Describe the three conditions that are generally present when fraud occurs, including the risk factors related to these conditions

These factors are sometimes called the fraud triangle and are:

1. Incentives or pressures exist to commit fraud
2. Opportunities exist due to poor management
3. Individuals rationalize, or justify, their behavior

33d Describe common accounting warning signs and methods for detecting each

The reading includes 15 examples of accounting warning signs and within each of these suggests calculations that the analyst can do or steps that can be taken to check whether these signs are present. Learn this list, but be aware that the questions on this section are likely to be applied. For example, a question might ask you to determine which ratio might be best to determine if operating cash flow is out of line with reported earnings and give the options.

(A) Days inventory on hand
(B) Operating cash flow/net income (correct)
(C) Current assets/Current liabilities

Reading 33 sample question
(Answers on p. 306)

Which of the following is most likely to be an example of improper revenue recognition?

(A) Bill and hold arrangements
(B) Deferred customer acquisition costs
(C) Extraordinary and non-recurring losses

This reading covers only one LOS and so is short. Don't spend a lot of time on this reading, but do make sure that you are able to explain how each of the four methods outlined in the LOS can be used by the unethical accountant to manipulate the picture regarding the cash position.

LEARNING OUTCOME STATEMENTS

Application LOS	Knowledge LOS
34 **Analyze** and describe the following ways to manipulate the cash flow statement: • Stretching out payables • Financing of payables • Securitization of receivables • Using stock buyback to offset dilution of earnings	

APPLICATION LEARNING OUTCOME STATEMENTS

34 Analyze and describe the following ways to manipulate the cash flow statement:
- Stretching out payables
- Financing of payables
- Securitization of receivables
- Using stock buyback to offset dilution of earnings

The LOS requires an understanding of how a fraudulent accountant could manipulate each of these areas in order to report a healthier cash position than actually exists.

Questions on this area could take the form of a brief description of one of these activities, followed by the requirement for you to identify which activity is taking place. Alternatively, the question could ask you which of the methods you would choose, if you had a desired outcome you were trying to achieve in the financial statements.

Reading 34 sample question
(Answers on p. 306)

Which of the following combinations would most likely be considered the business with the most sustainable cash flows?

(A) Firm A which has increasing accounts payable and an increased use of receivables securitization
(B) Firm B which has increasing accounts payable and a reduced use of receivables securitization
(C) Firm C which has decreasing accounts payable and a reduced use of receivables securitization

This reading contains a lot of contextual information which is very helpful to anyone who does not have an accounting background. The readings contain excellent examples to illustrate the points, so make the best use of them. You should start with the examples, for efficiency, as you probably know all the technical content from earlier readings. If you find that you are unsure about the basic principles as you work through these examples, read the text.

Remember that the exam questions are short. You are unlikely to be presented with a half-page of information about scenarios and then have to do lots of analysis. The questions will instead tend to focus on one area, testing that within a short scenario.

LEARNING OUTCOME STATEMENTS

Application LOS	Knowledge LOS
	35a **Evaluate** a company's past financial performance and explain how a company's strategy is reflected in past financial performance
	35b **Prepare** a basic projection of a company's future net income and cash flow
	35c **Describe** the role of financial statement analysis in assessing the credit quality of a potential debt investment
	35d **Describe** the use of financial statement analysis in screening for potential equity investments
	35e **Determmine and justify** appropriate analyst adjustments to a company's financial statements to facilitate comparison with another company

KNOWLEDGE LEARNING OUTCOME STATEMENTS

35a Evaluate a company's past financial performance and explain how a company's strategy is reflected in past financial performance

This LOS draws on all the ratio analysis that you have learned about in previous readings. The most efficient way to approach this section is to go straight into Examples 1 and 2 so that you can see how this works in a practical manner.

Bear in mind that the exam questions will be short and to-the-point, so expect brief information about a scenario on which you will base your decisions. This will simplify the questions greatly so that you are likely to be dealing with only a few ratios at any one time.

35b Prepare a basic projection of a company's future net income and cash flow

As the exam questions are multi-choice, you are unlikely to have to be able to put together a full forecast of net income and cash flow in the exam. Rather, you are likely to have to identify the best methods of putting forecasts together or to identify the best assumptions, given detailed information about a scenario.

For this reason, you should go straight to Examples 4 through 6 and be sure to make notes about the methods that are advocated in those examples. The rationale for employing certain methods is the important lesson to learn. All the technical content should be familiar to you already from the earlier readings and the ratios included in those sections.

35c Describe the role of financial statement analysis in assessing the credit quality of a potential debt investment

This LOS draws on some of the ratios that you have seen before in earlier readings. The readings provide an example of the ratios that Moody's uses to assess credit ratings in Example 7. Work through the example and check that you have retained the knowledge about the ratios.

The example is good to check that not only do you know what goes into calculating the ratios, but that you can also understand the implications of the analysis.

Example 8 tests similar knowledge and could easily be adapted into an exam-style question, although in the exam you would be given three options to choose from.

35d Describe the use of financial statement analysis in screening for potential equity investments

Screening involves the use of benchmark ratios to select stocks. It is a fairly simple process and so questions on this area are likely to be straightforward. Essentially, any stock that meets the benchmark criteria should be selected. Attempt Example 9 just to confirm that you understand some of the limitations involved in screening which are:

- Survivorship bias
- Look-ahead bias
- Data-snooping bias

35e Determine and justify appropriate analyst adjustments to a company's financial statements to facilitate comparison with another company

Key areas where the analyst will need to make adjustments are in:

- Investments
- Inventories

- PPE
- Goodwill
- Off-balance sheet financing

As you worked through the earlier readings, you will have noticed that areas where there are accounting choices would lead to inconsistencies in application between different companies. If different companies choose different methods, their accounts will not be comparable.

Although the examples given in the readings are detailed and long, they are useful for gaining an understanding of all the accounting elements covered in the earlier readings.

Reading 35 sample question
(Answers on p. 306)

Which of the following would least likely be the reason that an analyst would adjust a company's financial statement when comparing two companies' accounts? The companies:

(A) Operate in different sectors
(B) Have chosen different accounting policies
(C) Report their financial statements under different accounting rules

STUDY SESSION 11
CORPORATE FINANCE

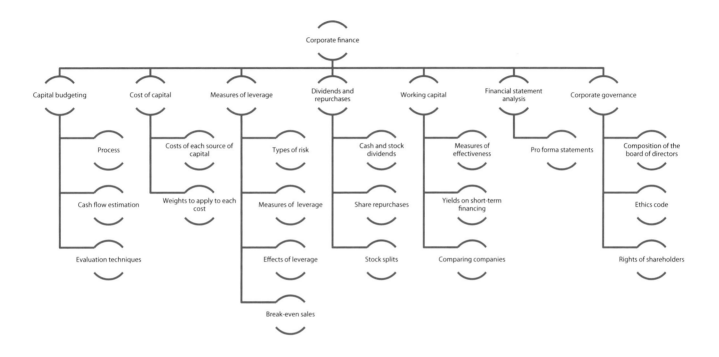

Topic:	Corporate Finance
Weight:	8%
Study sessions:	11
Readings:	36–41

THE BIG PICTURE

The Corporate Finance coverage is, basically, what you learn in a finance management course. The attention of the readings is on capital budgeting, cost of capital, leverage, dividends and repurchases, working capital, financial planning (that is, pro forma statements), and corporate governance. The corporate finance topic covers a lot of ground, with a diverse set of topics. With the exception of the corporate governance, you need to be able to both describe and calculate.

Though this is a lot of ground to cover, keep in mind throughout how all these financial management decisions affect what analysts and investors see in terms of financial statements and share value:

- How do capital budgeting decisions affect a company's value?
- What is the cost of capital and how does this interact with the company's capital structure and investment decisions?
- What is a company's business risk and financial risk? How do we measure these?
- Do dividends, stock repurchases, or stock splits matter? What is the relevance for the investor?
- How effective is a company in managing its working capital? How costly is its short-term borrowing? How does the company compare with its competitors?
- What is important to owners in a company's governance system?

Therefore, as you go through the readings, remember the perspectives of the financial analyst and the investor, and how the financial management decisions a company makes affect its value.

This reading recaps some of the basic quantitative methods you saw earlier on in your studies. The calculations of NPV and IRR that you learned in the Quantitative Methods section will be required in this section. However, whereas in the Quantitative Methods section you focused on the math and inputting the numbers into your calculator correctly, here you will be tested on your understanding of the underlying principles behind the calculations.

As you work through this section, it is advisable to keep asking yourself whether you fully understand why you are doing whatever it is you have to do in the calculations. A key requirement of this section is that you should be able to apply what you learn to the work done by analysts and so you should be able to identify problems that analysts face, as well as knowing the pure theory.

LEARNING OUTCOME STATEMENTS

Application LOS	Knowledge LOS
36d **Calculate** and interpret the results using each of the following methods to evaluate a single capital project: net present value (NPV), internal rate of return (IRR), payback period, discounted payback period, and profitability index (PI)	36a **Describe** the capital budgeting process, including the typical steps of the process, and distinguish among the various categories of capital projects
	36b **Describe** the basic principles of capital budgeting, including cash flow estimation
	36c **Explain** how the evaluation and selection of capital projects is affected by mutually exclusive projects, project sequencing, and capital rationing
	36e **Explain** the NPV profile, compare the NPV and IRR methods when evaluating independent and mutually exclusive projects, and describe the problems associated with each of the evaluation methods
	36f **Describe** and account for the relative popularity of the various capital budgeting methods and explain the reaction between NPV and company value and stock price
	36g **Describe** the expected relations among an investment's NPV, company value and share price

APPLICATION LEARNING OUTCOME STATEMENTS

36d Calculate and interpret the results using each of the following methods to evaluate a single capital project: net present value (NPV), internal rate of return (IRR), payback period, discounted payback period, and profitability index (PI)

You should already be able to do two of the calculations required by this LOS (NPV and IRR), so some of this section is a repeat of the Quantitative Methods reading.

However, there are more calculations to add into the mix and so you also need to make sure that you can calculate:

- Payback and discounted payback period – use Example 1 to test your calculation of NPV as well as your understanding of the payback period
- Profitability index – use Example 2 to confirm that you can calculate the PI

Bear in mind that although the LOS does not include Average Accounting Rate of Return as a required calculation, there is a numerical example of this other method of calculating returns and so you should have a look at this in Section 4.5.

KNOWLEDGE LEARNING OUTCOME STATEMENTS

36a Describe the capital budgeting process, including the typical steps of the process, and distinguish among the various categories of capital projects

Learn the capital budgeting process, which is summarized as:

1. Generating ideas
2. Analyzing individual proposals
3. Planning the capital budget
4. Monitoring and post-auditing

Also, you should be able to provide one-sentence summaries of the following types of capital budgeting projects:

- Replacement projects
- Expansion projects
- New product and services
- Regulatory projects
- "Pet" projects

36b Describe the basic principles of capital budgeting, including cash flow estimation

The basic principles will become second-nature the more calculations you do, but the key rules are:

- Base decisions on cash flows, not accounting profits
- Timing of the cash flows is crucial
- Base cash flows on opportunity costs
- Use after-tax cash flows
- Ignore financing costs

Learn each of these rules.

You should be able to explain each of the following terms and also explain why they are important, or how they affect the capital budgeting process and any associated calculations:

- Sunk cost
- Opportunity cost
- Incremental cash flow
- Externalities
- Conventional cash flow pattern
- Independent projects

Make notes as you read through these sections that explain, in your own words, what is meant by each of these terms.

36c Explain how the evaluation and selection of capital projects is affected by mutually exclusive projects, project sequencing, and capital rationing

As with the previous LOS, you should be able to explain each of the following terms and also explain why they are important, or how they affect, the capital budgeting process and any associated calculations:

- Mutually exclusive projects
- Independent projects
- Project sequencing
- Capital rationing

Once again, a tip to keep your study efficient and effective is to make sure that you can put these concepts into your own words. Write down what the term means, but also try to add some context. What would an analyst have to consider in each of these situations.

36e Explain the NPV profile, compare the NPV and IRR methods when evaluating independent and mutually exclusive projects, and describe the problems associated with each of the evaluation methods

The NPV profile is the graph of the project NPVs at various discount rates. There is an example in the CFA Institute readings in Example 3. Review this and note that where the NPV=0, the discount rate is 20%, which is also the IRR of the project.

Note that problems occur when the situation is not quite as simple as shown in Example 3. NPV and IRR analysis may lead to conflicting conclusions about a project. For example, NPV could be positive and yet IRR could be under the required rate of return for the company. The key rule is that for mutually exclusive projects, you should choose based on NPV. However, read through Section 4.8 so that you can fully appreciate the problems that you might see.

Other problems include projects that have either multiple or no IRRs. For the Level I exam, you just need to be aware that this could be a problem. No calculations are required.

36f Describe and account for the relative popularity of the various capital budgeting methods and explain the reaction between NPV and company value and stock price

Studies show that while NPV and IRR are widely used, especially by those with business degrees, the other methods are also very popular, especially in Europe. NPV is most closely related to stock prices.

36g Describe the expected relations among an investment's NPV, company value and share price

If a project has a positive NPV, it will be possible to calculate how much additional shareholder value is created. This can then be divided up between all the shares to work out an incremental additional value per share for the new project.

Work through Example 6 to confirm that you can do this calculation accurately before moving on to the Practice Problems.

Reading 36 sample questions
(Answers on p. 306)

FSC Inc is considering investing in a project requiring an initial cash outlay of $10m. The project is expected to generate the following cash flows:

Year 1: –$0.7m
Year 2: $2.8m
Year 3: $6.3m

The internal rate of return (IRR) of the project is closest to:

(A) –5.97%
(B) 5.97%
(C) 11%

This reading covers a lot of essential basic calculations that you will need to work through slowly. To this end you will need to spend relatively longer on this section than on the other readings in this Study Session.

Although there are many calculations to learn and to remember, the calculations themselves are relatively simple and straightforward.

As well as being able to do the calculations, a good portion of the questions are likely to focus on your understanding of the theory that goes into each of the calculations. So, as you work through the calculations, make sure that you are not simply learning and regurgitating the method without understanding it. It's important that you understand why you are doing what you are doing, because the questions could be narrative questions that test this knowledge.

LEARNING OUTCOME STATEMENTS

Application LOS	Knowledge LOS
37a **Calculate** and interpret the weighted average cost of capital (WACC) of a company	37b **Describe** how taxes affect the cost of capital from different capital sources
37f **Calculate** and interpret the cost of fixed rate debt capital using the yield-to-maturity approach and the debt-rating approach	37c **Explain** alternative methods of calculating the weights used in the WACC, including the use of the company's target capital structure
37g **Calculate** and interpret the cost of non-callable, non-convertible preferred stock	37d **Explain** how the marginal cost of capital and the investment opportunity schedule are used to determine the optimal capital budget
37h **Calculate** and interpret the cost of equity capital using the capital asset pricing model approach, the dividend discount model approach, and the bond-yield plus risk-premium approach	37e **Explain** the marginal cost of capital's role in determining the net present value of a project
37i **Calculate** and interpret the beta and the cost of capital for a project	37j **Explain** the country equity risk premium in the estimation of the cost of equity for a company located in a developing market
	37k **Describe** the marginal cost of capital schedule, explain why it may be upward-sloping with respect to additional capital, and calculate and interpret its break-points
	37l **Explain** and demonstrate the correct treatment of flotation costs

APPLICATION LEARNING OUTCOME STATEMENTS

37a Calculate and interpret the weighted average cost of capital (WACC) of a company

Draw on your knowledge of how to calculate a simple weighted average from the Quantitative Methods section for this LOS. You will need to be able to calculate weighted average costs of debt, equity and preferred stocks.

37f Calculate and interpret the cost of fixed rate debt capital using the yield-to-maturity approach and the debt-rating approach

The first method used to calculate the cost of debt is the yield-to-maturity approach that you have seen before in the Quantitative Methods and Fixed Income readings. If you have not studied this yet, it is advisable that you do so now because you will need to understand the principles behind the calculation in order to calculate the cost of debt.

Where the company has no reliable market price for its current debt, it might be necessary for an analyst to guess a comparable rate of interest on comparable companies' bonds with comparable maturity dates. This is called the debt-rating approach.

37g Calculate and interpret the cost of non-callable, non-convertible preferred stock

You have seen the basic principles at play in this calculation when pricing non-convertible preferred stocks in the Quantitative Methods section. If you rearrange this formula, you will be able to calculate the discount rate if you are given all other relevant information.

37h Calculate and interpret the cost of equity capital using the capital asset pricing model approach, the dividend discount model approach, and the bond-yield plus risk-premium approach

There are three methods for calculating the cost of equity:

1. Capital Asset Pricing Model
2. Dividend Discount Model
3. Bond-Yield plus Risk Premium

The Capital Asset Pricing Model approach reflects the fact that equity holders take on more risk than debt holders and therefore should require more return for their investment. The cost of equity is calculated by adding on a premium for the riskiness of the company's stocks.

Starting with the risk-free rate, a premium is then added on to reflect that equities are more risky than corporate bonds by calculating how much more risky the equity market is than the government bond market. Not every company is equally risky though, and so this premium is then fine-tuned by multiplying by a "riskiness factor" for the company's own stock, called the beta.

Using Gordon's Growth Model that you have seen previously, you can see that the rate used to discount the cash flows will be the company's cost of equity. You will need to review the formulae in Section 3.3.2 to make sure that the rearrangement makes sense to you and that you would be able to deal with simple numerical questions on this.

The last, and most simple, method for the purposes of the exam is simply to take the bond yield and add on a risk premium for equities. You are unlikely to have to calculate the risk premium for a given stock in the exam and so you only need to be able to add on the premium given to the bond yield.

37i Calculate and interpret the beta and the cost of capital for a project

In simple terms, beta is calculated by regressing the returns of a company's stocks against the market returns.

There are several things to consider:

- The time period for the regression
- Whether this is done daily, weekly or monthly
- Which market index to use
- Whether to adjust beta to reflect the regression to the mean of 1
- Small companies' betas may need to be adjusted

When calculating the beta for a private company, it is not possible to use a regression of the company's stock price because there isn't one. In this case, it is necessary to use comparable company analysis to infer a beta for the company using a beta from a similar company.

One problem with doing this is that the company that is used for the comparison is unlikely to have the same capital structure as the subject company. Because of this, the beta calculation should be adjusted to reflect the capital structure of the subject company. This process is known as the pure-play method and is shown in the calculations in Section 4.1. Read this section slowly and work through each step of the calculation so that you understand the steps involved.

Once you have done this, work Examples 9, 10, and 11, which will confirm your understanding and bring all the information together.

Knowledge learning outcome statements

37b Describe how taxes affect the cost of capital from different capital sources

The key fact to remember is that the finance cost of debt is always tax deductible, whereas dividend payments on common and preferred stock are not. For this reason, we use pre-tax costs for common and preferred stock and after-tax costs for the cost of debt.

37c Explain alternative methods of calculating the weights used in the WACC, including the use of the company's target capital structure

When you are working through the questions on this section, you should be looking for clues about how to work out the different proportions of debt and equity for the weighted average calculation.

In the first instance, you should be looking for the company's target capital structure. Analysts might not know this target though and so, in this case, they will have to adopt one of three methods:

- Assuming the current capital structure is the target
- Examine trends in the recent capital structure and infer a reasonable structure
- Use averages of comparable companies' structures

37d Explain how the marginal cost of capital and the investment opportunity schedule are used to determine the optimal capital budget

As a company takes on more and more projects, new opportunities will gradually decrease. As a company takes on more and more financing, it will become more expensive.

Use Figure 1 as a guide to see that the optimal capital budget is set where these two curves intersect.

37e Explain the marginal cost of capital's role in determining the net present value of a project

The MCC is the same as the WACC. You have seen before that the WACC is used in NPV calculations as the discount factor used to discount the cash flows back to their present value.

Bear in mind that as a company takes on new, and different, projects the WACC is likely to have to be adjusted to reflect the different levels of risk that the company is exposed to.

37j Explain the country equity risk premium in the estimation of the cost of equity for a company located in a developing market

Stock betas do not adequately capture country risk for companies located in developing markets. For this reason, it is necessary to add a country risk premium to the cost of equity.

One way of doing this is to add on the sovereign yield spread, which is the difference in yields between developed and developing nations. The other method is to enhance this calculation by adding in an additional spread to reflect the volatility of the equity market in the developing country relative to the sovereign bond market therein.

Work through Example 12 to see how this calculation is done.

Corporate Finance

37k Describe the marginal cost of capital schedule, explain why it may be upward-sloping with respect to additional capital, and calculate and interpret its break-points

As a company raises additional capital, the cost of such capital is likely to rise because the new providers of capital are exposed to more risk than the original providers of capital. Additional risk to the providers will be compensated for with additional returns to them, and hence the costs to the company will rise.

Figure 2 shows that these costs increase in a stepped manner. Review Table 3 and the numerical example that shows how debt break-points work, then work Example 13 which will test that you have understood the knowledge.

37l Explain and demonstrate the correct treatment of flotation costs

Flotation costs are the costs incurred by the company for investment bankers to help them raise capital. Flotation costs should be deducted as part of the net present value calculation by showing the expenses as a relevant cash outflow.

The only problem with this is that it can sometimes be difficult to estimate these costs.

Reading 37 sample questions
(Answers on p. 307)

1. Diddy Inc. currently pays a dividend of $1.50, which is expected to grow at 7%. If the current value of the shares, based on Gordon's Growth Model, is $25, which of the following is closest to the required rate of return?

(A) 10.42%
(B) 11.42%
(C) 13.42%

2. Given a beta of 1.4, a risk-free rate of 5.5%, and assuming a 10% market risk premium, the expected rate of return for this stock is closest to:

(A) 7.7%
(B) 11.8%
(C) 19.5%

This reading includes a number of calculations that analysts perform in order to establish the degree of risk that a company faces. By making some simple calculations, an analyst can compare peer companies' level of operating and financial risk. He or she can also compare how a company's risk profile changes over time.

For this reason, it is important not just to learn how to calculate these risks, but to understand how the results of the calculations would be interpreted in practice.

The best way to test whether you are able to interpret calculations is to try to write down, in one or two short sentences, the reasons why these calculations are important. If you find that you cannot do this, you need to revisit the text until you have a clearer idea about this.

LEARNING OUTCOME STATEMENTS

Application LOS	Knowledge LOS
38b **Calculate** and interpret the degree of operating leverage, the degree of financial leverage, and the degree of total leverage	38a **Define** and explain leverage, business risk, sales risk, operating risk, and financial risk and classify a risk, given a description
38d **Calculate** the breakeven quantity of sales and determine the company's net income at various sales levels	38c **Describe** the effect of financial leverage on a company's net income and return on equity
38e **Calculate** and interpret the operating breakeven quantity of sales	

APPLICATION LEARNING OUTCOME STATEMENTS

38b Calculate and interpret the degree of operating leverage, the degree of financial leverage, and the degree of total leverage

There are three calculations to learn:

1. Degree of operating leverage shows the proportion of a company's costs that are fixed. The more fixed costs a company has, the less flexible it is (fixed costs are harder to cut than variable costs are). The lower the proportion of fixed costs, the less operating risk a company has. The calculation provides us with an idea about how sensitive operating income is to changes in revenue.
2. Degree of financial leverage shows the effect of fixed financial costs on net income by calculating how sensitive net income is to a change in operating income. The greater the impact of fixed financial costs, the bigger impact there will be on net income, which is risky for the company.
3. Total leverage combines both operating leverage and financial leverage by analyzing the change in net income, given a specific change in units of the product the company sells.

38d Calculate the breakeven quantity of sales and determine the company's net income at various sales levels

Example 5 shows this calculation, which requires the application of the formula for the breakeven point.

This formula basically states that when revenue = all your costs, a company will break even. The complexity comes when the different type of costs are included. Fixed operating and financial costs do not vary with revenue, but variable costs do.

38e Calculate and interpret the operating breakeven quantity of sales

This LOS draws on the same information as the previous one. If you fully understand the equation for breakeven, then these calculations will not pose a problem. The key application will be that you will have to rearrange the formula to find revenue, rather than net income.

KNOWLEDGE LEARNING OUTCOME STATEMENTS

38a Define and explain leverage, business risk, sales risk, operating risk, and financial risk and classify a risk, given a description

This LOS is reasonably simple because it requires learning of risks. As you read through the section, do so actively. Compile a one-sentence definition of each of the types of risk so that you are able to correctly identify the risks, given definitions.

The questions will probably test your understanding by providing you with practical examples of a risk and asking you to classify it, so be prepared for this.

38c Describe the effect of financial leverage on a company's net income and return on equity

This LOS requires you to apply your knowledge about how to calculate the financial leverage and show that you understand what this means for the company. In order to test that you can do this, make sure that you could explain clearly why an analyst might calculate financial leverage. What are they looking for? How might they use this analysis to evaluate risk?

Reading 38 sample question
(Answers on p. 307)

A firm produces mops at a variable cost of $6 per mop. If the firm has fixed operating costs of $2m and sells the mops for $10 each, the operating breakeven point is closest to:

(A) 200,000 units
(B) 500,000 units
(C) 1,000,000 units

This reading covers some of the basics about how dividends "work" from a practical standpoint. In this section, you will learn about the reasons companies pay dividends, how share repurchases work and the payment methodology, among other things.

As this reading is quite practical, it is important that as you read through the text, you make notes about the processes involved so that you are actively learning as you read. If you do this, rather than simply read the text, then the likelihood that you will remember the content when you come back to study this section again nearer to the exam will increase.

LEARNING OUTCOME STATEMENTS

Application LOS	Knowledge LOS
39d **Calculate** and compare the effects of a share repurchase on earnings per share when 1) the repurchase is financed with a company's excess cash and 2) the company uses funded debt to finance the repurchase	39a **Describe** regular cash dividends, extra dividends, stock dividends, stock splits, and reverse stock splits, including their expected effect on a shareholder's wealth and a company's financial ratios
39e **Calculate** the effect of a share repurchase on book value per share	39b **Describe** dividend payment chronology, including the significance of declaration, holder-of-record, ex-dividend, and payment dates
39f **Explain** why a cash dividend and a share repurchase of the same amount are equivalent in terms of the effect on shareholder's wealth, all else being equal	39c **Compare** share repurchase methods

APPLICATION LEARNING OUTCOME STATEMENTS

39d Calculate and compare the effects of a share repurchase on earnings per share when 1) the repurchase is financed with a company's excess cash and 2) the company uses funded debt to finance the repurchase

A share repurchase could increase, decrease or have no effect on earnings per share. You need to be able to work the calculations on this LOS and so it is advisable that you work through Examples 6 (excess cash) and 7 (debt finance). Make sure that you learn the methods so that you can apply it to other calculations.

39e Calculate the effect of a share repurchase on book value per share

This LOS is reasonably straightforward. You need to be able to calculate the impact on book value per share as shown in Example 8. Make sure that you make a note of the method used in the example so that you can apply it to other scenarios.

39f Explain why a cash dividend and a share repurchase of the same amount are equivalent in terms of the effect on shareholder's wealth, all else being equal

Example 9 provides a numerical calculation to prove this LOS. Work through the calculation because it does help to understand the point about the equivalency of cash dividends and share repurchases.

You will also see an example of a share repurchase that transfers wealth. Although this is not specifically referred to in the LOS, do read through the numerical example because this information is not optional.

KNOWLEDGE LEARNING OUTCOME STATEMENTS

39a Describe regular cash dividends, extra dividends, stock dividends, stock splits, and reverse stock splits, including their expected effect on a shareholder's wealth and a company's financial ratios

A lot of this LOS involves reading and remembering facts from the text. There are no calculations and so it is important to keep your reading active.

As you work through all the definitions, fill out a table to make sure you are picking up the key points in order to answer the exam questions.

The table should look like this:

	What are they?	**How do they affect shareholder's wealth**	**How do they affect the company's financial ratios**
Example content			
Regular cash dividends	A quarterly or semi-annual cash payment to shareholders	Constant or growing dividends signal stability to investors. Good for investors who need regular income	They reduce equity and so will affect any ratio including average or absolute equity

39b Describe dividend payment chronology, including the significance of declaration, holder-of-record, ex-dividend, and payment dates

As the LOS suggests, there are four key dates associated with dividends and the payment thereof. You need to be able to explain what happens on each of these dates. If you can do this, there should be no need to learn the order in which each one happens; you should be able to use logic to work it out. However, if you have a good memory, it could save you time to also learn the order of payments.

Key dates that you need to explain are:

- Declaration date
- Ex-dividend date
- Holder-of-record date
- Payment date

Attempt Examples 3 and 4, which will test whether you have successfully understood all the key terms on this section.

39c Compare share repurchase methods

There are four main methods that you need to learn:

- Buying shares in the open market
- Buying back a fixed number of shares at a fixed price
- Dutch auction
- Repurchase at a negotiated price

Try Example 5 to test your understanding of these methods.

Reading 39 sample question
(Answers on p. 308)

Prior to a share repurchase, a company's book value per share (BVPS) exceeds its market price per share. After the share repurchase, the company's BVPS is most likely to:

(A) Increase
(B) Decrease
(C) Remain the same

Much of this reading will already be familiar to you from the financial statement analysis part of the readings. The notion of working capital, and most of the associated calculations, have already been introduced and you should know these. In this section, the materials focus on how you would appraise one company relative to another to determine whether management are running the company efficiently.

Once you know how to calculate the relevant metric, you already have an understanding of what goes into that calculation. This means that the implications and conclusions that you need to draw should come easily. For that reason, don't dwell too long on the calculations. Instead, make sure you note carefully the analysis that you haven't seen before and commit new lists of information to memory.

LEARNING OUTCOME STATEMENTS

Application LOS	Knowledge LOS
40b **Compare** a company's liquidity measures with those of peer companies	40a **Describe** primary and secondary sources of liquidity and factors that affect a company's liquidity position
40c **Evaluate** working capital effectiveness of a company based on its operating and cash conversion cycles, and compare the company's effectiveness with that of peer companies	40d **Explain** the effect of different types of cash flows on a company's net daily cash position
40e **Calculate** and interpret comparable yields on various securities, compare portfolio returns against a standard benchmark, and evaluate a company's short-term investment policy guidelines	40g **Evaluate** the choices of short-term funding available to a company and recommend a financing method
40f **Evaluate** a company's management of accounts receivable, inventory, and accounts payable over time and compared to peer companies	

APPLICATION LEARNING OUTCOME STATEMENTS

40b Compare a company's liquidity measures with those of peer companies

You have seen some of the liquidity measures included in this LOS in earlier sections on financial statement analysis. The ratios and calculations that you should be able to do are as follows:

* Current ratio
* Quick ratio
* Accounts receivable turnover

- Inventory turnover
- Number of days of receivables
- Number of days of inventory
- Number of days of payables
- Operating cycle
- Net operating cycle

You should know from your earlier studies how these ratios and calculations can help an analyst to evaluate the cash position of a company, and whether it is improving or not.

Using the same principles learned before, you can then compare the calculations from two peer companies to determine which has better cash management. If you feel comfortable with this from your earlier studies, move straight on to the next section. If you are a little rusty, review the formulae in this section before practicing the questions.

40c Evaluate working capital effectiveness of a company based on its operating and cash conversion cycles, and compare the company's effectiveness with that of peer companies

The net operating cycle (receivables days + inventory days − payables days) was first introduced in the financial statement analysis section of your studies. This is repeated here. An operating cycle works on similar principles but only includes receivables and inventory, not payables.

The quicker a company turns its assets into cash, the less time it will need financing (if at all) and so the shorter this period, usually the better.

40e Calculate and interpret comparable yields on various securities, compare portfolio returns against a standard benchmark, and evaluate a company's short-term investment policy guidelines

The information in this section should be read in conjunction with the fixed income sections. There is a lot of information in this section that you will have seen already when you learned about the types of fixed income investments. There is also some new information and you should spend a relatively high proportion of your time on this section.

Exhibit 7 provides an excellent summary of the different type of investments. Test your own knowledge about these investments by covering up the table and trying to fill in the detail yourself. You should be able to fill in at least 50% of this table based on the information you learned in the fixed income readings.

As some of this information requires you to apply the knowledge you used in the fixed income section, this exercise would be a good test of whether you have been able not only to learn the information, but also to apply it to different, unexpected, scenarios.

Once again, there are calculations included in this LOS that have been covered elsewhere (both in the Quantitative Methods readings and the Fixed Income readings). The calculations included here that you should know already are:

- Money market yield
- Bond equivalent yield
- Discount-basis yield

You need to be able to explain different strategies that managers use for investment, both passive and active.

Be able to explain each of the following methods:

- Passive strategy
- Matching strategy
- Mismatching strategy
- Laddering strategy

40f Evaluate a company's management of accounts receivable, inventory, and accounts payable over time and compared to peer companies

There is a lot of material in the CFA Institute readings about the management of each of these areas of working capital. The readings give some excellent context about working capital management as well as some practical information about how companies carry out these management techniques in real life.

As you read through this section, use the list below as a checklist of items that you need to understand. If you cannot explain any of the terms below in simple language, go back to the text and re-read until you can do so.

The key terms to explain are:

- Credit management policies
- Credit accounts
- Credit terms (including some examples)
- Credit scoring model
- Float factors
- Accounts receivable aging schedule
- Economic order quantity
- Just in time
- The three motives for holding inventories
- The four costs of holding inventories
- The cost of trade credit

Knowledge learning outcome statements

40a Describe primary and secondary sources of liquidity and factors that affect a company's liquidity position

Learn the list of primary sources of liquidity, which are those that do not tend to affect the company's operations:

- The company's cash balances
- Short-term funds (e.g. lines of credit)
- Cash flow management

Also be able to distinguish the secondary sources of liquidity:

- Negotiating debt contracts
- Liquidating assets
- Filing for bankruptcy

This section also requires you to learn the drags and pulls on liquidity, which are:

Drags on liquidity	Pulls on liquidity
Uncollected receivables	Making payments early
Obsolete inventory	Reduced credit limits
Tight credit	Limits on short-term lines of credit
	Low liquidity positions

Make sure that you can explain each of the above – make notes and be able to put all of these terms into your own words to test that you fully understand how these things affect the company's working capital position.

40d Explain the effect of different types of cash flows on a company's net daily cash position

Exhibit 6 provides a useful summary of the different time horizons that cash managers use within a business to manage the short- and long-term cash positions.

For more information about what companies' cash managers or treasury teams do each day, read Section 3.2 Monitoring cash uses and levels.

40g Evaluate the choices of short-term funding available to a company and recommend a financing method

Exhibit 15 summarizes the major short-term sources of financing instruments. You may be familiar with some of these instruments from the fixed income section of your studies, but review the table and make sure that you learn the key facts about each source.

Work through Example 7, which is designed to test that you are able to measure the cost of borrowing.

Reading 40 sample question
(Answers on p. 308)

MCD Inc. has a current ratio of 5.0 times and a quick ratio of 3.0 times. If the company's current liabilities are $200m, the inventory is closest to:

(A) 200
(B) 400
(C) 800

This reading is highly narrative. There are no calculations to do and no equations to learn. This means that to be efficient in your learning, you need to have a clear study plan for this section.

Approach the reading actively. Take a pen and some paper and make sure that you follow the advice below about how to do this. The more you can make notes and summarize the information concisely, the fewer times you will have to return to this section to re-read everything.

LEARNING OUTCOME STATEMENTS

Application LOS	Knowledge LOS
41b **Describe** practices related to board and committee independence, experience, compensation, external consultants, and frequency of elections, and determine whether they are supportive of shareowner protection	41a **Define** corporate governance
	41c **Describe** board independence and explain the importance of independent board members in corporate governance
	41d **Identify** factors that an analyst should consider when evaluating the qualifications of board members
	41e **Describe** the responsibilities of the audit, compensation, and nominations committees and identify factors an investor should consider when evaluating the quality of each committee
	41f **Explain** the provisions that should be included in a strong corporate code of ethics
	41g **Evaluate**, from a shareowner's perspective, company policies related to voting rules, shareowner-sponsored proposals, common stock classes, and takeover defenses

APPLICATION LEARNING OUTCOME STATEMENTS

41b Describe practices related to board and committee independence, experience, compensation, external consultants, and frequency of elections, and determine whether they are supportive of shareowner protection

The CFA Institute reading provides a summary of "rules" for good corporate governance throughout this section. They are included in bold, italicized text and really need to be learned. You cannot take a broad view of these rules, as the exam questions are likely to test the specific detail included within each one.

As you work through the rules, highlight the key facts, dates, frequencies, etc. You could make a one-page summary document for easy reference when you come back to study this section, or when you are practicing mock exams on this topic.

KNOWLEDGE LEARNING OUTCOME STATEMENTS

41a Define corporate governance

There are a number of different definitions of the very broad term "corporate governance" so be sure to make notes about the CFA Institute's chosen definition. Summarize the definition into a few key points so that you would recognize these things in a multi-choice scenario.

41c Describe board independence and explain the importance of independent board members in corporate governance

Put simply, board independence exists where the board are not biased. If the corporate governance rules outlined in the previous LOS are followed, then a company is likely to have an independent board. If not, then the independence of the board is probably compromised.

This is likely to increase the level of business, operating or financial risk within a company and a good analyst would have to use the results of investigations to determine what effect this might have on his or her calculations.

41d Identify factors that an analyst should consider when evaluating the qualifications of board members

There is a list of the relevant factors on page 244 which should be learned. Most of this is common sense but be sure to take note of the details in case the questions are particular about the details.

41e Describe the responsibilities of the audit, compensation, and nominations committees and identify factors an investor should consider when evaluating the quality of each committee

It is difficult to compile lists of governance requirements that are the same all around the world, and for this reason, there are specific country requirements included in these readings.

Because these are not "optional" sections, you should take note of the differences between countries. It's unlikely that the exam questions will go into too much specific detail about the different country requirements but the additional information can add color about the form and function of the board committees.

Once again, there is a long list of facts to learn on this section; be active in your reading so that you have helpful condensed notes to study from.

Corporate Finance

41f Explain the provisions that should be included in a strong corporate code of ethics

Review the section on management that starts on page 255. The section includes two main areas for study: the implementation of the code of ethics and also corporate transparency. Both of these sections include information that will help answer questions from this LOS.

41g Evaluate, from a shareowner's perspective, company policies related to voting rules, shareowner-sponsored proposals, common stock classes, and takeover defenses

This section is very heavy on detail and contains a lot of rules about good governance in the areas outlined above. Once again, this is a lot of learning points with few opportunities to practice questions in the manual.

A good approach to this section would be, once again, to make detailed notes and then to move straight in to practical question practice to make sure that you can answer the questions correctly.

To study efficiently, make sure that you have made summary notes that you can then refer to as you do your initial question practice. Near the time of the exam, you should be able to attempt the questions without your notes and score at least 70% in each test that you do.

Reading 41 sample question
(Answers on p. 308)

If the chief executive officer is also the chairman of the board, the independent board members should:

(A) Have a lead member
(B) Meet only with non-executive members
(C) Meet only when both executive and non-executive members are present

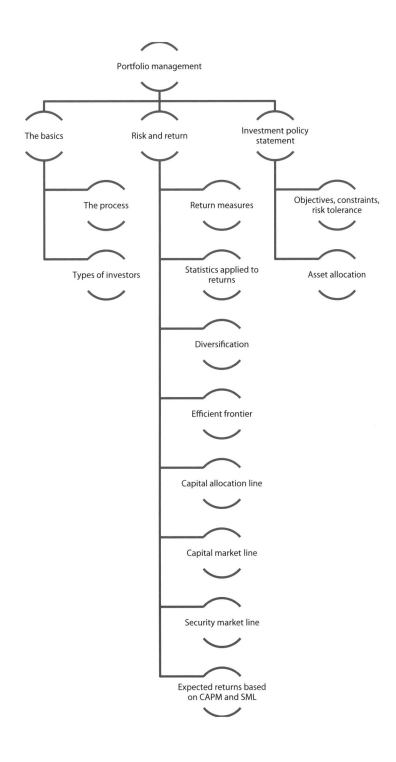

Portfolio management

The basics

Risk and return

Investment policy statement

The process

Return measures

Objectives, constraints, risk tolerance

Types of investors

Statistics applied to returns

Asset allocation

Diversification

Efficient frontier

Capital allocation line

Capital market line

Security market line

Expected returns based on CAPM and SML

Topic:	Portfolio Management
Weight:	5%
Study sessions:	12
Readings:	42–45

The big picture

The weight assigned to portfolio management, 5%, may appear relatively small, especially after you have covered the tools topics (Corporate Finance, Economics, Financial Reporting and Analysis, and Quantitative Methods), but this subject is essential for understanding the different asset classes in the study sessions that follow. Portfolio Management as a topic expands to be up to 15% of the Level II exam, and up to 55% of Level III. Therefore, mastering this topic is worth the investment of your time.

Portfolio management, planning, and construction

Investment decisions are typically made in the context of a portfolio, and the selection of investments for a portfolio is made considering the client's objectives, constraints, and risk tolerance. The selection includes not only the choice of asset classes, but of the specific assets within a class. An important element of managing a portfolio is the development of the investment policy statement, which is translating the client's objectives, constraints, and risk tolerance into the policy statement.

Risk and return

The development of the concepts of risk and return in these readings begins with the basic statistics applied to historical returns, and then progresses to encompass the concept of diversification from investing in assets whose returns are not perfectly, positively correlated. Though historical return information is useful in giving us a ballpark idea of returns and how they relate to one another, we are most interested in expected returns and risk when we make portfolio decisions. Therefore, portfolio theory focuses on expected returns and risk.

The next step in this development is to look at what happens when we form all possible portfolios, and what emerges is the efficient frontier – the set of portfolios that are superior (in terms of expected return and risk) to all other portfolios.

The capital asset pricing model (CAPM) picks up from the efficient frontier, combining the efficient frontier with borrowing and lending (that is, investing in a risk-free asset), and you end up with the set of portfolios that comprise the capital allocation line (CAL). If you then introduce the idea of market portfolio consisting of all investable risky assets (that is, the market portfolio), the capital allocation line becomes the capital market line (CML).

Expected returns on assets, according to the CAPM, are related to beta, which is a measure of the sensitivity of the return on an asset to changes in the return on the market portfolio (i.e. an elasticity measure). When we compare expected returns with beta, we arrive at the security market line (SML). Keep in mind that the CAPM describes the relation between expected returns on an asset and total risk (variance), whereas the SML describes the relation between expected returns on an asset and beta. Be prepared to insert numbers into the CAPM and the SML to estimate expected returns on an asset.

The first reading in Portfolio Management is purely narrative and gives an overview of the portfolio management process.

LEARNING OUTCOME STATEMENTS

Application LOS	Knowledge LOS
	42a **Describe** the portfolio approach to investing
	42b **Describe** types of investors and distinctive characteristics and needs of each
	42c **Describe** the steps in the portfolio management process
	42d **Describe** mutual funds and compare them with other pooled investment products

KNOWLEDGE LEARNING OUTCOME STATEMENTS

42a Describe the portfolio approach to investing

The portfolio approach to investing means considering the risk and return trade-off, and the ability to reduce portfolio risk through diversification. Sections 2.1–2.5 of the reading cover these basic ideas with some background examples, but you will see them in much more detail in Reading 43, so focus your attention there.

42b Describe types of investors and distinctive characteristics and needs of each

Section 3 of the reading covers this LOS and the table below summarizes the key facts that need to be committed to memory.

	Individual investors	Defined benefit schemes	Endowments and funds
Aims/characteristic	Children's education Major purchase Starting a business	Need to ensure sufficient assets to pay pension benefits	Provide financial support to a university and its students Charity
Time horizon	Varies by individual	Typically long term	Very long term
Risk tolerance	Varies by individual	Typically quite high	Typically high
Income needs	Growth – seeks capital gains Income – retirees	High for mature funds; low for growing funds	To meet spending commitments
Liquidity needs	Varies by individual	Typically quite low	Typically quite low

	Banks	Insurance	Investment companies
Aims/characteristics	Accept deposits and extend loans Invest excess reserves	Invest premiums to allow them to pay claims	Collective financial institution
Time horizon	Short term	Short term for property and casualty; long term for life	Varies by fund
Risk tolerance	Quite low	Typically quite low	Varies by fund
Income needs	To pay interest on deposits and operational expenses	Typically low	Varies by fund
Liquidity needs	High to meet repayment of deposits	High to meet claims	High to meet redemptions

42c Describe the steps in the portfolio management process

Section 4 of the reading lists the three steps of the portfolio management process. These should be committed to memory.

42d Describe mutual funds and compare them with other pooled investment products

This is another LOS with narrative information to commit to memory. Section 5.2 lists the characteristics of money market, bond, stock and hybrid/balanced funds.

In Section 5.3 four other investment vehicles are then compared to mutual funds. The key characteristics of exchange-traded funds (ETFs), separately managed accounts, hedge funds, and venture capital funds are discussed.

Note that ETFs, hedge funds, and venture capital are discussed in more detail in the alternative investments section.

Reading 42 sample question
(Answers on p. 308)

Which of the following investments are likely to trade at their net asset value per share?

(A) Closed-end mutual funds
(B) Open-end mutual funds
(C) Exchange-traded funds

Readings 43 and 44 cover modern portfolio theory and the vast majority of calculations and theoretical concepts in the Portfolio Management section are included within these two readings.

LEARNING OUTCOME STATEMENTS

Application LOS	Knowledge LOS
43a **Calculate** and interpret major return measures and describe their appropriate uses	43c **Describe** the characteristics of the major asset classes that investors consider in forming portfolios
43b **Calculate** and interpret the mean, variance, and covariance (or correlation) of asset returns based on historical data	
43d **Explain** risk aversion and its implications for portfolio selection	
43e **Calculate** and interpret portfolio standard deviation	
43f **Describe** the effect on a portfolio's risk of investing in assets that are less than perfectly correlated	
43g **Describe** and interpret the minimum-variance and efficient frontiers of risky assets and the global minimum-variance portfolio	
43h **Discuss** the selection of an optimal portfolio, given an investor's utility (or risk aversion) and the capital allocation line	

APPLICATION LEARNING OUTCOME STATEMENTS

43a Calculate and interpret major return measures and describe their appropriate uses

This LOS talks through a lot of concepts which have already been covered in the Quantitative Methods readings. The following points are all repeated from Quantitative Methods:

- Holding period return (yield)
- Arithmetic mean
- Geometric mean
- Money-weighted return
- Annualizing returns
- Weighted average return
- Real and nominal returns

In addition the terms gross and net returns are introduced to note that asset managers will charge fees on managed funds. The gross return is earned by the manager, and the net return paid to the investor after deduction of fees.

The idea of leveraged returns is also mentioned. If an investor borrows half the funds to make an investment then the returns earned are doubled (as are losses). Leverage can also be achieved through the use of futures contracts. If the margin deposit required to open a futures position is 20% then the returns earned will be 5× that of an investor who pays the full amount.

43b Calculate and interpret the mean, variance, and covariance (or correlation) of asset returns based on historical data

Again this is a repeat of familiar concepts from the Quantitative Methods material. Arithmetic mean is used as the measure of return on an asset and standard deviation (the square root of variance) as the standard measure of risk. The covariance is calculated in this reading as:

$$Cov(R_i, R_j) = \rho_{ij}\sigma_i\sigma_j$$

Where

$$Cov(R_i, R_j) \text{ is the covariance between two investments } i \text{ and } j$$

$$\rho_{ij} = \text{correlation between the two returns}$$

There is also a lot of material on the historical returns of various asset classes which is useful background information, but your focus should be the calculations above. This mean and variance framework assumes that returns are normally distributed and markets are efficient.

Note that kurtosis and skewness, as discussed in Quantitative Methods, violate the assumption of a normal distribution.

43d Explain risk aversion and its implications for portfolio selection

Risk aversion is a key assumption underpinning modern portfolio theory. The key point is that given two investments with the same expected return, a risk-averse investor will choose the investment with the lowest risk. In order to invest in an investment with a higher risk, the investor will require extra return.

Risk-neutral and risk-seeking investors are mentioned in Section 3.1 as a contrast to risk aversion. Risk-seekers choose higher risk and risk-neutral investors are indifferent between investments with the same return and different risks.

The concept of "utility" is introduced in Section 3.2. This is a measure of the satisfaction an investor obtains from different investments. For a risk-averse investor the investment with the same return but lower risk will have the higher utility.

A function that can be used to calculate the level of utility is given but there is not a specific requirement to calculate it in the LOS. The key is to understand that for a risk-averse investor, utility increases with expected return and decreases with risk.

Investments with the same utility can be plotted on a line known as an indifference curve. An investor strives to be on the highest indifference curve possible. Exhibit 11 shows the classic shape of an indifference curve.

Two key properties should be noted for a risk-averse investor. First, the curves are upward sloping – to take on extra risk the investor requires a higher return. Second, the curves are steeper at higher risk levels – the higher the risk, the higher the extra return required to compensate for the increase in risk.

Section 3.3 introduces the capital allocation line (CAL) for combinations of a risk-free and a risky asset. The formula to derive the line and its slope are given. Note that the slope is the Sharpe ratio.

Note that investors choose the combination of assets that lie on the highest indifference curve.

43e Calculate and interpret portfolio standard deviation

The risk of a two asset portfolio is calculated using the two asset risk formula which again should be familiar from Quantitative Methods.

43f Describe the effect on a portfolio's risk of investing in assets that are less than perfectly correlated

Unless assets are perfectly positively correlated, a combination of the two assets will have a standard deviation which is lower than the weighted average of the two individual assets.

Two assets which are perfectly negatively correlated can be combined to eliminate risk. Note that even with positive correlation, risk reduction is achieved unless the correlation is perfect (+1.0). Example 7 gives comprehensive practice on all the calculations.

43g Describe and interpret the minimum-variance and efficient frontiers of risky assets and the global minimum-variance portfolio

Due to the multi-choice nature of the exam, it is not possible for you to be asked to construct any of the diagrams referred to in this LOS, so rather than spending time learning how to construct them, make sure that you are able to describe them and justify their shape.

The key point for the minimum variance frontier is that it plots the portfolio of risky assets which gives the minimum variance for every possible return.

The global minimum-variance portfolio is the portfolio on this line which has the lowest variance.

The efficient frontier is a subset of the minimum variance frontier. It excludes the inefficient portfolios to the right of the global minimum-variance frontier. They are inefficient as a higher return could be obtained with lower risk in other portfolios to the left and above the global minimum-variance frontier.

43h Discuss the selection of an optimal portfolio, given an investor's utility (or risk aversion) and the capital allocation line

The key step to go from the efficient frontier to the CAL is the introduction of the risk-free asset. Recall from LOS 43d that any combination of a risk-free asset and a risky asset leads to a linear upward-sloping CAL.

Each point on the efficient frontier represents a risky portfolio. Each can be combined with the risk-free asset to give a CAL as demonstrated in Exhibit 23 in Section 5.3.

However, rational investors will all choose the CAL with the steepest slope, and hence the highest Sharpe ratio. This is the CAL which just touches the efficient frontier.

Finally, remember that every investor will choose to lie on the highest utility curve. This will be the curve which touches the capital allocation line. The key conclusion is that the point where the highest utility curve touches the capital allocation line is where the investor chooses to invest.

Note that the point chosen for an investor depends on the slope of indifference curves, which in turn depends on the level of risk aversion. The higher the level of risk aversion, the steeper the curves. This will lead to a portfolio being chosen to the left on the CAL, which means a higher weighting in the risk-free asset compared to a less risk-averse investor.

The idea that all investors choose a combination of the risk-free asset and a risky portfolio is known as the two fund separation theorem.

KNOWLEDGE LEARNING OUTCOME STATEMENTS

43c Describe the characteristics of the major asset classes that investors consider in forming portfolios

There is a great deal of historic information on the major asset classes. The task here is to identify the risk and returns on stocks, bonds, and T-bills. Stocks have a higher risk and return than bonds which in turn have a higher risk and return than T-bills.

Reading 43 sample questions
(Answers on p. 308)

1. A stock was bought for $192 and sold for $185 in the following year. During this period, the stock paid $14 in dividends. The total return over the holding period is closest to:

(A) –3.64%

(B) 3.64%

(C) 10.94%

2. An investor has two stocks in their portfolio, stock A and stock B. What is the variance of the portfolio given the following information about the two stocks?

Standard deviation A = 65%

Standard deviation B = 120%

Cor = –0.5

Weighting of asset A in the portfolio = 60%

(A) 0.1953

(B) 0.3259

(C) 0.5697

Readings 43 and 44 cover modern portfolio theory, and the vast majority of calculations and theoretical concepts in the Portfolio Management section are included within these two readings.

LEARNING OUTCOME STATEMENTS

Application LOS	Knowledge LOS
44a **Describe** the implications of combining a risk-free asset with a portfolio of risky assets	44d **Explain** return-generating models (including the market model) and their uses
44b **Explain** the capital allocation line (CAL) and the capital market line (CML)	
44c **Explain** systematic and non-systematic risk, including why an investor should not expect to receive additional return for bearing non-systematic risk	
44e **Calculate** and interpret beta	
44f **Explain** the capital asset pricing model (CAPM), including the required assumptions, and the security market line (SML)	
44g **Calculate** and **interpret** the expected return of an asset using the CAPM	
44h **Describe** and **demonstrate** applications of the CAPM and the SML	

APPLICATION LEARNING OUTCOME STATEMENTS

44a Describe the implications of combining a risk-free asset with a portfolio of risky assets

As discussed in Reading 43, all possible combinations of a risk-free asset and a portfolio of risky assets lie on a capital allocation line.

The key implication outlined in Section 2.2 is that investors can achieve a better risk-return trade off than is possible with any portfolio of risky assets in isolation. In other words, combinations of assets on the CAL lie outside the efficient frontier. All investors therefore will choose a point on this line.

44b Explain the CAL and the CML

Reading 43 introduced the CAL. Section 2.2 in this reading introduces the CML. It is illustrated in Exhibit 3 in Section 2.2.3.

The key point to explain is that the CML is a special case of the CAL where the risky portfolio chosen is the market portfolio. It is the steepest CAL (highest Sharpe ratio) which touches the efficient frontier and so will be chosen by all investors as long as they have homogenous expectations.

The calculations of risk, return, and the slope of the line are repeated again here, but have already been introduced in Reading 43. Example 1 is a useful tool in understanding how to construct the CML given market data, but is not an exam-style question.

The final point to discuss is the use of leverage in Section 2.2.4. Investors as we saw in Reading 43 choose the point on the CML which lies on an investor's highest indifference curve.

Those investors with a high level of risk aversion will lie far to the left of the market portfolio, with a mix of the risk-free and market portfolio.

Those investors with a lower level of risk aversion may lie to the right of the market portfolio. This is achieved using leverage. Investors borrow at the risk-free rate and invest in the market portfolio.

This is demonstrated comprehensively in Example 3.

44c Explain systematic and non-systematic risk, including why an investor should not expect to receive additional return for bearing non-systematic risk

Section 3.1 of the reading breaks total risk into systematic and non-systematic risk. The key point is to understand the factors that give rise to each and the fact that non-systematic risk is diversifiable.

It is the fact that it is diversifiable that means investors do not receive compensation for bearing the risk. As it is diversifiable, any investor exposed to systematic risk is choosing to be in that position. Example 4 covers the key points required.

44e Calculate and interpret beta

Section 3.2.4 introduces the calculation and interpretation of beta. The LOS specifically states calculate, so the calculation shown in the reading should be committed to memory. See Example 5.

The key to interpreting beta is to understand that it is a risk index where a beta of zero indicates a risk-free asset and a beta of one an asset with risk equal to the market. Stocks with a beta greater than one are riskier than the market, and those with a beta of less than one less risky than the market.

44f Explain the capital asset pricing model (CAPM), including the required assumptions, and the security market line (SML)

CAPM is a model for calculating the expected return on a stock given the risk-free rate, the market return, and the stock's beta.

The simple formula is given at the start of Section 4 and will become very familiar over the course of your studies both here and in the Equity section. There are numerous example questions at the end of the chapter which demonstrate the use of the formula as required in LOS 44g.

Note that (Rm – Rf) is often given directly in questions as the "market risk premium."

Section 4.1 then lists the six key assumptions which should be committed to memory.

Section 4.2 covers the SML and is simply the graphical representation of the CAPM equation. It is shown in Exhibit 7 and Example 7 demonstrates more classic calculations using the CAPM.

44g Calculate and interpret the expected return of an asset using the CAPM

This LOS simply involves using the CAPM formula from LOS 44f to calculate security returns.

44h Describe and demonstrate applications of the CAPM and the SML

The most straightforward use of the CAPM is to calculate expected return as above. This can then be compared to actual returns to assess the performance of a stock or security. The performance evaluation measures are covered in Section 4.3.2 and the calculation of the Sharpe ratio, Treynor ratio, M^2, and Jensen's alpha should all be practiced extensively.

Example 10 demonstrates the use of each.

In addition the SML can be used graphically to indicate whether securities are over or undervalued as shown in Exhibit 12. Again, practice this technique using the end of reading questions as much as possible.

Note that Section 5 identifies the limitations of the CAPM model (Section 5.2) and possible extensions to the model in Section 5.3. Although they are not specifically referred to in an LOS they are very much part of the general understanding of the CAPM model and should be committed to memory.

Knowledge learning outcome statements

44d Explain return-generating models (including the market model) and their uses

CAPM is a single-factor model that is used to calculate expected returns. This LOS briefly introduces multi-factor models covered in Section 3.2.1 and the market model in Section 3.2.3. Examples are given of each; it is important to note the inputs used in each model to derive the security return.

Reading 44 sample questions
(Answers on p. 309)

1. An investor believes stock G will rise from a current price of $40 per share to a price of $50 per share over the next year. The following information is used by the investor to assess investment opportunities:

RF = 4%
ERM = 15%
Beta = 1.5

According to the investor's belief regarding the stock price change, should the investor purchase the stock?

(A) No, because it is overvalued
(B) No, because it is undervalued
(C) Yes, because it is undervalued

2. The covariance between a risk-free asset and the market portfolio is:

(A) −1
(B) 0
(C) +1

This reading is a very descriptive section concerned with the process of constructing a portfolio of major asset classes to meet the varying needs of a range of clients.

LEARNING OUTCOME STATEMENTS

Application LOS	Knowledge LOS
	45a **Describe** the reasons for a written investment policy statement (IPS)
	45b **Describe** the major components of an IPS
	45c **Describe** risk and return objectives and how they may be developed for a client
	45d **Distinguish** between the willingness and the ability (capacity) to take risk in analyzing an investor's financial risk tolerance
	45e **Describe** the investment constraints of liquidity, time horizon, tax concerns, legal and regulatory factors, and unique circumstances and their implications for the choice of portfolio assets
	45f **Explain** the specification of asset classes in relation to asset allocation
	45g **Describe** the principles of portfolio construction and the role of asset allocation in relation to the IPS

KNOWLEDGE LEARNING OUTCOME STATEMENTS

45a Describe the reasons for a written investment policy statement (IPS)

Section 2.1 is a very short section outlining the reasons for having a well-defined IPS, all of which should be committed to memory.

45b Describe the major components of an IPS

Section 2.2 provides a list of nine major components of an IPS; again it is a simple case of learning the components and identifying their content and purpose.

45c Describe risk and return objectives and how they may be developed for a client

Risk objectives are covered in Section 2.2.1 and Example 1 is a good demonstration of applying the key learning outcomes. A key point in the discussion of risk objectives is the distinction between willingness and ability to take risk. Return objectives are then listed in Section 2.2.2 and the case study in Example 4 is a good application of the concepts.

45d Distinguish between the willingness and the ability (capacity) to take risk in analyzing an investor's financial risk tolerance

This is covered within the risk objectives discussion in LOS 45c.

45e Describe the investment constraints of liquidity, time horizon, tax concerns, legal and regulatory factors, and unique circumstances and their implications for the choice of portfolio assets

Sections 2.2.3 through 2.2.7 cover each of these constraints in turn. Example 7 is a good case study which identifies constraints and how each affects an investor's investment decisions.

Example 8 shows a brief example of an IPS to show how the information above can be pulled together.

45f Explain the specification of asset classes in relation to asset allocation

The key to meeting client objectives in the IPS is strategic asset allocation. Specifying asset classes is the first step. The introduction to Section 3 identifies an asset class as a category of assets that have similar characteristics, attributes, and risk-return relationships.

45g Describe the principles of portfolio construction and the role of asset allocation in relation to the IPS

The principles are described in Section 3.1, which discusses setting market expectations, Section 3.2 which discusses strategic asset allocation, and Section 3.3 which discusses risk budgeting.

Note that the risk and return calculations shown are those that have already been seen in the earlier Portfolio Management readings. The main task is to learn each of the steps in the process. Example 12 is a comprehensive look at the whole process.

Reading 45 sample question
(Answers on p. 309)

If an individual specifies they have a high level of risk tolerance and seek long-term wealth accumulation, what investment goal would they most likely have?

(A) Income generation
(B) Capital appreciation
(C) Preservation of capital

Equity

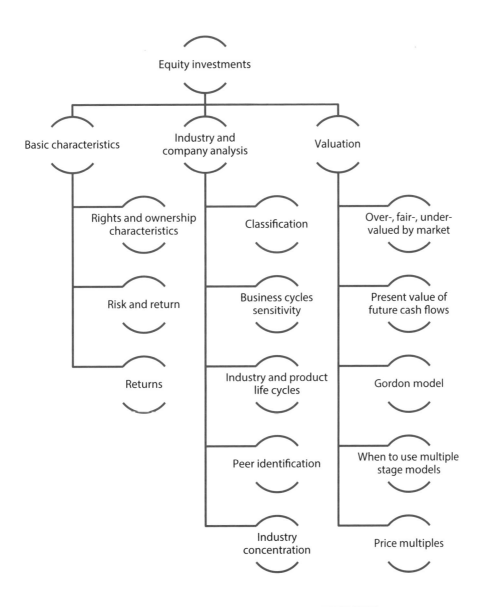

Topic:	Equity Investments and Valuation
Weight:	10%
Study sessions:	13–14
Readings:	46–51

The big picture

Equity investments comprise 10% of Level I, but increase up to 30% for Level II and then drop a bit to 15% at Level III. The focus of this topic at Level I is the description of equity securities, industry and company analysis, and valuation. The depth of the material is similar to what you experience in a principles of investments course.

Markets

The characteristics of markets in which investment decisions are made are important because markets affect valuation, and hence investment decision-making. You should have a basic understanding of the different types of markets and the role of regulation in the functioning of markets, and you should understand how market indices are constructed.

A key topic is that of market efficiency, because this affects the viability of technical analysis (see Reading 12) and valuation. The bottom line is that markets in developed countries are, at a minimum, semi-strong efficient, which means that prices in the market reflect all available information.

Description of equity securities

The descriptive material is straightforward: what are the basic characteristics of equity securities (and don't forget preferred stock)? Understand the securities can be publicly traded or privately held, and that an investor can invest in securities outside his/her country's borders through different means (e.g. direct investment, GDR).

When we refer to the value of an equity security, we are most often referring to the market value, not the book value. (Why? Recall in the financial reporting and analysis topic the issues with how assets are reported on the balance sheet – and how this affects reported book value of equity.)

Industry and company analysis

The valuation of an equity security depends on what is expected to occur in the future. The way we formulate expectations is to develop an understanding of the industry in which the company operates, and then consider how the company fits into that industry. The challenge is to first identify the company's industry, which is not always easy because companies rarely are a single line of businesses. Then once you identify the industry, you then analyze this industry in terms of the market concentration and competition, the life cycle of the industry and products, and the sensitivity of the industry to the business cycle (e.g. cyclical).

Valuation

The valuation component is primarily an application reading. You need to be familiar with the different models that are typically used in valuing equity securities. These include the dividend discount model (and the special case Gordon model and the two-stage model), the free cash flow discount model, and price multiples. The calculation LOSs are limited to the Gordon, two-stage dividend discount, and price multiples, however.

There looks to be an overwhelming amount to learn in this 80+ page reading. However, much of it is giving detailed background, which although it will inform your understanding, does not need to be learnt verbatim. You should read it through but make extensive use of the summaries as we have indicated below.

Apart from these summaries, you should make sure that you can calculate the leverage ratio, the initial margin requirements, and the stock value which would trigger a margin call, as asked for in LOS 46f. We go through these in detail below.

LEARNING OUTCOME STATEMENTS

Application LOS	Knowledge LOS
46a **Explain** the main functions of the financial system	46b **Describe** classifications of assets and markets
46d **Describe** types of financial intermediaries and the services that they provide	46c **Describe** the major types of securities, currencies, contracts, commodities, and real assets that trade in organized markets, including their distinguishing characteristics and major subtypes
46e **Compare** positions an investor can take in an asset	46i **Define** primary and secondary markets and explain how secondary markets support primary markets
46f **Calculate** and interpret the leverage ratio, the rate of return on a margin transaction, and the security price at which the investor would receive a margin call	46j **Describe** how securities, contracts, and currencies are traded in quote-driven markets, order-driven markets, and brokered markets
46g **Compare** execution, validity, and clearing instructions	46l **Describe** objectives of market regulation
46h **Compare** market orders with limit orders	
46k **Describe** characteristics of a well-functioning financial system	

APPLICATION LEARNING OUTCOME STATEMENTS

46a, k   Explain the main functions of the financial system; describe characteristics of a well-functioning financial system

Questions about the main functions are likely to ask which of the three options is or is not a function. The summary at the start of Section 2 is all you really need:

• The achievement of the purposes for which people use the financial system (six purposes listed above the summary)

- The discovery of the rates of return that equate aggregate savings with aggregate borrowings
- The allocation of capital to the best uses

The rest of Section 2 (eight pages) is worth reading through as it expands on these, but there is no need to take extensive notes.

The characteristics of a good, well-functioning market are gone through near the end of the reading in Section 9. It is worth reading through these two pages to get the idea but, in summary, the characteristics would be:

- Transparency (information is quickly and widely available)
- Liquidity (lots of buyers and sellers)
- Internal efficiency (transaction and settlement costs are low)
- External efficiency (the market adjusts quickly to new information)

46d Describe types of financial intermediaries and the services that they provide

Section 4 covers these and it is worth reading through to get the background, but all you need for the exam is to be able to identify the person or institution described. A useful summary is given at Section 4.8.

46e, f, g, h Compare positions an investor can take in an asset; calculate and interpret the leverage ratio, the rate of return on a margin transaction, and the security price at which the investor would receive a margin call; compare execution, validity, and clearing instructions and market orders with limit orders

This is the only area that contains any calculations in this reading, and from an exam point of view it is worth slowing down on Section 5 to make sure you understand how the different types of order work and to ensure you can calculate the leverage and margin call limits.

A long position describes the buyer and the short position, the seller; in many markets, both can borrow to achieve their position. The long borrows cash to fund the purchase, while the short borrows the asset in order to sell it. Short positions are more risky as the potential loss is unlimited and they will usually have to pass over the proceeds of the sale as collateral to the asset lender, who will give them a low rate of interest on this collateral.

A long position can magnify their returns by borrowing some of the funds needed, but as this increases the risk for the broker (who is usually the lender) there will be rules about the percentage which must be put up by the buyer. This is called margin and there is often an initial margin (the minimum level is set by the Fed in the US) and a maintenance margin which gives the level at which more funds must be put in.

Example

C buys 100 shares for $20 each; initial margin is 40% and maintenance margin is 25%.

	Originally	Stock price rises to $40	Stock price falls to $18	When a margin call occurs
C's money (margin)	800	2,800 (balance)	600 (balance)	25%
Broker (borrowed)	1,200	1,200	1,200	75% (balance)
Value of stock in account	2,000	4,000	1,800	100%

If the stock price doubles to $40, the stock in the account is worth $4,000. However, the broker is still only owed $1,200 so C's stake is now worth $2,800.

C's return = +2,000 / 800 = 2.50 or 250%

The stock value has increased by 100% so C's return = stock increase × 1 / 0.40

1 / 0.40 is called the leverage ratio and is 1 / (initial margin)

The greater the leverage ratio, the greater the magnification of gains (and losses!).

If the stock price falls to $18, the broker now only has $1,800 in the account to cover his loan of $1,200. He sets a limit (in this case 25%) of the stock value that must be financed by C. In this case C is now financing 33% of the value.

To calculate when C would have to pay more (a margin call), we must see what stock value leaves C with only 25% and the broker with 75%. As the broker is always owed $1,200, this will be when 75% of the stock price is equal to $1,200.

Thus the stock price must be 1,200 / 0.75 = $1,600.

Alternatively, we can use the formula:

$$[\text{Initial value}] \times (1 - \text{initial margin}) / (1 - \text{maintenance margin})$$

$$= \$2,000 \times (1 - 0.40) / (1 - 0.25) = \$1,600$$

Short positions also have to "post" margin; the initial margin is the same amount as it would be if they had *bought* the stock.

Types of order are more straightforward and are covered in Section 6. Briefly, you need to know the difference between:

- A market order (e.g. sell at best price when order reaches the trading floor)

- A limit order (e.g. sell at $20 or better)
- A stop (stop-loss) order (e.g. sell if the price drops to $18)
- Hidden orders / Iceberg orders (size of order is hidden from the public)
- GTC (good-till-cancelled) vs time limited orders (could be immediate or cancel, day orders, good on close, good on open, or time specific)

KNOWLEDGE LEARNING OUTCOME STATEMENTS

46b, c Describe classifications of assets and markets; describe the major types of securities, currencies, contracts, commodities, and real assets that trade in organized markets, including their distinguishing characteristics and major subtypes

These are gone through in great detail in the 25 pages of Section 3. Again, these pages are worth reading but much of the detail you will come across elsewhere in your studies (e.g. forwards, futures, swaps, and options are covered in Derivatives). Here, all we need is a summary of the assets and contracts available, and enough knowledge to recognize which is being described.

The main categories are:

Financial assets	Securities (debt, equity, shares in pooled investments)
	Currencies
	Contracts (forwards, futures, swaps, options)
Physical assets	Commodities (metals, energy, agriculturals)
	Real assets (tangible properties)

46i, j Define primary and secondary markets and explain how secondary markets support primary markets; describe how securities, contracts, and currencies are traded in quote-driven markets, order-driven markets, and brokered markets

These are looked at in Sections 8 and 9. You need to understand:

- The difference between primary (raising finance) and secondary (trading) markets and why a strong secondary market will help the primary market
- How the primary market can be used to raise finance and the meaning of underwriting, best effort offering, public offerings, private placements, shelf registrations, DRIPs and rights issues
- How the secondary market can be run as a call market or a continuous trading market
- The differences between quote-driven and order-driven markets (8.2) and brokered markets

46l Describe objectives of market regulation

Market regulation is covered in Section 10 and there is a useful summary of the six objectives (which is what the LOS wants you to know) at the end.

Reading 46 sample question
(Answers on p. 309)

A trader holds a short position in a stock currently trading at $10. He instructs his broker to buy the stock if it reaches $15. How could this order best be described?

(A) Stop loss order
(B) Market buy order
(C) Limit order

This reading is far more straightforward than it would initially appear. The calculations needed are generally quite simple – certainly simpler than the huge tables they produce as examples – while you only need a broad overview of the types of market indices rather than the detail they give. Do not get bogged down but use our introduction below and the summaries, which are scattered throughout the reading.

LEARNING OUTCOME STATEMENTS

Application LOS	Knowledge LOS
47a **Describe** a security market index	47f **Describe** rebalancing and reconstitution of an index
47b **Calculate** and interpret the value, price return, and total return of an index	47g **Describe** uses of security market indices
47c **Describe** the choices and issues in index construction and management	47h **Describe** types of equity indices
47d **Compare** the different weighting methods used in index construction	47i **Describe** types of fixed-income indices
47e **Calculate** and analyze the value and return of an index given its weighting method	47j **Describe** indices representing alternative investments
	47k **Compare** types of security market indices

APPLICATION LEARNING OUTCOME STATEMENTS

47a, b Describe a security market index; calculate and interpret the value, price return, and total return of an index

A security market index helps track the change in value of a market, market segment, or asset class. The value is regularly calculated using market prices of the individual securities.

The price return looks at the change in the market value.

The total return looks at the change in the market value and the reinvestment of the income received since inception.

47c, d, e Describe the choices and issues in index construction and management; compare the different weighting methods used in index construction; calculate and analyze the value and return of an index given its weighting method

The reading in this area can become a little overwhelming with formulae and tables of numbers. Questions will be simpler and more like the example below, so make sure you understand it.

There are three main construction methods and you have to be able to apply them, discuss their differences, and their drawbacks.

Example

Suppose we have three investments in the index as follows:

	Number of shares	Opening price	Closing price	Percentage return
A	100	$80	$90	12.5%
B	1,000	$20	$30	50%
C	10,000	$1	$3	200%

1. Price-weighted

   We weight each investment based purely on the stock price:

   $\times 100 = 122$

2. Market value-weighted

   We weight each investment by the total market capitalization:

   $\times 100 = 182$

3. Unweighted (equal weighted)

   We average the individual percentage returns:

   $\times 100 = 187.5$

Price-weighted indices are biased towards those stocks with the higher prices (A in our example).

Market value-weighted indices are biased towards those stocks with the higher market capitalizations (B and C in our example).

Unweighted indices give equal weight to all stocks but probably do not give a reasonable representation of the market.

Float-adjusted market capitalization weightings only include the value of the shares in its market float (those shares which are available to the investing public); this is felt to be a fairer reflection of what is available to an investor.

KNOWLEDGE LEARNING OUTCOME STATEMENTS

47f Describe rebalancing and reconstitution of an index

This is covered in Section 3.3 and you just need to know what they are:

- Rebalancing = adjusting the weights (needed as stock prices and market caps change)
- Reconstitution = changing the items included in the index (depends on criteria for index)

Equity

47g Describe uses of security market indices

This is in the two pages of Section 4 and you should read them through as you may well get the odd question on this. It starts with a summary list and then explains each one in more detail.

47h, i, j, k Describe types of equity indices; describe types of fixed-income indices; describe indices representing alternative investments; compare types of security market indices

Although there is a lot of detail in Sections 5, 6, and 7 about the different types of index used around the world, you only need to know:

Equity	Difference between broad market, multi-market, sector, and style indices
	Typical style indices
Fixed Income	Relative illiquidity creates problems
	Different indices can reflect different dimensions
Commodities	No market cap so index providers must create their own weighting method
Real Estate	Appraisal, repeat sales, or REIT indices
	Highly illiquid market with infrequent transactions and pricing information
Hedge Funds	Rely on voluntary co-operation of hedge funds to provide data
	Unregulated so they can choose what data to reveal and to whom

Reading 47 sample question
(Answers on p. 309)

Which of the following is likely to be correct of a price-weighted index?

(A) It can be tracked by overweighting lower-priced stocks
(B) It can be tracked by investing equal values in the components
(C) It can be tracked by investing in an equal number of shares in the components

There are no calculations in this reading and it is easy to let your attention drift! Use the summaries and the questions at the back of the reading to keep you focused on what is important. The main areas revolve around the Efficient Market Hypothesis which we explain below.

LEARNING OUTCOME STATEMENTS

Application LOS	Knowledge LOS
48a **Describe** market efficiency and related concepts, including their importance to investment practitioners	48b **Distinguish** between market value and intrinsic value
48d **Contrast** the weak-form, semi-strong form, and strong-form market efficiency	48c **Explain** factors affecting a market's efficiency
48e **Explain** the implications of each form of market efficiency for fundamental analysis, technical analysis, and the choice between active and passive portfolio management	48g **Contrast** the behavioral finance view of investor behavior to that of traditional finance
48f **Describe** selected market anomalies	

APPLICATION LEARNING OUTCOME STATEMENTS

48a, d, e Explain market efficiency and related concepts, including their importance to investment practitioners; contrast the weak-form, semi-strong form, and strong-form market efficiency; explain the implications of each form of market efficiency for fundamental analysis, technical analysis, and the choice between active and passive portfolio management

Market efficiency (strictly informational efficiency) relates to the extent to which market prices reflect available information.

The Efficient Market Hypothesis describes three levels of forms of efficiency:

Form	Market price will definitely reflect:	Investor could NOT *consistently* beat the market using:
Weak	All historical data about stock price movements and volumes	Analysis of stock market movements (Chartism or technical analysis)
Semi-strong	All public information	Analysis of any public information, including in-depth analysis of company and its prospects (fundamental analysis)
Strong	All information (public and private)	Any information (including inside information)

Evidence suggests that in developed countries securities markets are semi-strong but that security markets in developing countries may not be semi-strong and may not even be weakly efficient. Strong form is not in evidence, which is why restrictions on insider dealing are necessary.

This would suggest that passive portfolio management (hold the index) is more beneficial on average than active management as active managers will be unable to consistently beat the market but will charge higher fees.

48f Describe selected market anomalies

There are some anomalies which appear to misprice securities. A comprehensive list of these appears in Exhibit 3; however, they can be broadly grouped as follows:

- Calendar effects: buying or selling (which impacts on prices) is driven by the time of year or week or day rather than new information
- Momentum and overreaction: prices rise (and fall) beyond what the new information would suggest
- Size or value effect: small, low P/E or market to book value ratios or high dividend yield companies can outperform other stocks
- Closed-end investment fund discounts, earnings surprises, and behavior of share price on an IPO

Although the reading quotes a number of studies which purport to show that these are not really anomalies, you only need you know what they are.

KNOWLEDGE LEARNING OUTCOME STATEMENTS

48b, c Distinguish between market value and intrinsic value; explain factors affecting a market's efficiency

In the context of the exam, this is less important but it is worth reading quickly through Sections 2.2, 2.3, and 2.4. The market value is what an asset can be bought or sold for at the moment; intrinsic (fundamental) value is the value if investors had complete knowledge of the asset's characteristics.

Factors that affect a market's efficiency include:

- Number of market participants (the more the better)
- Information available and the cost (the more and the cheaper, the better)
- Limits to trading (the fewer limits, the better)
- Transaction costs (the lower, the better)

48g Contrast the behavioral finance view of investor behavior to that of traditional finance

This seeks to explain the market implications of psychological factors in individual rational and irrational behavior. You only have to know some of the broad ideas:

Loss aversion	Dislikes losses more than likes gains (i.e. asymmetrical)
Overconfidence	Leads to overreaction
Representation Gambler's fallacy	Assume future is similar to present or recent past
Mental accounting Narrow framing	Treat each investment separately
Conservatism Disposition effect	Slow to react and realize gains (but not losses)
Herding Information cascade	Following the crowd in trading or acting on information gleaned from others

Reading 48 sample question
(Answers on p. 310)

An analyst believes that security prices fully reflect all publicly available information but do not reflect all private information. According to the Efficient Market Hypothesis, the analyst's beliefs support the:

(A) Weak form
(B) Semi-strong form
(C) Strong form

Equity

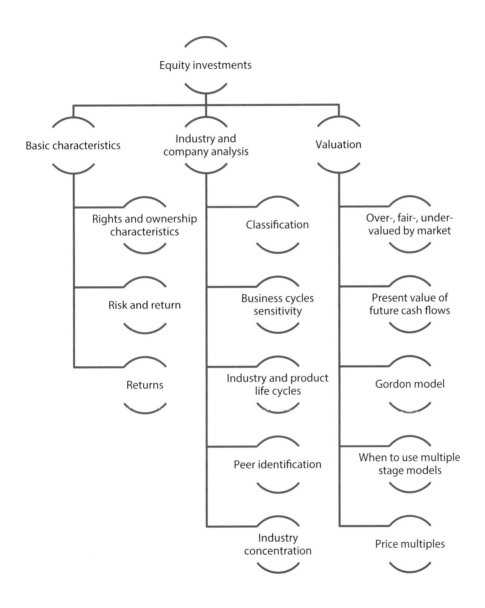

Topic:	Equity Investments and Valuation
Weight:	10%
Study sessions:	13–14
Readings:	46–51

This reading gives an overview of the different types of equity securities, and how they are traded. Much of the detail will probably be familiar to you, but you should make sure you know about the three primary types of private equity investment and the methods of investing in overseas equity.

LEARNING OUTCOME STATEMENTS

Application LOS	Knowledge LOS
49a **Describe** characteristics of types of equity securities	49e **Compare** the risk and return characteristics of types of equity securities
49b **Describe** differences in voting rights and other ownership characteristics among different equity classes	49g **Distinguish** between the market value and book value of equity securities
49c **Distinguish** between public and private equity securities	49h **Compare** a company's cost of equity, its (accounting) return on equity, and investors' required rates of return
49d **Describe** methods for investing in non-domestic equity securities	
49f **Explain** the role of equity securities in the financing of a company's assets	

APPLICATION LEARNING OUTCOME STATEMENTS

49a, b, f Describe characteristics of types of equity securities; describe differences in voting rights and other ownership characteristics among different equity classes; explain the role of equity securities in the financing of a company's assets

Section 3 describes how equity helps companies in their financing; it then goes on to discuss the different types of equity securities and their characteristics as well as the voting rights of different equity classes.

The reading has a lot of detail but you only need to understand:

- Common stock, different classes and voting rights, callable and putable common shares
- Preference stock, cumulative and non-cumulative

49c Distinguish between public and private equity securities

Although the reading only has two pages on this (Section 4), it is worth slowing down on this, as questions may well be asked about:

- The three primary types of private equity investment
- How a venture capitalist will realize their investment
- Which companies are likely targets for a leveraged buy-out
- The reduction in perceived short-term pressure for private equity firms
- The impact on effective corporate governance

49d Describe methods for investing in non-domestic equity securities

Section 5 starts with a historical perspective but we only need the methods available. These are:

- Direct investing in overseas markets (difficult, possibly expensive, and risky)
- Depositary receipts

For example, a bank with an office in Moscow has it buy some Russian equity and then issues receipts in New York. These may represent a number of or a fraction of shares but their value is directly linked to the value of the Russian equity deposited in the bank's Moscow office.

Sponsored DR = Russian company has direct involvement *and the buyers of the DR, rather than the bank, have voting rights*.

American Depositary Receipts (ADRs) are issued in the US in USD and there are three "levels" (Exhibit 16 gives details and you should know whether it is capital raising, the level of listing fees, and what trading is allowed).

Global Depositary Receipts (GDRs) are issued outside the US, mostly in USD but also in GBP or EUR. They can only be sold directly to institutions in the US (not to individuals and not on an exchange).

- Global registered share
- Basket of listed Depositary Receipts – a type of exchange-traded fund (ETF)

Knowledge learning outcome statements

49e Compare the risk and return characteristics of types of equity securities

Risk and return are directly related and we go into more detail in the Study Session on Corporate Finance.

Here, all we need is a comparison of common stock and preference stock, which is given in Section 6.2.

49g, h Distinguish between the market value and book value of equity securities; compare a company's cost of equity, its (accounting) return on equity, and investors' required rates of return

These are covered in Section 7, but are also covered in the Study Sessions on Corporate Finance and Financial Reporting and Analysis. You may need to calculate them in the exam so you should be familiar with the formulae.

The book value is the value of the equity in the company's balance sheet, divided by the number of shares. This may differ from the market's estimate of its intrinsic value, which is the present value of the future cash flows anticipated.

The cost of equity can be viewed as the minimum rate of return required by investors. A failure to deliver this would result in selling of the stock, a fall in the price, and a consequent increase in the return earned on an investment in the stock.

Reading 49 sample question
(Answers on p. 310)

Which of the following statements regarding preference shares is least accurate?

(A) Preference shares make fixed periodic payments to investors
(B) Preference shares can have put or call features
(C) Preference shares usually carry voting rights

This reading is unusual in that, despite there being no numbers, there is not much factual information to learn off by heart. Instead you need to understand the tools that could be used for analyzing an industry's prospects and apply them in questions.

The reading has numerous examples of application which are useful, but remember they are only examples – you don't have to learn them! Once you have a broad grasp of the methods, go through the questions at the end of the reading as they will give you a clearer idea of what is expected.

Learning outcome statements

Application LOS	Knowledge LOS
50a **Explain** the uses of industry analysis and the relation of industry analysis to company analysis	50b **Compare** methods by which companies can be grouped, current industry classification systems, and classify a company, given a description of its activities and the classification system
50c **Explain** factors that affect the sensitivity of a company to the business cycle and the uses and limitations of industry and company descriptors such as "growth," "defensive," and "cyclical"	50d **Explain** the relation of "peer group," as used in equity valuation, to a company's industry classification
50e **Describe** the elements that need to be covered in a thorough industry analysis	50j **Describe** demographic, governmental, social, and technological influences on industry growth, profitability, and risk
50f **Describe** the principles of strategic analysis of an industry	50k **Describe** the elements that should be covered in a thorough company analysis
50g **Explain** the effects of barriers to entry, industry concentration, industry capacity, and market share stability on pricing power and return on capital	
50h **Describe** product and industry life cycle models, classify an industry as to life cycle phase (e.g. embryonic, growth, shakeout, maturity, or decline) based on a description of it, and describe the limitations of the life cycle concept in forecasting industry performance	
50i **Compare** characteristics of representative industries from the various economic sectors	

KEY LEARNING OUTCOME STATEMENTS

50a Explain the uses of industry analysis and the relation of industry analysis to company analysis

Industry analysis is the analysis of a particular sector and is useful for

- Understanding a company's business and business environment
- Identifying active investment opportunities
- Helping to quantify the proportion of a portfolio's returns which are attributable to sector selection

50 c, e, f, g, h, i, j Explain factors that affect the sensitivity of a company to the business cycle and the uses and limitations of industry and company descriptors such as "growth," "defensive," and "cyclical" , Describe the elements that need to be covered in a thorough industry analysis, Describe the principles of strategic analysis of an industry, Explain the effects of barriers to entry, industry concentration, industry capacity, and market share stability on pricing power and return on capital, Describe product and industry life cycle models, classify an industry as to life cycle phase (e.g. embryonic, growth, shakeout, maturity, or decline) based on a description of it, and describe the limitations of the life cycle concept in forecasting industry performance, Describe product and industry life cycle models, classify an industry as to life cycle phase (e.g. embryonic, growth, shakeout, maturity, or decline) based on a description of it, and describe the limitations of the life cycle concept in forecasting industry performance, Compare characteristics of representative industries from the various economic sectors, Describe demographic, governmental, social, and technological influences on industry growth, profitability, and risk

This is the heart of the reading and discusses some of the methods that can be used to analyze an industry. The industry prospects (and those of a company in the industry) can be affected by factors outside the industry, factors inside the industry, and the stage of life of the industry. No single factor is going to be persuasive on its own but all the more significant factors have to be taken together. This may then lead to a tentative conclusion on whether companies operating in this industry are likely to do well in the future.

The reading explains the factors with lots of examples. This makes it easier to understand but do not get lost in them or feel you have to learn them.

Key Internal Factors (5.1) – Strategic Analysis
- The threat of substitute products (these would reduce demand and prices)
- The threat of new entrants (these would increase capacity and reduce prices)
- The bargaining power of customers (high power can exert downward pressure on prices)
- The bargaining power of suppliers (high power can exert upward pressure on costs)
- The intensity of rivalry among incumbents (higher intensity leads to pressure on prices)

You need to be able to identify which of three possible industries has, for example, high bargaining power of customers.

Equity

Stage of Life of the Industry (5.1.5.1)

You need to be able to recognize from a description what stage an industry is in, or conversely state what you'd expect to happen to prices, profits, and competition at the different stages.

Key External Factors (5.2)

These include macroeconomic, technological, demographic, governmental and social influences. The end of Exhibit 7 and Exhibit 8 use these (although strangely this is before they have been explained in the text). Again, you need to be able to say whether these are major influences for a particular industry.

Lastly, the state of the economy may or may not be a major influence on the industry; business cycle sensitivities are discussed in Section 3.2.

KNOWLEDGE LEARNING OUTCOME STATEMENTS

50b, d Compare methods by which companies can be grouped, current industry classification systems, and classify a company, given a description of its activities and the classification system; explain the relation of "peer group," as used in equity valuation, to a company's industry classification

You should have a broad awareness of these, which are explained in Section 3 over two to three pages. In addition, you should realize that classifications are already produced by a number of organizations (including government agencies), as detailed in Sections 4.1 and 4.2, although you do not have to learn them.

You should concentrate on the strengths and weaknesses of the current systems available (4.3) and how you might go about constructing a peer group for comparative performance assessment (4.4).

50k Describe the elements that should be covered in a thorough company analysis

A summary of these is given at the start of Section 6.1 but you should read through Exhibit 8, not to memorize all the points but to get an idea of what sort of things might be included in the six areas.

Reading 50 sample question
(Answers on p. 310)

Which of the following is least likely to be included in the fundamental analysis of a company?

(A) Charting
(B) Market analysis
(C) Industry analysis

The last reading in the Study Sessions on Equity is arguably the most important; your exam is bound to have some questions in the area of equity valuation. It is entirely focused on estimating the value of a company or a share and identifying the strengths and weaknesses of each method.

You should take some time to practice the calculations, using the questions at the back of the reading, and ensure that you understand the methodologies. These will all be tested again at Level II so it is well worth putting in the effort now.

LEARNING OUTCOME STATEMENTS

Application LOS	Knowledge LOS
51c **Explain** the rationale for using present-value of cash flow models to value equity and describe the dividend discount and free-cash-flow-to-equity models	51a **Evaluate** whether a security, given its current market price and a value estimate, is overvalued, fairly valued, or undervalued by the market
51e **Calculate** and interpret the intrinsic value of an equity security based on the Gordon (constant) growth dividend discount model or a two-stage dividend discount model, as appropriate	51b **Describe** major categories of equity valuation models
51g **Explain** the rationale for using price multiples to value equity and distinguish between multiples based on comparables versus multiples based on fundamentals	51d **Calculate** the intrinsic value of a non-callable, non-convertible preferred stock
51h **Calculate** and interpret the following multiples: price to earnings, price to an estimate of operating cash flow, price to sales, and price to book value	51f **Identify** companies for which the constant growth or multistage dividend discount model is appropriate
51i **Explain** the use of enterprise value multiples in equity valuation and demonstrate the use of enterprise value multiples to estimate equity value	51k **Explain** the advantages and disadvantages of each category of valuation model
51j **Explain** asset-based valuation models and demonstrate the use of asset-based models to calculate equity value	

APPLICATION LEARNING OUTCOME STATEMENTS

51c, e Explain the rationale for using present-value of cash flow models to value equity and describe the dividend discount and free-cash-flow-to-equity models; calculate and interpret the intrinsic value of an equity security based on the Gordon (constant) growth dividend discount model or a two-stage dividend discount model, as appropriate

This is the most important part of the reading and you should expect some calculation questions in the exam. Sections 4, 4.2, and 4.3 go through the derivation and apply it to numerous examples. You should work through these examples carefully to ensure you understand, as well as all the questions at the end of the reading.

You do not need to be able to reproduce the derivation but only use the formulae in a valuation:

- Share held for a set period and resale price estimated:
  Discount projected dividends and resale price at cost of equity
- No resale price estimated or no definite end to holding period:
  $P = D_1 / (k_e - g)$
- High growth or uneven cash dividends in first few years, followed by steady growth in perpetuity: discount the first few years individually and add the present value of the perpetuity

Notice that some investors prefer to use the dividend *capacity* rather than actual dividends paid, calculated as:

$$\text{Free Cash Flow to Equity} = \text{CFO} - \text{Cash needed for reinvestment in capital assets} + \text{Net funds borrowed in year}$$

Occasionally, growth may have to be estimated using ROE × retention rate as seen in the Financial Reporting and Analysis Study Sessions.

51g, h, i Explain the rationale for using price multiples to value equity and distinguish between multiples based on comparables versus multiples based on fundamentals; calculate and interpret the following multiples: price to earnings, price to an estimate of operating cash flow, price to sales, and price to book value; explain the use of enterprise value multiples in equity valuation and demonstrate the use of enterprise value multiples to estimate equity value

A multiplier model, such the P/E ratio model, takes an item in the company's balance sheet or income statement (such as earnings per share) and multiplies it to estimate the share value. The reading explains it well in Section 5; notice in particular:

- The multiple can be deduced from what are thought to be similar other companies (comparables) or from estimates of the pay-out ratio, cost of equity and growth prospects (justified)
- Multiples can relate to forecast items in next time's accounts (leading) or in last time's accounts (trailing) as long as they are derived in the same manner
- In the justified P/E ratio, increased risk increases k_e and reduces value, while increased estimated growth increases value (subject to the impact on the pay-out ratio)

- Enterprise value (EV) = value of equity + value of debt
- EV multiples can be used, such as EV / EBITDA but the value of the debt will then be needed to estimate the value of the equity; this can cause problems

51j Explain asset-based valuation models and demonstrate the use of asset-based models to calculate equity value

These are discussed in Section 6. They are relatively easy to do, using either balance sheet values or potential resale values for assets and liabilities.

However, the balance sheet does not usually capture all of the value drivers of the business value, such as customer goodwill, contacts, and reputation. As a result, it will usually produce a lower valuation than other methods and may be misleading for a service business which is a going concern.

KNOWLEDGE LEARNING OUTCOME STATEMENTS

51a Evaluate whether a security, given its current market price and a value estimate, is overvalued, fairly valued, or undervalued by the market

This is quite simple and is demonstrated in Section 2. If the value estimated exceeds the current market value, the analyst thinks it is undervalued by the market. In questions, this can sometimes be the final conclusion after carrying out a valuation.

51b, f, k Describe major categories of equity valuation models; identify companies for which the constant growth or multistage dividend discount model is appropriate; explain the advantages and disadvantages of each category of valuation model

The general categories (discounted cash flow, multiplier, and asset valuations) are described in Section 3, but by the time you have worked through the rest of the reading, much of what is said will seem obvious.

The appropriateness of the dividend growth models to different companies is discussed in the three paragraphs between Exhibit 8 and Exhibit 9 in Section 4.3, which is easy to overlook! It's worth reading through.

No valuation is a perfect estimate, which is why a number of different methods are often used. You should notice the advantages and disadvantages of each method as you read; these mostly revolve around:

- Simplicity of use
- Simplicity and appropriateness of assumptions made
- Difficulty in estimating inputs

51d Calculate the intrinsic value of a non-callable, non-convertible preferred stock

This is looked at briefly in Section 4.1; it is like common stock but there is no growth in the dividend. As g = 0, the calculation is relatively simple.

Reading 51 sample questions
(Answers on p. 310)

1. A company has a $100 par preferred stock. The annual dividend is $3.50. The required return is 7%. The company's earnings are forecast to grow at 3%. Corporation tax is 40%. The value of preferred stock is closest to:

    (A) $50
    (B) $51.50
    (C) $83.33

2. Kevin follows the PQR Limited stock and as per his estimates this company will have a period of supernormal growth rate of 15% for the next three years. Thereafter, the dividend growth rate will be 5%. The company's cost of equity capital is 10%.

    Other relevant market information about the company is as follows:

    1. Current market price per share = $16.75
    2. Dividend per share = $1.10
    3. Current risk-free rate = 4%

    Based on the above information, using the two-stage dividend discount model, value of the stock of PQR Limited is closest to:

    (A) $30.00
    (B) $37.35
    (C) $45.2

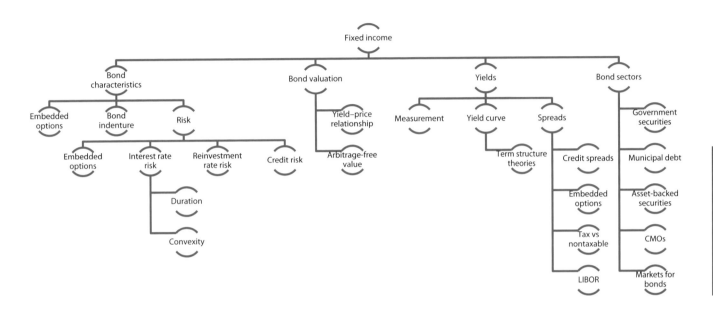

Topic:	Fixed Income
Weight:	12%
Study sessions:	15–16
Readings:	52–59

THE BIG PICTURE

The Fixed Income topic covers a lot of ground, starting with the features of fixed income instruments, continuing on to valuation, spot rates, and interest rate risk. Because of the importance of fixed income in the next two levels, you should think about getting a solid foundation in fixed income now so that you are prepared for the more advanced concept and calculations.

OVERVIEW AND FEATURES OF FIXED INCOME INSTRUMENTS

Keep in mind that bonds are only one type of fixed income security. You should be prepared to describe the many types of fixed income securities (such as mortgage-back securities), but the primary focus of the Level I material is on bonds. Throughout the Fixed Income topic, you should have a keen understanding of the relationship between yield and value.

Valuing a bond as the discounted value of coupon cash flows and the maturity value, all discounted at the yield to maturity, produces a bond value that is not appropriate because by using a single yield to maturity you are assuming that the yield curve is flat, which is rare. Therefore, you should understand the concept and calculations of spot and forward rates, and how to value a bond using forward rates; this bond value is the arbitrage-free value of the bond.

RISKS

There are many different types of risks when investing in bonds, and you should be able to relate these risks to a bond's features. The risks include interest rate risk, reinvestment rate risk, currency risk, inflation risk, and call risk. For example, you should be able to reason that when comparing two bonds that are identical in terms of all features except for the coupon rate, the bond with the higher coupon has lower interest rate risk as measured by duration.

The only calculations that you are responsible for in this topic are the calculations of duration, dollar duration, and the estimated change in the value of bond given duration, though you are responsible for the duration calculation for both an individual bond and bond portfolio. In this context, you should focus on effective duration, though having gone through the gory detail on a Macaulay duration problem may help you understand the concept of duration – the idea that it is a cash-flow weighted measure.

The effect of an embedded option (e.g. call option) on the value of a bond requires an understanding of the key determinants of an option's value: price of the underlying, exercise price, time to expiration, opportunity cost, and volatility. As you look at the different embedded options, keep in mind these five parameters and how they affect the value of the embedded option. Also, bear in mind the perspective of the option: if the option is held by the bond issuer (e.g. call option), then it reduces the value of the bond to the investor; if the option is held by the investor (e.g. put option), then it enhances the value of the bond to the investor.

The first reading in Fixed Income is quite short and very narrative. There are some simple calculations, but most of the material is descriptive.

LEARNING OUTCOME STATEMENTS

Application LOS	Knowledge LOS
52b Describe the basic features of a bond, the various coupon rate structures, and the structure of floating-rate securities	**52a Explain** the purposes of a bond's indenture and describe affirmative or negative covenants
52e Identify common options embedded in a bond issue, explain the importance of embedded options, and identify whether an option benefits the issuer or the bondholder	**52c Define** accrued interest, full price, and clean price
	52d Explain the provisions for redemption and retirement of bonds
	52f Describe methods used by institutional investors in the bond market to finance the purchase of a security (i.e. margin buying and repurchase agreements)

APPLICATION LEARNING OUTCOME STATEMENTS

52b Describe the basic features of a bond, the various coupon rate structures, and the structure of floating-rate securities

This is a straightforward reading introducing the basic terminology used to describe bonds.

Par value	Coupon rate	Price
• Amount repaid at maturity • Also known as principal, maturity or face value	• Multiply by par value to get cash coupon payment received • Also known as nominal rate	• Bond may trade above or below its par value

The various coupon structures shown below need to be learned and described, but the vast majority of calculations in the later readings are based on a fixed coupon.

Zero coupon	Step-up notes	Deferred coupon
• No coupon payments are made • Return is all capital gain • Must trade below par	• Coupon rate increases over time	• Payments deferred for a number of years • Later payment higher to compensate for delay

Floating rate securities, sometimes called variable rate securities, are the final type of structure which needs to be studied. As the name suggests, the coupon is variable, typically being a reference rate plus a quoted margin. Inverse floaters pay a coupon which increases when the reference rate decreases, allowing investors to benefit from a belief that rates will fall.

Floaters may have a maximum interest rate, known as a cap, which benefits the issuer. A minimum rate, or floor, benefits the holder. Both can be set up using options – this is covered in the derivatives material.

52e Identify common options embedded in a bond issue, explain the importance of embedded options, and identify whether an option benefits the issuer or the bondholder

The presence of an embedded option will affect the value of a bond. Those which benefit the investor make the bond more attractive to buy and so increase the bond price. Those which benefit the issuer make it less attractive and so decrease the bond price. All the options listed below need to be identified as benefitting the holder or issuer.

Call and refunding	• Right to pay back early • Benefits issuer • Refunding involves callling a bond using proceeds from a cheaper issuer
Prepayment	• Benefits issuer • Right to repay an amortizing security early • Common for mortgage-backed securities
Accelerated sinking fund	• Benefits issuer • A portion of the bond is returned each year if the bond is issued with a sinking fund provision • An accelerated sinking fund provision gives the issuer the right to retire more of the principal than scheduled
Cap on a floater	• Benefits issuer • Specifies maximum interest to be paid on a floating rate security
Conversion	• Benefits holder • Right to receive common stock instead of principal at maturity
Put provision	• Benefits holder • Right to have the bond redeemed early
Floor on a floater	• Benefits holder • Specifies minimum interest to be received by holder

KNOWLEDGE LEARNING OUTCOME STATEMENTS

Reading 52 begins the coverage of duration and interest rate risk, but this is all covered again in detail in Study Session 16.

52a Explain the purposes of a bond's indenture and describe affirmative or negative covenants

The indenture of the bond lists the terms of the bond issue. An affirmative covenant describes actions that the borrower promises to do, while negative describe limitations and restrictions on the borrower's activities. Affirmative includes paying interest, taxes, and other claims, to maintain property in good working order and to submit regular reports. Negative imposes limitations on borrowing and incurring additional debt.

52c Define accrued interest, full price, and clean price

As the coupon interest is paid at regular intervals, typically every six months, anyone buying a bond between coupon dates must pay the accrued interest to the holder. The full price including this accrued interest is known as the dirty price. The clean price is the price quoted, and excludes accrued interest.

52d Explain the provisions for redemption and retirement of bonds

Non-amortizing bonds pay interest only, and the principal is redeemed at maturity. Amortizing securities pay principal and interest over the life of the instrument. Other provisions for redemption are call options and sinking fund provisions, both covered in LOS 52e.

52f Describe methods used by institutional investors in the bond market to finance the purchase of a security (i.e. margin buying and repurchase agreements)

Margin buying involves borrowing funds from a broker who has in turn borrowed from a bank. Note the call money rate is the rate charged by the bank to the broker. A repurchase agreement (repo) involves selling and repurchasing a security at a higher price. The difference in price is the interest charge. Both methods are defined succinctly in Sections 11.1 and 11.2 of the reading.

Reading 52 sample questions
(Answers on p. 311)

1. If an investor sells a bond at par prior to maturity she will make a capital gain if:

    (A) She bought the bond at a premium
    (B) Interest rates at the date of sale are higher than interest rates at the time the bond was issued
    (C) Interest rates at the date of sale are lower than interest rates at the time the bond was issued

2. Which of the following embedded options is most likely to benefit the bondholder?

    (A) Calls and sinking fund provisions
    (B) Caps on floating rate bonds
    (C) Put and conversion provisions

This is a largely descriptive reading on the risks of investing in bonds. The calculations on duration and price relationships are covered in more detail in Study Session 16.

LEARNING OUTCOME STATEMENTS

Application LOS	Knowledge LOS
53b **Identify** the relations among a bond's coupon rate, the yield required by the market, and the bond's price relative to par value (i.e. discount, premium, or equal to par)	53a **Explain** the risks associated with investing in bonds
53c **Explain** how a bond maturity, coupon, embedded options and yield level affect its interest rate risk	53d **Identify** the relation of the price of a callable bond to the price of an option-free bond and the price of the embedded call option
53e **Explain** the interest rate risk of a floating-rate security and why its price may differ from par value	53f **Calculate** and interpret the duration and dollar duration of a bond
53g **Describe** yield-curve risk and explain why duration does not account for yield curve risk	53j **Describe** types of credit risk and the meaning and role of credit ratings
53h **Explain** the disadvantages of a callable or prepayable security to an investor	53k **Explain** liquidity risk and why it might be important to investors even if they expect to hold a security to the maturity date
53i **Identify** the factors that affect the reinvestment risk of a security and explain why prepayable amortizing securities expose investors to greater reinvestment risk than non-amortizing securities	53l **Describe** the exchange rate risk an investor faces when a bond makes payments in a foreign currency
53n **Explain** how yield volatility affects the price of a bond with an embedded option and how changes in volatility affect the value of a callable bond and a putable bond	53m **Explain** inflation risk
	53o **Describe** sovereign risk and types of event risk

APPLICATION LEARNING OUTCOME STATEMENTS

53b Identify the relations among a bond's coupon rate, the yield required by the market, and the bond's price relative to par value (i.e. discount, premium, or equal to par)

This is a fundamental set of relationships which can be tested descriptively or with a calculation. It is also covered in detail in Study Session 16.

53c Explain how a bond maturity, coupon, embedded options and yield level affect its interest rate risk

Interest rate risk is covered in detail in Reading 59. The key relationships covered in this LOS are as below. Note that the presence of an embedded call option, or the presence of an embedded put option, both lower interest rate risk.

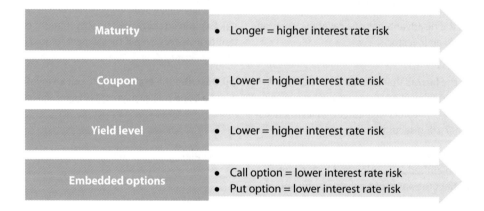

53e Explain the interest rate risk of a floating-rate security and why its price may differ from par value

Interest rate risk is explained in detail in Study Session 16. The key point here is that the periodic resetting of the coupon means that interest rate risk is lower for floating rate bonds. They may, however, differ from par for three reasons:

1. Between reset dates required return may be different to market return. The longer it is until reset, the larger the movement away from par. The price will be equal to par at the reset date as the coupon is set equal to the yield (see LOS 53b)

2. Required margins may change. If the margin offered over the benchmark is lower than the market requires, the price will fall below par, and vice versa

3. Floating rate may be capped. If the benchmark + margin is above the cap, the investor receives the cap rate and the price will fall below par

53g Describe yield-curve risk and explain why duration does not account for yield curve risk

If duration is used to assess the effect of a change in yields on a bond portfolio, it assumes that the yield-curve shift is parallel. Yield-curve risk is the risk that the shift is non-parallel, i.e. different maturities experience different changes in yields. In this case, duration will not give an accurate measure on the price change of the portfolio. Yield curves and duration are covered in detail elsewhere in the readings.

53h Explain the disadvantages of a callable or prepayable security to an investor

There are three disadvantages listed:

1. The cash flow pattern is uncertain
2. The bond is likely to be called when interest rates are low, meaning that the investor receives cash that will have to be reinvested at low yields
3. Price appreciation of callable bonds is restricted

Points 2 and 3 are explained in more detail in Study Session 16.

53i Identify the factors that affect the reinvestment risk of a security and explain why prepayable amortizing securities expose investors to greater reinvestment risk than non-amortizing securities

This LOS defines and explains reinvestment risk – the risk that proceeds from the bond cannot be reinvested at the expected rate. The greater the proceeds during the life of the bond, the greater the reinvestment risk. This means higher coupon and amortizing bonds have higher reinvestment risk. Again there is more detail on quantifying this risk in Study Session 16.

53n Explain how yield volatility affects the price of a bond with an embedded option and how changes in volatility affect the value of a callable bond and a putable bond

The key to this LOS is to distinguish the impact of yield volatility from the impact of yield levels. An increase in volatility increases the value of both put and call options (as seen in the Derivatives Study Sessions). This will decrease the value of a callable bond, but increase the value of a putable bond.

Knowledge learning outcome statements

53a Explain the risks associated with investing in bonds

All the risks are covered in detail in the later LOS. The only real use of this LOS is to provide a list of the risks that are covered.

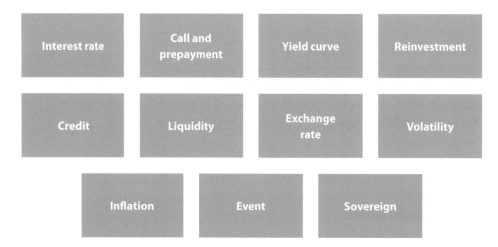

53d Identify the relation of the price of a callable bond to the price of an option-free bond and the price of the embedded call option

The impact of call options on the price of a bond is covered in detail in Study Session 16. Only the fact that the call option is unattractive to investors and hence reduces the price of the bond is given here, and hence the relationship:

$$\text{Price callable} = \text{Price option-free} - \text{price of call}$$

53f Calculate and interpret the duration and dollar duration of a bond

Although this is a key concept in the syllabus, it is covered in detail in Study Session 16.

53j Describe types of credit risk and the meaning and role of credit ratings

Although there is a detailed list of the actual credit ratings given in the material, the key takeaway point from the LOS are the three types of credit risk – default, credit spread, and downgrade. Default and downgrade are very straightforward, and credit spread is explained in the yield curve material.

53k Explain liquidity risk and why it might be important to investors even if they expect to hold a security to the maturity date

The LOS defines liquidity risk – having to sell a bond at a price below the value indicated by a recent transaction

– and then makes the distinction between investors who intend to sell the bond before it matures and those who intend to hold until maturity. Wider bid–ask spreads indicate higher liquidity risk.

Those who intend to sell are exposed to liquidity risk. Those who hold until maturity are also exposed if they are required to mark their portfolio to market periodically, e.g. mutual funds.

53l Describe the exchange rate risk an investor faces when a bond makes payments in a foreign currency

Bonds that pay in a foreign currency expose the investor to foreign currency risk. This is covered in a very short section in this session, but foreign exchange risk generally is covered in much more detail in Economics.

53m Explain inflation risk

An increase in inflation decreases the value of a fixed set of cash flows.

53o Describe sovereign risk and types of event risk

Sovereign risk is broken down in the reading into willingness of a foreign government to pay, and the ability to pay.

Three types of event risk are identified – natural disasters, takeovers, and regulatory change.

Reading 53 sample question
(Answers on p. 311)

1. A 5%, four-year annual-pay corporate bond yielding 3% is priced at $107.434. If yields fall by 50 basis points to 2.5%, the bond's price will increase to $109.405. If yields increase by 50 basis points to 3.5%, the price of the bond will fall to $105.509. Compute the effective duration of the bond.

    (A) 1.8
    (B) 3.6
    (C) 3.8

2. Consider the bond below. Which answer is closest to its price relative to par and what is the most likely ranking of its coupon rate and yield?

    Price: 110
    Coupon: 10

    (A) Premium, coupon greater than yield
    (B) Discount, yield greater than coupon
    (C) Premium, yield greater than coupon

This is another reading with a large amount of knowledge to memorize. The focus is on learning the different types of bond instrument available.

LEARNING OUTCOME STATEMENTS

Application LOS	Knowledge LOS
54c **Describe** how stripped Treasury securities are created and distinguish between coupon strips and principal strips	54a **Describe** the features, credit risk characteristics, and distribution methods for government securities
54e **Describe** the types and characteristics of mortgage-backed securities, and explain the cash flow and prepayment risk for each type	54b **Describe** the types of securities issued by the US Department of the Treasury (e.g. bills, notes, bonds, and inflation protection securities), and differentiate between on-the-run and off-the-run Treasury securities
54f **Explain** the motivation for creating a collateralized mortgage obligation	54d **Describe** the types and characteristics of securities issued by US federal agencies
54i **Define** an asset-backed security, describe the role of a special purpose vehicle in an asset-backed security's transaction, state the motivation for a corporation to issue an asset-backed security, and describe the types of external credit enhancements for asset-backed securities	54g **Describe** the types of securities issued by municipalities in the United States, and distinguish between tax-backed debt and revenue bonds
	54h **Describe** the characteristics and motivation for the various types of debt issued by corporations (including corporate bonds, medium-term notes, structured notes, commercial paper, negotiable CDs, and banker's acceptances)
	54j **Describe** collateralized debt obligations
	54k **Describe** the mechanisms available for placing bonds in the primary market and distinguish between the primary and secondary markets for bonds

APPLICATION LEARNING OUTCOME STATEMENTS

54c Describe how stripped Treasury securities are created and distinguish between coupon strips and principal strips

The key point to the strips LOS is to identify that coupon and principal strips are single cash flows that are direct obligations of the US government. Each flow represents either a single coupon payment or the principal payment from a Treasury note or bond, as shown below.

The resulting strips are single cash flows and hence effectively zero coupon bonds. This two-year semi-annual bond is stripped down to four coupon strips and one principal strip. The other point to note is that non-US entities are often taxed on interest during the life of the strip even though no cash flow is received until maturity.

54e Describe the types and characteristics of mortgage-backed securities, and explain the cash flow and prepayment risk for each type

The key to this LOS is to identify the risks associated with, and the differences between, mortgage passthrough securities and collateralized mortgage obligations (CMO).

The securities considered are agency securities created from a pool of fixed-rate, level-payment, fully amortizing mortgages. Holders of mortgage passthroughs receive regular payments made up of interest, principal repayments, and principal prepayments.

The prepayment is analogous to a call option on a corporate bond. It means investors receive excess cash when mortgage rates drop and mortgages are prepaid. This is an unattractive feature of mortgage passthroughs.

54f State the motivation for creating a collateralized mortgage obligation

The advantage of a CMO is that the securities are arranged into prepayment tranches. The early tranches receive all prepayments until they are fully paid off. This means that later tranches are protected from prepayments.

The key term to grasp is redistribution. The early tranches absorb the prepayments until they are fully paid off and so have a high risk of being paid back early, whereas the later tranches have protection and a low risk of being paid off early. There is no overall reduction in prepayment risk, it has just been redistributed.

54i Define an asset-backed security, describe the role of a special purpose vehicle in an asset-backed security's transaction, state the motivation for a corporation to issue an asset-backed security, and describe the types of external credit enhancements for asset-backed securities

The key to this LOS is understanding the motivation for the issue of an asset-backed security via a special purpose vehicle.

The originator sells high-quality assets to the special purpose vehicle which then issues securities backed by the assets. As the vehicle does not have any operating risk and no other obligations, the securities issued have a higher credit rating. The higher the credit rating, the lower the yield that has to be paid, which is ultimately the motivation for the originating company.

External credit enhancements are listed in Section 7.2 of the reading and it is an easy list to learn.

KNOWLEDGE LEARNING OUTCOME STATEMENTS

54a Describe the features, credit risk characteristics, and distribution methods for government securities

Section 3 of the reading discusses government debt. US government debt is still used throughout the syllabus as a benchmark risk-free rate, meaning it has no credit risk. Overseas debt, however, may have risk.

There are four distribution methods described in Section 3.2, which should be committed to memory.

54b Describe the types of securities issued by the US Department of the Treasury (e.g. bills, notes, bonds, and inflation protection securities), and differentiate between on-the-run and off-the-run Treasury securities

Treasury bills mature in less than 12 months, pay no coupon, and hence are issued at a discount. Treasury notes pay a coupon and mature in no more than 10 years. Treasury bonds pay coupons and mature in more than 10 years.

Inflation protected securities (TIPS) pay a fixed coupon but the principal is adjusted in line with inflation so that investors get a higher return with higher inflation.

54d Describe the types and characteristics of securities issued by US federal agencies

The reading covers Fannie Mae and Freddie Mac very briefly, stating that they issue debentures and discount notes.

The agencies also provide liquidity to the market through the issue of mortgage passthrough securities. The nature of these securities is covered in LOS 54e.

54g Describe the types of securities issued by municipalities in the United States, and distinguish between tax-backed debt and revenue bonds

Section 5 of the reading covers state and local government issues in the US. These bonds are known as municipalities. Examples of tax backed and revenue backed are given in Sections 5.1 and 5.2 respectively.

54h Describe the characteristics and motivation for the various types of debt issued by corporations (including corporate bonds, medium-term notes, structured notes, commercial paper, negotiable CDs, and banker's acceptances)

Section 6 of the reading covers the six different securities that need to be described. The key points are as follows:

Corporate bonds	• May be secured or unsecured • May have credit enhancements via third party or letter of credit
Medium-term notes (MTN)	• Offered continuously • Medium term is misleading, they can have a wide range of maturities
Structured notes	• MTN combined with a derivative
Commercial paper	• Short term, most commonly less than 50 days maturity • Often rolled over
Negotiable CDs	• Certificate of deposit issued by banks (deposit-taking institutions) • Negotiable allows the initial depositor to sell before the maturity date
Banker's acceptances	• Used to facilitate trade

54j Describe collateralized debt obligations

The introduction to CDOs is a very short section with less than a page of information to learn. Key terms are collateralized bond obligations (CBOs) if they are backed by bonds, CLOs if they are backed by loans.

If the motivation of the sponsor is to make a spread between yields on the underlying and yield on the CDO, it is referred to as an arbitrage transaction. If the motivation is to remove assets from the sponsor's balance sheet, it is referred to as a balance sheet transaction.

54k Describe the mechanisms available for placing bonds in the primary market and distinguish between the primary and secondary markets for bonds

Section 9 covers the final LOS of the reading. The mechanisms for placing in the primary market that need to be memorized are bought deal, auction process, and private placement.

The secondary market provides liquidity to the primary market and is described briefly in Section 9.2.

Fixed Income

Reading 54 sample question
(Answers on p. 312)

An institutional portfolio manager makes the following statements regarding Treasury inflation-protected securities (TIPS).

- Statement 1: "TIPS make semi-annual coupon payments at a rate fixed at issuance of the bonds"
- Statement 2: "TIPS coupons are paid semi-annually as a percentage of the inflation-adjusted face value of the bond"

Which of these statements is/are most accurate?

(A) Statement 1
(B) Statement 2
(C) Both statements 1 and 2

This reading introduces a lot of concepts which will be used extensively in Study Session 16 to value bonds. Be aware that Section 6 of the reading on swap spreads is marked optional and hence is not examinable.

LEARNING OUTCOME STATEMENTS

Application LOS	Knowledge LOS
55e **Calculate** and **compare** yield spread measures	55a **Identify** the interest rate policy tools available to a central bank
55f **Describe** credit spreads and relationships between credit spreads and economic conditions	55b **Describe** a yield curve and the various shapes of the yield curve
55g **Describe** how embedded options affect yield spreads	55c **Explain** the basic theories of the term structure of interest rates and describe the implications of each theory for the shape of the yield curve
55i **Calculate** the after-tax yield of a taxable security and the tax-equivalent yield of a tax-exempt security	55d **Define** a spot rate
	55h **Explain** how liquidity and issue size affects the yield spread of a bond relative to other similar securities
	55j **Define** LIBOR and explain its importance to funded investors who borrow short term

APPLICATION LEARNING OUTCOME STATEMENTS

55e Calculate and compare yield spread measures

There are three yield spread measures which need to be calculated:

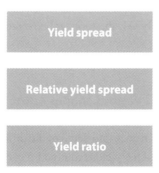

Section 4.1 has excellent examples of each simple calculation.

55f Describe credit spreads and relationshipsbetween credit spreads and economic conditions

Section 4.2 defines intermarket and intramarket spreads, but there is much more information to cover on credit spreads in Section 4.3. There are a lot of illustrations on past credit spreads, but the key point to understand is that they widen in a recession and narrow in a boom.

In a recession investors reject corporate risk and invest in Treasuries, driving Treasury prices up and yields down, and at the same time corporate prices down and yields up. The opposite is true in a boom period.

55g Describe how embedded options affect yield spreads

Options which favor the issuer increase yield spreads as the investor demands an extra yield to compensate for the option. Those which favor the investor reduce spreads for the opposite reason. This relationship is covered in detail in Study Session 16 on valuation.

Also note that the prepayment option on a mortgage-backed security increases yield spreads as it is similar to a call option on a corporate bond.

55i Calculate the after-tax yield of a taxable security and the tax-equivalent yield of a tax-exempt security

Section 4.6.1 shows examples of the two calculations required for this LOS. Both calculations allow a comparison between taxable and tax-exempt bonds. Practice question 3 demonstrates exactly how each calculation works.

KNOWLEDGE LEARNING OUTCOME STATEMENTS

55a Identify the interest rate policy tools available to a central bank

Section 2 addresses this LOS very briefly. All the tools are covered in much more detail in the Economics section.

55b Describe a yield curve and the various shapes of the yield curve

This LOS is a precursor to LOS 55c, which goes into detail of the different theories of term structure. The term structure is the graphical representation of the yields required for each maturity. An upward-sloping (normal) curve means longer maturities require higher yields. A downward-sloping (inverted) curve means longer maturities require lower yields.

55c Explain the basic theories of the term structure of interest rates and describe the implications of each theory for the shape of the yield curve

There are three basic theories, covered in Section 3.2.1. The pure expectations theory states that the yield curve will follow an investor's expectations. An upward sloping curve reflects an expectation that rates will rise, etc.

The liquidity preference theory is the most tricky. It states that longer maturities require a premium to compensate for higher interest rate risk (note: not liquidity risk). This premium is added to the expectations theory to give the shape of the yield curve. Note that under the liquidity preference theory the yield curve may still be downward sloping. If expectations were for rates to fall, then the liquidity premium may simply make the curve less downward sloping. A flat or upward curve under the pure expectations theory will lead to a steeper upward sloping curve under the liquidity preference theory.

The market segmentation theory is also covered, stating that the shape of the curve is dictated by supply and demand at each maturity point, and that certain investors prefer different maturity ranges. For example, a large demand from banks for short maturities and a large demand from pension funds for long maturities may result in a humped curve. The large demand at either end of the curve drags yields down.

55d Define a spot rate

The yield on a zero coupon bond is known as a spot rate. It is the correct rate to use to discount a single cash flow from time t to today. It is used extensively in Study Session 16 and can be studied there.

55h Explain how liquidity and issue size affects the yield spread of a bond relative to other similar securities

Increased liquidity (hence lower liquidity risk) and higher issue size both reduce yield spread.

55j Define LIBOR and explain its importance to funded investors who borrow short term

LIBOR is the interest rate at which banks borrow from each other in the London interbank market. This is the benchmark borrowing cost for short-term investors. Institutions will have to pay LIBOR plus a spread depending on their credit rating, and then will look to earn in excess of this rate on their investments.

Fixed Income

Reading 55 sample question
(Answers on p. 312)

A bond analyst makes the following statements on the shape of the yield curve.

- Statement 1: "The normal yield curve is flat"
- Statement 2: "The inverted yield curve is upward sloping"

Which of these statements is/are least accurate?

(A) Statement 1
(B) Statement 2
(C) Both statements 1 and 2

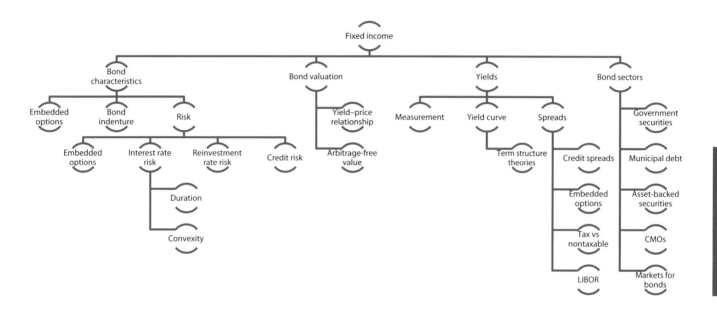

Topic:	Fixed Income
Weight:	12%
Study sessions:	15–16
Readings:	52–59

Fixed Income

This reading introduces a lot of concepts which will be used extensively in Study Session 16 to value bonds. Be aware that Section 6 of the reading on swap spreads is marked optional and hence is not examinable.

LEARNING OUTCOME STATEMENTS

Application LOS	Knowledge LOS
56a **Explain** the steps in the bond valuation process	56b **Describe** types of bonds for which estimating the expected cash flows is difficult
56c **Calculate** the value of a bond (coupon and zero-coupon)	56d **Explain** how the price of a bond changes if the discount rate changes and as the bond approaches its maturity date
56e **Calculate** the change in value of a bond given a change in its discount rate	
56f **Explain** and demonstrate the use of the arbitrage-free valuation approach and describe how a dealer can generate an arbitrage profit if a bond is mispriced	

APPLICATION LEARNING OUTCOME STATEMENTS

56a Explain the steps in the bond valuation process

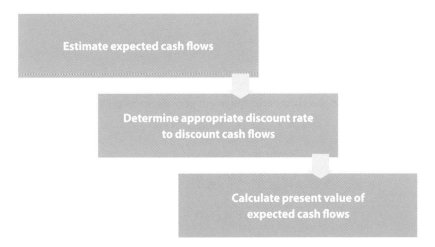

56c Calculate the value of a bond (coupon and zero-coupon)

This section brings out the calculation of present values from the Quantitative Methods section. The assumption unless told otherwise in the exam is that corporate bonds are semi-annual, fixed-income coupons with a par value of $1,000.

Example – Coupon paying
10 year, 5% coupon, yielding 7%

If the question does not tell us otherwise, we presume a semi-annual coupon and a $1,000 par value. This bond therefore pays $25 every 6 months for 10 years (20 coupon payments). At maturity it will pay back the par value of $1,000. The yield is the return the investor is getting and is always quoted on an annual basis. This information can be used to calculate the price using the TVM buttons:

$$N = 20$$

$$I/Y = 3.5$$

$$PMT = 25$$

$$FV = 1,000$$

$$CPT\ PV = -857.88$$

Note that the 5% quoted coupon was annual, and 2.5% is received every six months. Similarly, the yield was quoted as 7% annually but is applied as 3.5% every six months.

To value a zero coupon bond, the same method can be used, but the payment will be zero. Alternatively, as the bond will pay out only a single cash flow – the par value at maturity – the single cash flow can be discounted to present value.

Either way, the key point to remember when valuing a zero coupon bond is that payment periods are semi-annual. Even though the coupon is zero, yields quoted on an annual basis must still be applied semi-annually.

Example – Zero coupon
10 year, zero coupon, yielding 6%

It must be assumed that the bond has six monthly payment periods, so using the TVM function:

$$N = 20$$

$$I/Y = 3.0$$

$$PMT = 0$$

$$FV = 1,000$$

$$CPT\ PV = -553.68$$

Alternatively, discount 1,000 by 3% for 20 periods, $1,000/(1.03)^{20} = 53.68$.

Note that the zero will always trade at a discount to par.

56e Calculate the change in value of a bond given a change in its discount rate

The discount rate used to get the price of the bond is input into the TVM buttons as I/Y. To see the effect of a change in the discount rate, we simply recalculate the value using a new I/Y.

As the discount rate increases, the present value of cash flows, and hence the price of the bond, decreases. Interest rates and bond prices are inversely related: as one rises, the other falls. This amount the price moves by is measured using duration and convexity.

56f Explain and demonstrate the use of the arbitrage-free valuation approach and describe how a dealer can generate an arbitrage profit if a bond is mispriced

The key to the arbitrage opportunity is breaking down a bond into individual cash flows. A two-year semi-annual coupon bond pays four coupons and the par at value at maturity. These five cash flows can be broken down and valued individually. The sum of the value of each cash flow should be equal to the value of the whole bond as they are an equivalent set of cash flows. If the sum is different there is an arbitrage opportunity.

Section 4.2 demonstrates this process using Treasuries and strips (as discussed in LOS 55c). Each strip represents a single cash flow. The discount rate used to get the present value of the strip is known as a spot rate – the rate used to discount a single cash flow from a future point in time back to today.

An exam question may present a set of strips and the spot rates required to calculate their present values. Once calculated and added up, the total is compared to the value of the bond.

If the value of the bond is lower than the total of the strips, the bond should be purchased, broken down into individual strips (stripped) and the strips sold. If the value of the bond is higher than the total of the strips, the strips should be purchased, added together (reconstituted), and sold as a bond.

Example
2 year, 5% Treasury bond is priced at $945.84

Spot rates are as follows:

	Spot rate
6 month	4%
1 year	6%
18 months	7%
2 years	8%

Discount rate	Cash flow $	Present value $
4%/2 =2.0%	25.00	$25/(1.02) = 24.51$
6%/2 = 3.0%	25.00	$25/(1.03)^2 = 23.56$
7%/2 = 3.5%	25.00	$25/(1.035)^3 = 22.55$
8%/2 = 4.0%	1025.00	$1025/(1.04)^4 = 876.17$
	Total value of strips	946.79

As the total value of the bond is higher than the total value of the strips, the bond should be purchased for $945.84, stripped, and the strips sold for $946.79, netting an arbitrage profit of $0.95.

The bond price would be arbitrage free if it were $946.79.

Knowledge learning outcome statements

56b Describe types of bonds for which estimating the expected cash flows is difficult

Bonds may contain an option to change the date of principal repayment. The coupon payment may vary according to a reference rate or it may be convertible. All present issues in trying to predict cash flows.

56d Explain how the price of a bond changes if the discount rate changes and as the bond approaches its maturity date

As seen earlier, an increase in the discount rate leads to a decrease in the price, and vice versa.

As a bond approaches maturity, its value approaches par. So assuming interest rates remain constant, a bond issued at a premium will gradually fall to its par value and a bond issued at a discount will gradually rise to par value.

Reading 56 sample question
(Answers on p. 312)

Given the following spot rate curve:

Spot rates
- 1-yr zero = 8.50%
- 2-yr zero = 7.75%
- 3-yr zero = 7.25%
- 4-yr zero = 7.35%
- 5-yr zero = 7.45%

What will be the market price of a three-year, 8% annual coupon rate bond?

(A) $1,018.09
(B) $1,021.76
(C) $1,111.11

LEARNING OUTCOME STATEMENTS

Application LOS	Knowledge LOS
57b **Calculate and interpret** traditional yield measures for fixed-rate bonds and explain their limitations and assumptions	57a **Describe** the sources of return from investing in a bond
57c **Explain** the reinvestment assumption implicit in calculating yield to maturity and describe the factors that affect reinvestment risk	
57d **Calculate** and **interpret** the bond equivalent yield of an annual-pay bond and the annual-pay yield of a semi-annual pay bond	
57e **Describe** the calculation of the theoretical Treasury spot rate curve and calculate the value of a bond using spot rates	
57f **Explain** nominal, zero-volatility, and option-adjusted spread, and the relations among these spreads and option cost	
57g **Explain** a forward rate and calculate spot rates from forward rates, forward rates from spot rates, and the value of a bond using forward rates	

APPLICATION LEARNING OUTCOME STATEMENTS

57b Calculate and interpret the traditional yield measures for fixed-rate bonds and explain their limitations and assumptions

Section 3 of the reading covers the different types of yield calculation required. The most heavily used is yield to maturity. This is calculated as I/Y on the BAII plus.

Example
10 year, 5% coupon, price 857.88
N = 20
PV = –857.88 (note the PV must be put in as a negative or the calculator will show "Error 5")
PMT = 25
FV = 1,000
CPT I/Y = 3.5

Important discussion points are the assumptions that underlie the YTM.

It will not be realized unless the yield is constant throughout the life of the bond. Reinvestment risk (see LOS 57C) is the risk that this is not the case.

The bond will be held until maturity.

If the bond contains a call option, then a yield to call (YTC) may be calculated assuming the bond is called. On the calculator replace FV with the call value and N with the periods until call.

Note, a bond may be non-refundable for a period, meaning it cannot be called using funds raised from a cheaper issue. A yield to first refunding calculates the yield to the first date when the bond can be called using funds from a cheaper issue.

If the bond contains a put option, then a yield to put can be calculated. The yield to worst is the lowest of all the yields calculated.

The advantage of the yields above is that they take into account time to maturity and current price, which is why they are most popular.

The current yield takes into account the current price but not time to maturity. Calculated as

Annual Coupon/Price

The nominal yield is simply the coupon rate. It does not take into account the price or time to maturity.

The following relationship always holds and is also examinable.

Bonds priced above par:

Bonds priced below par:

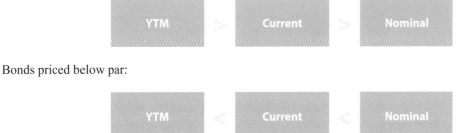

57c Explain the reinvestment assumption implicit in calculating yield to maturity and describe the factors that affect reinvestment risk

The two assumptions from LOS 57b are both required for the yield to be realized. The risk is that yields change or the bond is not held until maturity. The risk of yields changing is that income received over the life of the bond cannot be reinvested at the YTM.

If yields fall, then the realized yield will be lower than the YTM. If yields rise, the realized yield will be higher than the YTM.

The larger the cash flows over the life of the bond, the higher the reinvestment risk. Larger cash flows occur when the coupon is higher, the maturity is longer, or there is an option to get principal back earlier.

57d Calculate and interpret the bond equivalent yield of an annual-pay bond and the annual-pay yield of a semi-annual-pay bond

Bond equivalent yields (as discussed in Quantitative Methods) are a simple arithmetic doubling of the semi-annual effective yield. The annual yield on an annual pay bond is therefore not a BEY. It must be first turned into a semi-annual effective yield and then doubled. This is demonstrated with examples in Section 3.2.4 and can also be done using the ICONV function on the BAII plus.

57e Describe the calculation of the theoretical Treasury spot rate curve and calculate the value of a bond using spot rates

The process of bootstrapping is used to derive the curve. This process is explained and illustrated in Section 4.1 of the reading. Note the LOS asks for a description rather than a calculation. However, it is a requirement to be able to use spot rates to value a bond.

The bootstrapping process involves using a zero coupon bond to derive the spot rate for period one, and then successive on-the-run treasuries to discover subsequent rates. There is a detailed example in the section which should be reviewed for understanding but not recalculated.

The focus should be on valuing bonds using spot rates. Each cash flow from the bond is valued at the appropriate spot rate and discounted to present value. The total PV of the cash flows is the bond value. This is the exact process performed on the strips in LOS 56f.

57f Explain nominal, zero-volatility, and option-adjusted spreads, and the relations among these spreads and option cost

The spread is the difference between the yield on a benchmark Treasury and another bond. The nominal spread is the difference in the yield to maturity of the two bonds. It is important to note the key drawbacks – this spread assumes the yield is constant over the life of the bond, i.e. it does not take into account the shape of the yield curve. Second, if the bond has an embedded option, a change in volatility may alter the cash flows.

The z-spread is the difference in spot rates required to discount a benchmark Treasury bond and another bond. This takes into account the shape of the yield curve. The calculation is not a requirement of the LOS but is demonstrated in Section 4.2.1. It is important to note that the z-spread will be equal to the nominal spread only if the yield curve is flat. If it is not flat, steeper curves and longer maturities increase the difference.

The option-adjusted spread (OAS) is the z-spread adjusted for the effect of the option in the bond. That is to say the effect of the option is removed to get from the z-spread to the OAS. The table in Section 4.2.3 summarizes this key information. The nominal and z-spreads show the spread over the Treasury benchmark to compensate the investor for the extra credit, liquidity, and option risk. The OAS shows only the compensation for the extra credit and liquidity risk.

Two key points follow on from this. The difference between the z-spread and the OAS is the option cost (in yield), and the OAS for a callable bond will be lower than the z-spread as the option cost is positive (the OAS for a putable bond will be larger than the z-spread).

The formula given in Section 4.2.2.3 is the key to remembering this relationship.

57g Explain a forward rate and calculate spot rates from forward rates, forward rates from spot rates, and the value of a bond using forward rates

A forward rate shows the return an investor would receive between two future dates. Contrast this to a spot rate, which shows the return an investor would receive between today and a future date. Spot rates can be used to calculate forward rates, and vice versa. The key is to understand the assumption that investing today for two years should yield the same return as investing today for one year, then reinvesting at year one for another year.

In terms of forwards and spots, this is the same as saying that the two-year spot rate is equivalent to the one-year spot rate combined with the one-year forward rate one year from now.

This forward rate would be written as $_1f_1$ meaning a rate which lasts for one period and starts one period from now.

A forward which lasts for one period and starts two periods from now would be written as $_1f_2$. There are numerous examples covering the calculation of forwards from spots in Section 5.2. It is useful to note that an approximate answer to these calculations can be arrived at very quickly if the effect of compounding is ignored.

Example
S1 = 5%
S2 = 6%
Calculate $_1f_1$

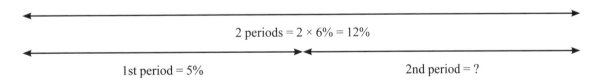

2 periods = 2 × 6% = 12%

1st period = 5%   2nd period = ?

If the relationship described above holds, then investing at s_2 rate for two years should yield the same as investing for the first period at s_1 and the second period at $_1f_1$.

$_1f_1$ must therefore be 7% so that 5% + 7% = 12%, the two-period return.

The answer will be slightly different when compounding is taken into account, as demonstrated below:

$$(1+s_2)^2 = (1+s_1)(1+{_1}f_1)$$

$$1.06^2 = 1.05(1+{_1}f_1)$$

$$(1+{_1}f_1) = 1.06^2/1.05 = 1.0701.$$

$${_1}f_1 = 7.01\%$$

Valuing a bond using forward rates is exactly the same process as valuing a bond using spots. The key point is that a forward can be used to derive the spot rates necessary to discount each cash flow on the bond.

In the example above, a cash flow of $25 arising after two periods could be discounted at s_2, giving:

$$PV = \$25/(1.06)^2 = \$22.25$$

Or it could be discounted by ${_1}f_1$ then s_1, giving:

$$PV = \$25/(1.0701)(1.05) = \$22.25$$

There are several practice questions which cover this method at the end of the reading.

Knowledge learning outcome statements

57a Describe the sources of return from investing in a bond

There are three sources of return. The coupon is the cash coupon paid. The capital gain or loss is the difference between the price paid and the par value paid back at maturity. A bond purchased at a discount will lead to a capital gain, a bond purchased at a premium a capital loss.

The third source of return is the interest received on reinvesting income during the life of the bond, e.g. the interest earned on reinvesting coupons. The variation in this reinvestment income is reinvestment risk and discussed in LOS 57c.

Reading 57 sample question
(Answers on p. 312)

A 20-year, 10% bond that pays interest annually is discounted priced to yield 12%, i.e. the discount rate is 12%. However, interest payments will be invested at 10%. The realized compound yield on this bond is closest to:

(A) <10.0%
(B) >12.0%
(C) Between 10.0% and 12.0%

This reading contains the key calculations for duration.

LEARNING OUTCOME STATEMENTS

Application LOS	Knowledge LOS
58b **Describe** the price volatility characteristics for option-free, callable, prepayable, and putable bonds when interest rates change	58a **Distinguish** between the full valuation approach (the scenario analysis approach) and the duration/convexity approach for measuring interest rate risk, and explain the advantage of using the full valuation approach
58c **Describe** positive convexity, negative convexity, and their relation to bond price and yield	58f **Distinguish** among the alternative definitions of duration, and explain why effective duration is the most appropriate measure of interest rate risk for bonds with embedded options
58d **Calculate and interpret** the effective duration of a bond, given information about how the bond's price will increase and decrease for given changes in interest rates	58i **Distinguish** between modified convexity and effective convexity
58e **Calculate** the approximate percentage price change for a bond, given the bond's effective duration and a specified change in yield	58k **Describe** the impact of yield volatility on the interest rate risk of a bond
58g **Calculate** the duration of a portfolio, given the duration of the bonds comprising the portfolio, and explain the limitations of portfolio duration	
58h **Describe the convexity measure of a bond and estimate** a bond's percentage price change, given the bond's duration and convexity and a specified change in interest rates	
58j **Calculate** the price value of a basis point (PVBP), and explain its relationship to duration	

APPLICATION LEARNING OUTCOME STATEMENTS

58c Describe positive convexity, negative convexity, and their relation to bond price and yield

The key outcome of the LOS is to identify the basic relationship between yields and bond prices, and then identify which types of convexity are displayed by option-free, callable, and putable bonds.

The price of option-free bonds falls as yields rise, but the relationship is not linear. When plotted on a graph the relationship is curved – the relationship gets steeper at lower yields and flatter at higher yields. This is positive convexity. Exhibits 5 and 6 in Section 3.1 demonstrate this relationship.

At lower yields for a callable bond, the curve flattens off due to the price ceiling at the call price. The lower the yield, the higher the bond price, and the more likely it is that the bond will be called. This is negative convexity. Exhibit 10 in Section 3.2 demonstrates negative convexity.

At higher yields for a putable bond, the curve flattens due to the floor at the put price. The higher the yield, the lower the bond price, and the more likely it is that the bond will be put. This is positive convexity at this end of the curve. Exhibit 13 in Section 3.2 demonstrates this relationship.

For exam-standard questions, you should be able to identify when callable and putable bonds demonstrate negative and positive convexity, and why.

58b Describe the price volatility characteristics for option-free, callable, prepayable, and putable bonds when interest rates change

This follows on from the LOS above. Given that the callable bond displays negative convexity at low yields, the increase in price is limited. It therefore has lower price volatility than option-free bonds, i.e. lower interest rate risk.

The putable bond shows more positive convexity than an option-free bond at high yields, and hence its price does not drop as much as an option-free bond at high yields, i.e. it also has lower interest rate risk.

The key point is that both callable and putable bonds display lower price volatility, i.e. have lower interest rate risk than an option-free bond.

The prepayment option on a prepayble security such as a mortgage-backed security is similar to a call option. Again this will reduce price volatility due to negative convexity at low yields.

These relationships are all shown on price/yield diagrams in Exhibits 9–13 in Section 3.

58d Calculate and interpret the effective duration of a bond, given information about how the bond's price will increase and decrease for given changes in interest rates

Calculating duration is a common question in the practice material, but it is equally important to interpret the result.

Questions will state an initial bond price (Po), a bond price if yields decline, and a bond price if yields rise. Duration is then calculated as:

Price when yields decline – Price when yields rise

$$2 \times \text{Initial Price} \times \text{Change in yield}$$

Key points to note are that the change in yield should be included as a decimal, and is the change in yield either side of the initial yield, i.e. if yields are increased by 50bp and decreased by 50bp to get the new bond prices, the change in yield should be input into the formula as 0.005. Note that the result of this calculation is known as effective duration. Other measures are discussed in LOS 58f.

Section 4.1 contains a walkthrough calculation and practice questions, all of which should be attempted.

The duration figure calculated using this method is known as effective duration. It states the approximate percentage change in price for a 1% change in yield.

A duration of 3.2 would therefore mean a 1% change in yield would lead to a 3.2% change in the price of the bond. A 2% change in yield would lead to a 6.4% change in the price of the bond, and so on.

Crucially, the change in price predicted by duration is only approximate. It assumes that the relationship between yields and prices is linear, when in fact it is convex. The larger the yield change, the less accurate the prediction. This is illustrated in Section 4.3.

Due to the positive convexity of the relationship between prices and yields, duration is higher at low yield levels. This is illustrated by the very steep curve at low yields.

Duration is also higher for bonds with longer maturities and lower coupons. This is because the cash flows are received further into the future and hence the price (present value) is more sensitive to a change in interest rates (discount rate).

58e Calculate the approximate percentage price change for a bond, given the bond's effective duration and a specified change in yield

This LOS is mostly a repeat of LOS 58d. Once we have calculated duration, the interpretation allows us to calculate the movement in the price of a bond. Note that if yields increase, bond prices fall, and vice versa. The following formula is given in the readings and may help with remembering this key negative relationship:

$$\% \text{ Change in bond price} = -\text{Duration} \times \text{change yield} \times 100$$

So for a 0.5% increase in yields and a bond with a duration of 6.8, the approximate change in price would be $-6.8 \times 0.005 \times 100 = -3.4$ – an approximate drop in price of 3.4%.

58g Calculate the duration of a portfolio, given the duration of the bonds comprising the portfolio, and explain the limitations of portfolio duration

The key point of this LOS is that the duration of a portfolio is the weighted average duration of the bonds within the portfolio. The bonds should be weighted by market value. Section 4.8 contains a comprehensive walkthrough example if you need a reminder on weighted average calculations.

Fixed Income

The critical limitation of this measure is that it assumes a parallel shift in the yield curve, i.e. yields shift by the same amount for every bond within the portfolio. Portfolio duration will not correctly measure the change in value for a non-parallel shift (this is yield curve risk).

58h Describe the convexity measure of a bond and estimate a bond's percentage price change, given the bond's duration and convexity and a specified change in interest rates

Convexity is a measure which is used to correct the error in the estimate of price change using duration.

Although the formula is given in Section 5, the key focus of the LOS is on calculating the price change of a bond using convexity if it is given. The estimate of price change using duration assumes a linear relationship between yields and prices. The convexity adjustment corrects for some of this error. The adjustment required is:

$$\text{Convexity} \times \text{Change in yield}^2 \times 100$$

Practice question 3 in Section 5.1 shows several examples of calculating bond price changes using a given duration and convexity.

58j Calculate the price value of a basis point (PVBP), and explain its relationship to duration

PVBP is an extension of duration. Rather than stating the change in price as a percentage which duration allows us to do immediately (e.g. a duration of 4.1 means a 4.1% change in price for a 1% change in yield), PVBP measures the dollar value change in bond price for a 1 basis point change in yield. It can be calculated as:

$$\text{Duration} \times 0.0001 \times \text{Bond price}$$

For a bond priced at $102 and a duration of 5.2, this means a PVBP of $0.05304. The PVBP is always stated as a positive dollar amount. Obviously if yields increase, then this amount would be deducted from the initial price to get the new bond price.

KNOWLEDGE LEARNING OUTCOME STATEMENTS

58a Distinguish between the full valuation approach (the scenario analysis approach) and the duration/convexity approach for measuring interest rate risk, and explain the advantage of using the full valuation approach

As discussed in the application LOS, the duration and convexity measures only approximate the price change in the bond. Notably, if a portfolio duration is used, the assumed yield change must be a parallel shift.

The full valuation approach involves changing yields by different amounts for each bond using different scenarios. This will give a more accurate prediction but is very time consuming, hence the common use of portfolio duration.

58f Distinguish among the alternative definitions of duration, and explain why effective duration is the most appropriate measure of interest rate risk for bonds with embedded options

The calculation LOS in this reading require the calculation of effective duration.

Modified duration is a measure of duration that ignores the potential change in cash flows given a change in yield. Bonds which contain options may well have a change in cash flows when yields change, hence modified duration is suitable if there are embedded options in the bonds.

Macaulay duration measures the average time until cash flows are received for a bond in present value terms. The key point, however, is that it also ignores the possible changes in cash flows, so again is not suitable for bonds with embedded options.

58i Distinguish between modified convexity and effective convexity

Just as it is possible to calculate modified duration, which ignores the possibility of a change in cash flows, it is also possible to calculate modified convexity, which also ignores them.

58k Describe the impact of yield volatility on the interest rate risk of a bond

All calculations of interest rate risk so far have assumed a given volatility. The higher the volatility, the higher the interest rate risk for a given duration.

Reading 58 sample question
(Answers on p. 312)

A bond with a par value of $1,000, a 7% coupon paid semi-annually and 15 years to maturity is currently trading at $1,100. If the yield decreases by 150 basis points, the bond's price will increase to $1,300, and if the yield increases by 150 basis points, the price will decrease to $900. What is the approximate percentage change in price for a 1% change in rates?

(A) 10.12%
(B) 11.12%
(C) 12.12%

Fixed Income

LEARNING OUTCOME STATEMENTS

Application LOS	Knowledge LOS
59d **Explain** risks in relying on ratings from credit rating agencies	59a **Describe** credit risk and credit-related risks affecting corporate bonds
59f **Calculate** and interpret financial ratios used in credit analysis	59b **Describe** seniority rankings of corporate debt and explain the potential violation of the priority of claims in a bankruptcy proceeding
59g **Evaluate** the credit quality of a corporate bond issuer and a bond of that issuer, given key financial ratios of the issuer and the industry	59c **Distinguish** between corporate issuer credit ratings and issue credit ratings and describe the rating agency practice of "notching"
59i **Calculate** the return impact of spread changes	59e **Explain** the components of traditional credit analysis
59j **Explain** special considerations when evaluating the credit of high yield, sovereign, and municipal debt issuers and issues	59h **Describe** factors that influence the level and volatility of yield spreads

APPLICATION LEARNING OUTCOME STATEMENTS

59d Explain risks in relying on ratings from credit rating agencies

The risks are listed as points 1 through 4 in Section 4.3. Focus on learning these points rather than spending much time on the history of defaults, which is just in there to point out that historically credit ratings have generally been accurate (sub-prime crisis aside). There are six exam-style questions to attempt in Example 4.

59f Calculate and interpret financial ratios used in credit analysis

Section 5.2.1 on capacity contains a large case study on the evaluation of credit quality in Example 6. The ratios given should be largely familiar from FRA, so focus on how they are applied using Exhibits 10–13. This is good practice on the understanding of financial statements and ratio calculation.

59g Evaluate the credit quality of a corporate bond issuer and a bond of that issuer, given key financial ratios of the issuer and the industry

This LOS follows directly on from 59f. The case study in Section 5.2.1 uses the ratios calculated to assess the credit quality of the issuer. Make sure you are comfortable with reaching the conclusions – again this depends on an understanding of financial accounts and ratio analysis. For example, you should be aware that higher leverage and lower coverage will both lead to lower credit ratings.

59i Calculate the return impact of spread changes

These calculations are covered after Example 8 in Section 6. The change in spread is just a change in interest rates, so the calculations here are very similar to the modified duration and modified convexity calculations from the earlier reading. There is an example given in the text that you should make sure you're comfortable with before attempting Example 9.

59j Explain special considerations when evaluating the credit of high yield, sovereign, and municipal debt issuers and issues

High yield issuers are covered extensively in Section 7.1. Most of the points are intuitive; higher yields result from higher rsk businesses, and the sources of higher risk are fairly intuitive so review these quickly and note any that you didn't think were obvious. To specifically address the special considerations, focus on the paragraphs on liquidity, financial projections, debt structure, corporate structure and covenant analysis.

In Section 7.2, the key considerations for sovereign debt are both ability (as usual in credit analysis) but also willingness to pay. Note the key points listed under the headings political and economic profile, and flexibility and performance profile.

Municipal debt in Section 7.3 is broken down into general obligation bonds and revenue bonds. For general obligation, the special considerations revolve around the ability of the issuer to raise taxes and cover the cash flows. Specific risk factors that are mentioned include reliance on one or two types of tax, and hidden pension scheme deficits. Revenue bonds are covered briefly, their repayment depends on the revenues generated by a specific project, hence credit analysis must focus on the project as well as the terms of the issue.

KNOWLEDGE LEARNING OUTCOME STATEMENTS

59a Describe credit risk and credit-related risks affecting corporate bonds

This LOS breaks credit risk into default risk, as seen in other readings, and loss severity (loss given default). Ensure you can use the probability of default multiplied by the loss given default to work out the expected loss. There is an example given in Section 2.

In addition you should take away the term "spread risk" and be able to break it down into credit migration (downgrade) risk and market liquidity risk. The crisis of 2008 is referenced specifically here and that may be a good anecdote to help you remember the key points. Example 1 at the end of Section 2 contains three questions covering this LOS.

59b Describe seniority rankings of corporate debt and explain the potential violation of the priority of claims in a bankruptcy proceeding

Section 3.2 covers seniority ranking. There is a flow chart in Exhibit 1 that lists out the rankings. Section 3.3 then highlights the fact that different rankings have different recovery rates. It also notes that these rates vary within the credit cycle and by industry.

The final part of the section covers the second part of the LOS. Although secured should have priority over unsecured, and senior over junior, this is not always the case. There a couple of questions covering this LOS in Example 3.

59c Distinguish between corporate issuer credit ratings and issue credit ratings, and describe the rating agency practice of "notching"

Section 4.2 of the reading distinguishes between the issuer rating and the issue rating. It also covers notching and introduces the terms "cross default provisions" and "structural subordination," which you should note.

59e Explain the components of traditional credit analysis

Section 5 addresses the 4 c's of traditional credit analysis – capacity, collateral, covenants and character. You should note the key points that are addressed under each of these headings in Sections 5.2.1 through 5.2.4.

By far the largest section is Section 5.2.1 on capacity. Note that all of the ratio calculations in here are covered in LOS 59g, so use Exhibits 10–13 and Example 6 to address that LOS. Focus on the three questions in Example 7 for this LOS.

59h Describe factors that influence the level and volatility of yield spreads

Section 6 introduces yields and spreads, both of which should familiar terms from earlier readings. Move quickly through the historic information linking higher yields to higher risk, and focus on the bullet point list of five factors that influence spreads. Attempt the questions in Example 8 – the rest of this section then deals with LOS 59i.

Reading 59 sample question
(Answers on p. 313)

1. A corporate bond suffers a 75 bps widening in spread due a downgrade by the rating agencies. The bond has a modified duration of 8.3 and convexity of 78.2. The return impact from the 75 bps spread widening is closest to:

    (A) 6.44%
    (B) 5.80%
    (C) 6.01%

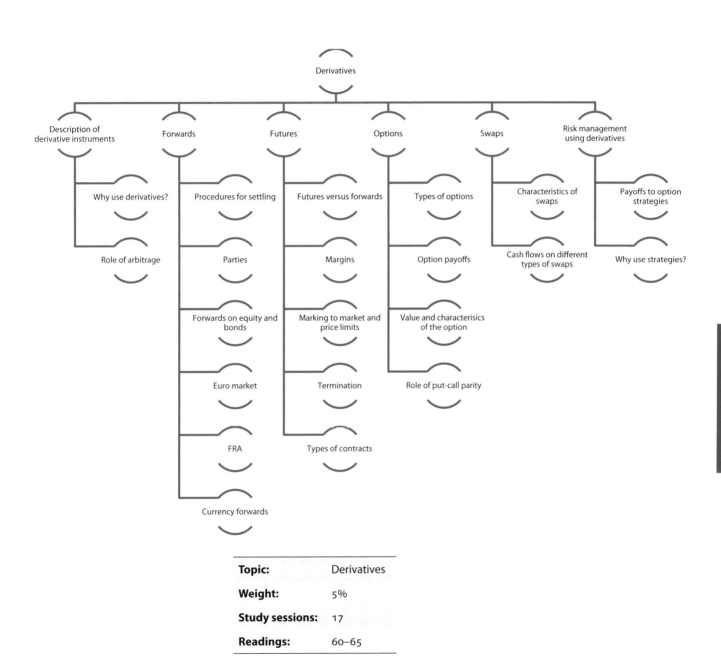

Topic:	Derivatives
Weight:	5%
Study sessions:	17
Readings:	60–65

THE BIG PICTURE

Derivatives is only 5% of the Level I exam, but there is a lot of material to cover – six readings. This topic has the potential to be 15% of the Level II and Level III exams, so it is a good idea to get a solid foundation in derivatives at this level. And that is what this material is all about: introducing you to different types of derivatives, their characteristics, why you would use them, and what is the payoff from using a strategy involving derivatives. You will notice that you are introduced to both the derivative instrument and the market in which it trades – so be sure not to overlook the market dimension.

FORWARDS AND FUTURES

Forwards and futures are contracts that allow you to lock in a future price for the sale or purchase of something, where this something may be a commodity, a security, an index, or a currency. Forwards and futures are similar in terms of why and how you take positions, but forwards are customized contracts, whereas futures contracts are standardized and traded on exchanges. The difference in these markets is important in terms of the LOS. In the case of forwards, the attention is focused on the process of settling the contracts and how these contracts can be devised. In the case of futures, the attention is on the market issues of price limits, margins, and the different types of futures contracts.

OPTIONS AND RISK MANAGEMENT

The readings covering options are very detailed and the LOS are descriptive [keywords: define, explain, compare]. You should be able to distinguish between an American option and a European option, and you should be able to identify the moneyness (i.e. in-, at-, or out-of-the-money) of an option based on the price of the underlying and the strike price. Though the calculations pertaining to options are limited to intrinsic value, minimum and maximum values, and payoffs, you should still make sure you understand how the key elements of the option (exercise price, time to expiration, volatility, and interest rates) and the value of the underlying stock affect the value of an option (that is, positive or negative).

The risk management reading focuses solely on options, and you should practice diagramming the basic strategies that involve both calls and puts using a payoff diagram (that is payoff versus price of the underlying). Though this may seem daunting at first, if you get in the habit of calculating the payoff at each value of the underlying for each leg of the strategy, and then adding this up across the legs for each price of the underlying, you will be able to disentangle almost any strategy.

SWAPS

The coverage of swaps is primarily descriptive, with some calculations for the cash flows that are exchanged with currency, equity, and plain vanilla interest rate swaps. The key to sorting this out is to lay out a timeline and indicate at each settlement point the amount that each party must "pay" – and then net these to determine who pays what to whom.

At first sight, the study session on Derivatives may seem a lot of work for 5% of the syllabus. However, you will find that at Level I the emphasis is on understanding the basics of the more common derivatives, and the questions, both written descriptions and simple numbers, are not hard. In addition, getting on top of the basics of forwards, futures, swaps, and options here will pay dividends in your Level II and Level III studies, when you will look at valuing the instruments and using them to hedge.

This first reading is an introduction to derivatives and their markets. It is interesting to read through but as far as the exam is concerned, you only have to remember a few key facts. These relate to definitions of the main types of derivatives, the difference between over-the-counter (OTC) and exchange-traded, the purposes and criticisms of derivative markets, and explaining how arbitrage between markets can help in setting a fair price.

LEARNING OUTCOME STATEMENTS

Application LOS	Knowledge LOS
60a **Define** a derivative and distinguish between exchange-traded and over-the-counter derivatives	60c **Define** forward contracts, future contracts, options (calls and puts), and swaps and compare their basic characteristics
60b **Contrast** forward commitments and contingent claims	
60d **Describe** the purposes of and controversies related to derivative markets	60e **Explain** arbitrage and the role it plays in determining prices and promoting market efficiency

APPLICATION LEARNING OUTCOME STATEMENTS

60a Define a derivative and distinguish between exchange-traded and over-the-counter derivatives

Questions can be as simple as spotting the correct (or fullest) definition. A derivative is a financial contract which has a return derived from the return of another asset (the "underlying").

Some derivatives can be bought or sold on an exchange (exchange-traded) and some are agreed privately between two parties outside any exchange (over-the-counter, usually OTC for short). The main differences are:

Exchange-traded	OTC
Only available for more popular derivatives (as the exchange needs volume to maintain liquidity)	In theory, you may be able to find another party to enter any derivative transaction
To enhance liquidity, the contracts are standardized – standard amounts (and specification where relevant) of the underlying and standard delivery dates	The contract can be tailored to the individual requirements of the parties
In order to reduce the risk (and hence increase liquidity), the exchange takes the other side of all the contracts, virtually eliminating counterparty risk (this is looked at in more detail in Reading 62)	There is a risk that the other party does not fulfill its obligations (counterparty risk)

Derivatives

60b Contrast forward commitments and contingent claims

In summary, forwards, futures and swaps are forward commitments, whereas options are contingent claims. All of these instruments will be covered in more detail in later LOSs, but Sections 2.1 and 2.2 give an overview of commitments and contingent claims respectively.

The most efficient approach is to cover the other LOSs first, then come back to this summary and simply check that you have picked up the main points.

60d Describe the purposes of and controversies related to derivative markets

This LOS often gives rise to practice questions that ask you to spot the answer which is NOT a purpose or NOT a controversy, so read the question carefully!

The reading goes through the purposes in Section 5 and the controversies in Section 6, but to summarize:

Purposes of derivatives markets:

- Provide price discovery as to price a derivative we need to have an idea of the price of the underlying
- Make markets in the underlying asset more efficient as the ability to replicate the transaction using derivatives means there is a check on the price
- Help risk management by giving certainty about the price of an underlying in the future (hedging)
- Lower transaction costs as it is cheaper to invest, for example, in a stock index future than to buy all the stocks in the index

Controversies of derivatives markets:

- Dangerous for unknowledgeable investors as they can be used inappropriately, leading to large losses
- "Like gambling" – seen as an unfair criticism as they can be used to manage risk, which benefits society

KNOWLEDGE LEARNING OUTCOME STATEMENTS

60c Define forward contracts, future contracts, options (calls and puts), and swaps and compare their basic characteristics

These are simple definitions which you need to be able to distinguish between. The details and terminology of options can be left until Reading 63.

- Forward commitment = agreement between two parties to buy/sell an asset at a specified price on a specified date in the future
- Forward contract = a forward commitment created in the OTC market
- Futures contract = a standardized forward commitment which is created and traded on an exchange
- Swap = a series of forward commitments in one OTC contract

- Option = a contract that gives one party the right (but not the obligation) to buy or sell an asset at a set price at a set future date or over a future period; this party pays the other party a premium to get this right
- Contingent claim = a contract with a payment which is dependent upon a future event occurring; this includes, but is not limited to, options

60e Explain arbitrage and the role it plays in determining prices and promoting market efficiency

Arbitrage means buying and selling an asset at two different prices at the same time so that a riskless profit can be made without investing any money. In the context of derivatives it means that the underlying could be bought now with borrowed money and held, or the investor could enter a forward commitment to buy the asset in the future. If the overall cost of these two is not the same, the combined actions of many investors taking part in this arbitrage opportunity will force the prices to an equilibrium in which there is no arbitrage opportunity.

Reading 60 sample questions
(Answers on p. 313)

1. The current price of silver is $300 per ounce and the risk-free rate is 6%. Assuming a market in equilibrium, the three-month forward price of silver should be closest to:

   (A) $300.00
   (B) $304.50
   (C) $318.00

2. Which of the following does not represent an example of a contingent claim?

   (A) Warrants
   (B) Options on futures
   (C) Futures

The main issues in this reading are first understanding broadly how a forward contract works and the default risk this entails, and second being able to calculate the compensation payment under a forward rate agreement (FRA).

This calculation of the FRA compensation is not difficult once you can see what it is trying to do, and you should practice it as it is highly likely to appear in your exam.

Notice that Section 2 on the structure of global forward markets, while useful in gaining an understanding of the background, does not feature in any of the LOS.

LEARNING OUTCOME STATEMENTS

Application LOS	Knowledge LOS
61a **Explain** delivery/settlement and default risk for both long and short positions in a forward contract	61c **Distinguish** between a dealer and an end user of a forward contract
61b **Describe** the procedures for settling a forward contract at expiration, and how termination prior to expiration can affect credit risk	61d **Describe** the characteristics of equity forward contracts and forward contracts on zero-coupon and coupon bonds
61f **Describe** forward rate agreements (FRAs) and calculate the gain/loss on a FRA	61e **Describe** the characteristics of the Eurodollar time deposit market, and define LIBOR and Euribor
61g **Calculate** and interpret the payoff of a FRA and explain each of the component terms of the payoff formula	61h **Describe** the characteristics of currency forward contracts

APPLICATION LEARNING OUTCOME STATEMENTS

61a, b Explain delivery/settlement and default risk for both long and short positions in a forward contract; describe the procedures for settling a forward contract at expiration, and how termination prior to expiration can affect credit risk

This is quite a useful section and is covered in Sections 1.1, 1.2, and 1.3. It gives a good summary of how forward contracts work and what the risks are. It's important that you grasp these, so make sure you spend enough time to understand them.

The buyer is called the long, and the seller is the short. The contract will be settled by the short delivering the relevant asset to the long on the appropriate day ("delivery") or, if allowed under the contract terms, by cash settlement. Cash settlement tends to be built into those contracts where delivery would be difficult (because the item doesn't exist or is restricted in its supply).

Example

Suppose the forward price agreed is $150.

Cash price of underlying asset at maturity of forward contract	Under delivery	Under cash settlement
$160	Short delivers asset and receives $150 (loses $10)	Short pays long $10 so long only has to spend $150 to buy asset
$130	Short delivers asset and receives $150 (gains $20)	Long pays short $20 so that long spends $150 in total ($130 to put asset in the market and $20 to short)

A contract can be terminated before it matures by entering an opposite transaction for the same asset at the same future date. However, if the new transaction is not with the same counterparty, there is a chance that one or both will default on the contract (credit risk). If the new transaction is with the same counterparty as the original contract, they can agree to offset the transactions and eliminate the credit risk. In this case there will be a net cash settlement on the difference between the two contract prices.

61f, g Describe forward rate agreements (FRAs) and calculate the gain/loss on a FRA; calculate and interpret the payoff and explain each of the component terms of the payoff formula

This is the only calculation in this reading and you should therefore make sure you are able to work out the compensation and which party is to pay which. It is more straightforward than the formula (not really worth trying to memorize) would suggest and it is often tested.

A forward rate agreement (FRA) is a forward contract that relates to the interest rate in a future period. A 3 × 9, for example, is looking at LIBOR for a six-month period (notice NOT a nine-month period) which starts in three months' time. (For a brief explanation of LIBOR and Eurodollar deposits see LOS 61e below.)

In three months' time, the six-month LIBOR is compared with the rate in the FRA and compensation is paid by the seller (short) to the buyer (long) if LIBOR exceeds the FRA rate and by the buyer to the seller if LIBOR is less than the FRA rate.

Suppose the FRA rate was 4% and had a notional principal of $10m and the actual number of days in the six-month period was 183. If LIBOR turns out to be 4.3%, the compensation received by the buyer would, at first sight, be:

$$\$10m \times (0.043 - 0.04) \times 183/360 = \$15,250$$

If the buyer had a borrowing arranged at the start of the relevant period at LIBOR + margin, this would compensate him if LIBOR was in excess of 4%; in the same way, if LIBOR was less than 4%, he would have to pay the seller. The borrower has thus effectively fixed LIBOR at 4%. An investor would *sell* a FRA to fix LIBOR.

There is, however, a final complication before we can identify the payoff. The compensation is for interest paid, which would normally be at the end of the six-month period, so a smaller amount is received (or paid) at the start of the period, as soon as LIBOR is known. This is the compensation as calculated above but discounted back 183 days by the current six-month LIBOR rate:

$$\text{Payoff} = \$15,250 / (1 + 0.043 \times 183/360) = \$14,924$$

KNOWLEDGE LEARNING OUTCOME STATEMENTS

61c Distinguish between a dealer and an end user of a forward contract

A dealer is a financial institution that offers forward contracts, while the end user needs the forward contract, often for hedging purposes. Easy marks if it comes up!

61d Describe the characteristics of equity forward contracts and forward contracts on zero-coupon and coupon bonds

The LOS only says **describe** so you won't have to do any calculations on these; you just need to know broadly what they are.

An equity forward contract is an agreement to buy or sell a specific equity, a specific portfolio, or an index at a specified price on a specific future date.

In the same way, forward contracts can be arranged on zero-coupon or coupon paying bonds.

As holding the underlying may generate additional cash flows such as dividends, which are not available to the holder of the forward contract, the price of the forward contract is adjusted to take this into account (no calculations involving this until you hit Level II!).

61e Describe the characteristics of the Eurodollar time deposit market, and define LIBOR and Euribor

A Eurodollar time deposit is a fixed (short) term investment denominated in dollars but outside the United States. It pays back the investment and interest, which is *quoted* on an annualized basis.

So a 40-day $10m investment at 3% will actually pay out at the end:

$$\$10m \times (1 + 0.03 \times 40/360) = \$10,003,333$$

LIBOR is the London Interbank Offer Rate and is the average rate at which London banks will lend Eurodollars for different lengths of time. Euribor is the Frankfurt average bank rate for euro-denominated time deposits.

61h Describe the characteristics of currency forward contracts

A currency forward contract is an agreement to buy or sell a specified amount of a certain currency on a specific future date. In other words, this amounts to agreeing an exchange rate for a future transaction and is looked at more fully in Study Session 6. Occasionally, currency is not exchanged and a compensation payment is made by one party to the other (this can happen if the foreign currency cannot be obtained as it's subject to restrictions).

Reading 61 sample question
(Answers on p. 313)

Megan Bourke is a corporate treasurer with PB Industries. She is of the opinion that interest rate volatility is about to increase over the next four months and is concerned about protecting a receipt of $10m which her firm is due to receive in one month's time.

She enters into a 1 × 4 FRA where she will receive a fixed rate of 5.75%. LIBOR one month later was 5.85%. Which of the following is closest to payoff resulting from the FRA?

(A) Pay $2,463.96
(B) Pay $2,500.00
(C) Receive $4,932.18

The important areas to understand, as they are a frequent source of exam questions, are calculating the daily profit or loss as the futures price changes (relatively easy) and the idea of margin. Margin can be very confusing (especially as there are three different types), so make sure you read the introduction below before drowning in the six pages covered by Section 3 in the reading.

Questions on margin are likely to be descriptive rather than calculation (apart from the profit or loss mentioned above), so if you follow our explanation below, you should be able to tackle any questions.

As usual there is some background information about exchanges and volumes and their history, but these are not in any LOS.

LEARNING OUTCOME STATEMENTS

Application LOS	**Knowledge LOS**
62a **Describe** the characteristics of futures contracts	62f **Describe** the characteristics of the following types of futures contracts: Treasury bill, Eurodollar, Treasury bond, stock index, and currency
62b **Compare** futures contracts and forward contracts	
62c **Distinguish** between margin in the securities markets and margin in the futures markets, and explain the role of initial margin, maintenance margin, variation margin, and settlement in futures trading	
62d **Describe** price limits and the process of marking to market, and calculate and interpret the margin balance, given the previous day's balance and the change in the futures price	
62e **Describe** how a futures contract can be terminated at or prior to expiration	

APPLICATION LEARNING OUTCOME STATEMENTS

62a,b Describe the characteristics of futures contracts; compare futures contracts and forward contracts

As noted in Reading 60, futures are like forward contracts but are exchange-traded and standardized in terms of asset specification, quantity, and timings. There is hardly any credit risk as the exchange itself takes the other side in all transactions (see LOS 62c, d, e below).

62c,d,e Distinguish between margin in the securities markets and margin in the futures markets, and explain the role of initial margin, maintenance margin, variation margin, and settlement in futures trading; describe price limits and the process of marking to market, and calculate and interpret the margin balance, given the previous day's balance and the change in the futures price; describe how a futures contract can be terminated at or prior to expiration

This can sound confusing until you realize what is going on; once you do, however, the questions will become relatively straightforward.

The starting point is that to encourage people to deal on an exchange and create liquidity, the exchange must try to reduce the credit risk for participants. To do this, the exchange becomes the counterparty in all transactions.

Example

A agrees to sell an asset in three months' time to B for $100

Recorded: A sells to the exchange for $100 (short position)

  B buys from the exchange for $100 (long position)

If, after three months, the cash price is $60, then A has made a profit of $40 and B a loss of $40. This can be achieved in two ways, depending on the exchange and the underlying asset. A could buy the asset for $60 and deliver it to the exchange (or its warehouse) and be paid $100 while B could collect it for $100 and sell it on the open market for $60 (or, of course, B might use it in its business if it is a commodity, but then it has suffered an "opportunity loss" as it could have bought it more cheaply). Alternatively, the $100 could be compared with the current asset price and $40 taken from B and $40 paid to A. This is very similar to the process we saw in Reading 61 for forward contracts.

Unlike with a forward contract, though, if A wanted, it could easily take its profit at any time before the future matures. Suppose, after two months, the market price was $70. A could go onto the market and enter a long position (a contract to buy the asset) for the same future date. As the counterparty is the same (the exchange), the transactions are netted and A takes the $30 profit. A forward contract holder would find this difficult as it is unlikely they would be able to enter an opposite transaction with the same counterparty. Without this, there would be no offsetting possible and no payment of the net profit.

However, the exchange now has credit risk in that B, currently losing, may not make the payment required. To remove this risk, every day the "open" positions are "marked to market," that is the value of the position is recorded as if it had been done at the end of the trading day (strictly the average over a closing period) and any profit added to and any loss subtracted from A's and B's accounts. B (if he makes a loss on the day's change) must pay in money and A can take money out.

But what if B cannot or will not pay? Both A and B have to make deposits when they first enter the futures contract and profits and losses are added to or subtracted from this. If the funds go below a certain level, they must be topped up. All of these are called margin.

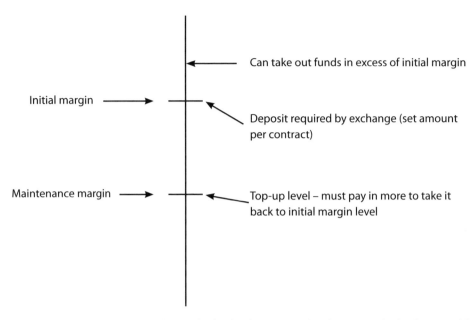

The LOS also wants you to distinguish margin in the futures market from margin in the securities market. Margin in the securities market is the amount of the investor's own money used in a purchase; the rest is borrowed (this is looked at in Study Session 13). Margin in the futures market does not mean that borrowed funds are being used as there is no cash needed for a purchase (the commitment is for a future date). Rather it is a deposit to guard against credit risk.

KNOWLEDGE LEARNING OUTCOME STATEMENTS

62f Describe the characteristics of the following types of futures contracts: Treasury bill, Eurodollar, Treasury bond, stock index, and currency

These are mentioned in Section 6 of the reading and you should read through them to get the broad idea of how they work. Any questions are likely to be simple and descriptive (with the exception of the IMM index mentioned below). There is no need to memorize every last detail on these pages, but make sure you understand in each case what the underlying asset is.

Notice that:

- If a 90-day T-bill or Eurodollar future is quoted at 96.00 (the IMM Index), then a future over $1m face value will actually cost:

$$\$1m \, (1 - 0.04 \times 90/360) = \$990,000$$

- A future over a US Treasury bond does not specify the exact bond to be delivered in order to stop any price distortion in the bond market. Each possible bond which could be delivered is given a conversion factor to calculate how much must be delivered to satisfy the contract

Reading 62 sample question
(Answers on p. 314)

A short seller came in and sold ten Eurodollar contracts at 94.75. The next day, the contract was trading at 94.87. What is his current unrealized profit and loss on the trade?

Tick size = 1 basis point
Tick value = $25

(A) A profit of $3,000.00
(B) A loss of $3,000.00
(C) A loss of $32,500.00

This reading, at nearly 50 pages including the questions, can look quite daunting, but we can break it down into three main areas – basic terminology, types of options, and value estimates.

By far the most important, as far as questions are concerned, are the value estimates, so do not spend too much time trying to memorize the features of all the different financial options.

Section 5 on value estimates itself looks at four areas:

- The factors that influence the value of an option
- The value of an option at expiration; this is also asked for in Reading 65 so you get two benefits if you can master this
- The minimum and maximum values for a put and a call option
- Put–call parity, which links the value of a put option, the value of a call option, the strike price, and the price of the underlying

Our introduction below should help you make sense of the 20 pages – they spend some time putting together the arguments, but you will need only the conclusions in questions.

LEARNING OUTCOME STATEMENTS

Application LOS	Knowledge LOS
63a **Describe** call and put options	63d **Compare** exchange-traded options and over-the-counter options
63b **Distinguish** between European and American options	63e **Identify** the types of options in terms of the underlying instruments
63c **Define** the concept of moneyness of an option	63f **Compare** interest rate options with forward rate agreements (FRAs)
63h **Calculate** and interpret option payoffs and explain how interest rate options differ from other types of options	63g **Define** interest rate caps, floors, and collars
63j **Determine** the minimum and maximum values of European options and American options	63i **Define** intrinsic value and time value, and explain their relationship
63k **Calculate** and interpret the lowest prices of European and American calls and puts based on the rules for minimum values and lower bounds	63l **Explain** how option prices are affected by the exercise price and the time to expiration
63m **Explain** put–call parity for European options, and explain how put–call parity is related to arbitrage and the construction of synthetic options	63o **Determine** the directional effect of an interest rate change or volatility change on an option's price
63n **Explain** how cash flows on the underlying asset affect put–call parity and the lower bounds of option prices	

APPLICATION LEARNING OUTCOME STATEMENTS

63a, b, c Describe call and put options; distinguish between European and American options; define the concept of moneyness of an option

Options have their own terminology, which we just have to know:

- Call = option to buy something at a set price at or before a certain date
- Put = option to sell something at a set price at or before a certain date
- Strike/exercise price = the price agreed in the option
- Premium = the amount paid to buy the put or call option
- Long/buyer = pays the premium and has the choice whether to then use the put or call option
- Short/seller = receives the premium and has to go through with the contract if, and only if, the long decides to exercise
- European option = can be exercised only at a specific date in the future, after which it will expire
- American option = can be exercised at any time until it expires
- *In the money = the underlying exceeds the strike price (call) or the underlying is less than the strike (put). This is called intrinsic value (see LOS 63i, l, o)
- *Out of the money = the underlying is less than the strike price (call) or the underlying is more than the strike (put)
- *At the money = the underlying price is equal to the strike price

*These will be clearer after looking at the payoffs for different options in LOS 63h below.

63h Calculate and interpret option payoffs and explain how interest rate options differ from other types of options

The payoffs at expiration for the long and short position for call and put options are all shown in Exhibit 5.

You don't need to be able to explain the logic, but you do need to be able to find the value at expiration given the strike price and the price of the underlying (here a stock) at expiration. To start with it may be worth making a quick sketch to make sure you're thinking about it the right way, but after a bit of practice it should start to make sense and you probably won't need to draw it. It is well worth practicing this type of question as it is one of the few LOS in this reading which asks for calculations.

Notice that the long and short positions are mirror images of each other and that although call options have no maximum to the positive value to the long and negative value to the short, put options have a limit on both.

Interest rate options and their payoffs are dealt with below in LOS 63e, f, g.

63j, k Determine the minimum and maximum values of European options and American options; calculate and interpret the lowest prices of European and American calls and puts based on the rules for minimum values and lower bounds

This can be confusing, so although it is worth reading through, do not get bogged down. It is here because we don't attempt an option valuation until Level II, but they want you to have an idea of the limits to any option value.

You really only need the conclusions, so if you get a bit lost, skip ahead or use the summary we have here. The minimums are broadly based around the intrinsic value but adjusted in the case of European options as they cannot be exercised early. LOS 63k says that you might be asked to feed data into the formula in order to arrive at a maximum or minimum, but it should be a relatively simple task once you know the formula.

	European call	American call	European put	American put
Minimum	Max of zero and $S - X / (1 + r)^T$	Max of zero and $S - X / (1 + r)^T$	Max of zero and $X / (1 + r)^T - S$	Max of zero and $X - S$
Maximum	S	S	$X / (1 + r)^T$	X

where S = current price of underlying and $X / (1 + r)^T$ = PV of the strike price.

Notice that the American option must always be worth at least as much as an equivalent European option. As it can be exercised at any time, the American put option minimum value does not discount back the strike price as it does not have to wait until expiry to receive it. However, although the same logic would apply to the American call option, $(S - X)$ would actually be smaller than $[S - X / (1 + r)^T]$ and it must be worth at least as much as the European call option, so we leave the minimum as $[S - X / (1 + r)^T]$.

63m, n Explain put–call parity for European options, and explain how put–call parity is related to arbitrage and the construction of synthetic options; explain how cash flows on the underlying asset affect put–call parity and the lower bounds of option prices

Put–call parity is very useful and it will crop up in questions at Level I and Level II. Notice at this level, only explanations are needed and not calculations.

The proof is not hard to follow and is laid out in Section 5.5.1, but you will not be asked to prove it, only explain its use. You need to learn the formula as you are bound to need it in your exam.

It says that for a European call and a European put with the same strike price over the same underlying and the same expiry date:

$$c_0 + X / (1 + r)^T = p_0 + S_0$$

where:

- c_0 is the current value of the call option
- $X / (1 + r)^T$ is the PV of the strike price
- p_0 is the current value of the put option
- S_0 is the current value of the underlying

This can be used in three ways:

1. If we know the other values, we can estimate the value of a call option or a put option (NB: this is its *full* value before expiration, not just the intrinsic value)
2. We can advise how to replicate one of the items without actually holding it. These are called synthetics:

$$\text{Synthetic call} = p_0 + S_0 - X / (1 + r)^T$$

So buy a put, hold the underlying, and borrow the PV of the strike price

$$\text{Synthetic put} = c_0 - S_0 + X / (1 + r)^T$$

So buy a call, short the underlying, and invest the PV of the strike price

$$\text{Synthetic underlying} = c_0 - p_0 + X / (1 + r)^T$$

So buy a call, sell a put, and invest the PV of the strike price
3. If the equation doesn't hold, there is an arbitrage opportunity. We would sell the item or combination with the higher price and buy the one with the lower price

KNOWLEDGE LEARNING OUTCOME STATEMENTS

63d Compare exchange-traded options and over-the-counter options

Options can be either OTC or exchange-traded, but unlike forward contracts and futures, they are both still called options. When dealing in exchange-traded options, the seller will have to pay initial margin and be subject to variation and maintenance margin as he may incur losses; the buyer will not if he pays the premium upfront. It's not likely you'll get much in the way of a question on this.

63e, f, g Identify the types of options in terms of the underlying instruments; compare interest rate options with forward rate agreements (FRAs); define interest rate caps, floors, and collars

Options can be purchased over a range of underlyings. Although we concentrate on financial options over things such as a stock, an index, a bond, an interest rate, or a currency, options on commodities and even the weather can be purchased. A quick read through Section 4 to get the idea of what is on offer is all that's needed. However, notice in particular the following:

- An OTC interest rate option is effectively an option over a FRA (a *borrower* wants the option to *buy* an FRA so buys an interest rate *call* option). If the FRA would produce a receipt, the holder of the option will exercise the option, but if it would produce a payment, he will not (and will only have lost the option premium). However, any compensation will be received at the *end* of the relevant period, not the beginning (unlike a normal FRA)
- A whole series of interest rate call options, bought to limit the interest rate for a borrower over a number of periods, is called a cap, and a series of interest rate put options for an investor is called a floor. A cap for a borrower can be very expensive in terms of the option premium payable, so he may sell put options to offset the cost. This will give a collar, which has both a cap and a floor, at minimal, and possibly zero, cost. An investor could also have a collar by buying the put options he wants to provide a minimum interest rate and selling call options to create a cap

63i, l, o Define intrinsic value and time value, and explain their relationship; explain how option prices are affected by the exercise price and the time to expiration; determine the directional effect of an interest rate change or volatility change on an option's price

Although valuation of options is left until Level II, you need to understand the two basic components of the value, and to be able to state whether the value would increase or decrease if one of the variables below changes. Notice that the effect is similar whether we are talking about call or put options *except in the case of a change in interest rates.*

The value of an option can be split into two parts:

Intrinsic value: for a call option = the maximum of zero or (strike price – underlying price). For a put option = the maximum of zero or (underlying price – strike price).

Time value: this is the additional amount payable for an option before its expiry date. This arises because there is still hope that the price of the underlying will move in such a way that the payoff increases. It is affected by:

- Time left before expiry: the longer there is left, the more valuable the option (except for European put options deeply "in the money" as the only way is down!)
- Volatility of the price of the underlying: the more volatile the price, the more valuable the option
- Interest rate: an increase in the interest rate will *increase* the value of a call option (think of it as a deferred payment for a guaranteed purchase, meaning that we can earn interest on our money before we exercise the option and purchase the underlying) and will *decrease* the value of a put option
- Exercise price: a call option with a lower strike price will be worth more than an identical call option with a higher strike. The reverse is true for put options

Reading 63 sample questions
(Answers on p. 314)

1. If interest rates rise, what is the likely effect on equity option premiums?

    (A) Call prices rise and put prices fall
    (B) Put prices rise and call prices fall
    (C) Call prices rise and put prices remain unchanged

2. If the 250 call is 15p, the stock is at 200p, short term-interest rates are 8%, and there are 250 days until expiry, the price of the European-style put using put–call parity is closest to:

    (A) 49.97p
    (B) 50.97p
    (C) 52.16p

Swaps can sound complicated and if you're not familiar with them already it is easy to get confused in this reading. However, the underlying idea is not difficult and the overview of each LOS below should help you grasp what is going on. The questions are not really terribly hard and once you get the idea, they should not cause you any real problems. The important thing is not to get bogged down by the detail in this reading.

The best start to answering nearly all swap questions is to sketch a rough diagram of the cash flows involved.

LEARNING OUTCOME STATEMENTS

Application LOS	Knowledge LOS
64a **Describe** the characteristics of swap contracts and explain how swaps are terminated	
64b **Describe**, calculate, and interpret the payments of currency swaps, plain vanilla interest rate swaps, and equity swaps	

APPLICATION LEARNING OUTCOME STATEMENTS

64a Describe the characteristics of swap contracts and explain how swaps are terminated

Swaps are agreements to exchange a series of cash flows in the future and normally at least one of these is uncertain (being dependent on LIBOR, an exchange rate, or the return on an index, for example).

Being OTC contracts, to terminate a swap a party will have to enter an equal and opposite transaction with the same counterparty. As estimates of the future cash flows will have changed, this will result in a payment or a receipt.

Alternatively, the party may be able to sell the contract to a third party or pay them to take it (but it will need permission from the counterparty).

64b Describe, calculate, and interpret the payments of currency swaps, plain vanilla interest rate swaps, and equity swaps

Interest rate swaps exchange interest cash flows and a plain vanilla one is where a fixed rate is exchanged for a variable rate (often LIBOR). A net payment is made by one party to the other each period.

Example

A company takes out a loan of $100m for 10 years at LIBOR + 2% and enters a pay-fixed, receive floating swap at 4% against LIBOR on a notional principal of $100m.

Overall, the company has fixed its borrowings at 6% (2% + 4%).

The net payment on the swap each period will depend on what LIBOR turns out to be each time. Suppose the swap payments are semi-annual and on 1 January and 1 July each year:

6-month LIBOR on 1 January	Payment/Receipt on following 1 July
3%	Company pays $100m × 1% × 6/12 = $500,000
4%	No payment or receipt
5%	Company receives $100m × 1% × 6/12 = $500,000

Notice that unlike a FRA (effectively a one-period swap), swaps normally settle at the *end* of each period.

A currency swap is like an interest rate swap but the two sets of cash flows are in different currencies. There is no netting of the interest payments, so each party pays the other, and normally the principals are exchanged at the beginning and returned at the end of the swap.

An equity swap is where at least one party pays the return on a particular stock or a stock index. Notice that if the index goes *down*, one party can be making a payment under both "legs" (this is a favorite exam trick when asking about equity swaps).

Example

A pays 4% and B pays the return on an index, with notional principal $100m and annual payments.

Return on index	Payment
6%	B pays A a net 2% × $100m = $2m
4%	No net payment
2%	A pays B a net 2% × $100m = $2m
-5%	A pays B 4% *and* 5%, i.e. 9% × $100m = $9m

Reading 64 sample question
(Answers on p. 315)

ABC Inc. has entered into a "plain-vanilla" interest rate swap on $1m notional principal. Their counterparty, XYZ Inc., receives a fixed rate of 9% on payments that occur at 90-day intervals. Eight payments remain, with the next one due in exactly 90 days. On the other side of the swap, ABC Inc. receives payments based on the LIBOR rate. Describe the transaction between ABC and XYZ at the end of the seventh period if the LIBOR rate is 11%.

(A) ABC Inc. pays $5,000
(B) ABC Inc. receives $5,000
(C) XYZ Inc. receives $22,500

There are many different combinations of options, but you only have to be comfortable with buying or selling call or put options on their own and a "covered call" (owning the underlying asset and selling a call option) and a "protective put" (owning the underlying asset and buying a put option). All the questions on these (which are mostly numerical) can be answered by being familiar with the graph of each, so there are six graphs to learn and understand.

LEARNING OUTCOME STATEMENTS

Application LOS	Knowledge LOS
65a **Determine** the value at expiration, the profit, maximum profit, maximum loss, breakeven underlying price at expiration, and payoff graph of the strategies of buying and selling calls and puts and determine the potential outcomes for investors using these strategies	
65b **Determine** the value at expiration, profit, maximum profit, maximum loss, breakeven underlying price at expiration, and payoff graph of the strategies of a covered call strategy and a protective put strategy, and explain the risk management application of each strategy	

APPLICATION LEARNING OUTCOME STATEMENTS

65a, b Determine the value at expiration, profit, maximum profit, maximum loss, breakeven underlying price at expiration, and payoff graph of the strategies of buying and selling calls and puts and of a covered call and protective put strategy; explain the risk management application of the covered call and protective put strategy

Notice that all of the calculations (value, profit, maximum profit, maximum loss, and breakeven price) are all at expiration so that there is no time value and only the intrinsic value is relevant.

The key diagrams are Exhibits:

- 2 (buy a call)
- 3 (sell a call)
- 4 (buy a put)
- 5 (sell a put)
- 6 covered call (= buy underlying and sell a call)
- 7 protective put (= buy underlying and buy a put)

Four of these have been done before in Reading 63, so only the last two are new.

It is generally simpler to sketch the graph quickly, label the strike price, premium, and underlying asset price at expiry, and then read off the required information, but if you prefer a summary, the main points are (at expiration):

	Long call	Short call	Long put	Short put	Covered call	Protective put
Value	+ Max (o or S–X)	– Max (o or S–X)	+ Max (o or X–S)	– Max (o or X–S)	+ Min (S or X)	+ Max (S or X)
Profit or loss	Value – Pr	Value + Pr	Value – Pr	Value + Pr	Value – S_0 + Pr	Value – S_0 – Pr
Max profit	Infinite	Pr	X – Pr	Pr	X – S_0 + Pr	Infinite
Max loss	Pr	Infinite	Pr	X – Pr	S_0 – Pr	S_0 – X + Pr
Breakeven price	X + Pr	X + Pr	X – Pr	X – Pr	S_0 – Pr	S_0 + Pr

where X = exercise or strike price, Pr = premium, S = price of underlying at expiration, S_0 = original price of underlying

Notice that the short call is a mirror image of a long call and a short put is a mirror image of a long put.

Reading 65 sample question
(Answers on p. 315)

Which of the following is correct regarding a call option?

(A) The writer pays a premium to the holder
(B) It can be used to hedge a short underlying position
(C) The holder of a call has unlimited downside potential

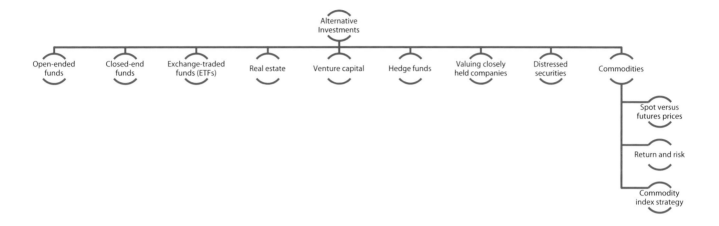

Topic:	Alternative Investments
Weight:	3%
Study sessions:	18
Readings:	66–67

THE BIG PICTURE

Alternative Investments is a tiny portion of the Level I curriculum, but these investments count towards up to 15% of the curriculum at Levels II and III. The key to alternative investments is to know the basic characteristics of each, and to be prepared to compare those investments.

Each of the investments discussed in these readings has a characteristic that is brought out by an LOS. For example, for real estate investments we pay attention to the net operating income, whereas for investments in closely held companies we use comparable valuation, but need to make adjustments, such as adding a premium for closely held or subtracting the discount for a minority interest. Heed the LOSs and look for the characteristic that is the focus of the relevant LOS.

There is special focus on commodities, so it is a good idea to understand the relationship between the spot and the forward prices, the risk and return for commodity investments, and the construction of a commodity index.

There are only two readings in Study Session 18. This is the bigger of the two, covering a wide range of alternative investments. Most of the work involves learning lists of facts about different investments. The real estate material includes some NPV calculations, the basis of which should be familiar from earlier study sessions.

LEARNING OUTCOME STATEMENTS

Application LOS	Knowledge LOS
66a **Compare** alternative investments with traditional investments	66b **Describe** categories of alternative investments
66c **Describe** potential benefits of alternative investments in the context of portfolio management	66e **Describe** issues in valuing, and calculating returns on, hedge funds, private equity, real estate, and commodities
66g **Describe** risk management of alternative investments	66d **Describe** hedge funds, private equity, real estate, commodities, and other alternative investments, including, as applicable, strategies, sub-categories, potential benefits and risks, fee structures, and due diligence
	66f **Describe**, calculate, and interpret management and incentive fees and net-of-fees returns to hedge funds

APPLICATION LEARNING OUTCOME STATEMENTS

66a Compare alternative investments with traditional investments

The reading begins with an introduction in Section 1 and an overview of alternatives at the start of Section 2. Although this is mostly knowledge, you must be able to apply this to questions that ask you why an investor may be interested in alternative rather than traditional investments.

The key points to take from the introduction are that investors are looking for positive returns throughout the economic cycle and diversification of risk.

Section 2 provides a list of six bullet points highlighting the characteristics of alternatives. Focus on these facts rather than the historic performance information.

66c Describe potential benefits of alternative investments in the context of portfolio management

As mentioned in the earlier LOS, the main advantage that investors see in the alternative sector is the diversification of risk whilst still collecting returns. Section 2.2 addresses the general strategies for achieving this return under the headings absolute return, market segmentation and concentrated portfolios. The main perceived benefit is the low correlation with the traditional sector. This is covered in Section 2.3.

66g Describe risk management of alternative investments

Section 8 covers risk management of alternatives. The point of the section is that the traditional risk management controls and measures are often not appropriate due to the non traditional nature of alternative investments. This section should be read in conjunction with the study session on portfolio management which covers traditional measures of risk.

Once you are comfortable with those traditional measures, the points made in this section should be fairly straightforward. The illiquidity of many investments and the non-normal nature of returns, for example, mean that the Sharpe ratio and standard deviation may not be appropriate measures.

For these reasons, throrough due diligence becomes more important than ever, and this is mentioned in a straightforward manner.

KNOWLEDGE LEARNING OUTCOME STATEMENTS

66b Describe categories of alternative investments

Section 2.1 provides a five-bullet-point list of categories of alternative investments. Most are covered in more detail in other LOSs, so review this at the end of your work on this reading to make sure you've picked up the main points.

66d, e, f Describe hedge funds, private equity, real estate, commodities, and other alternative investments, including, as applicable, strategies, sub-categories, potential benefits and risks, fee structures, and due diligence, Describe issues in valuing, and calculating returns on, hedge funds, private equity, real estate, and commodities, Describe, calculate, and interpret management and incentive fees and net-of-fees returns to hedge funds

This is the main part of the reading and involves a lot of fact learning. For each of the five alternative investment categories identified, you need to commit to memory the facts pertaining to each point in the LOS. Most of your time should be spent on hedge funds, private equity and real estate.

Hedge funds are covered in Section 3. Note that there is a large amount of material on fee structures and Example 2 provides exercises in the calculation of fees, so make sure you can work those numbers to specifically cover LOS f.

Private equity is covered in Section 4, and starts by defining leveraged buyouts, venture capital, development capital and distressed investing. You need to cover the investing strategies of each category, which are covered in Sections 4.2.1 through 4.2.3.

Sections 5 and 6 then cover real estate and commodities, respectively. Of the two sections, spend more time on real estate as there is an entire reading to come (Reading 67) on commodities. Once you have been through Reading 67, check Section 6 here to see if there are any additional points you need to pick up.

Finally, Section 7 briefly covers other alternatives and focuses almost exclusively on collectibles (e.g. art, stamps). Most of the points are intuititve so don't spend much time here.

Reading 66 sample question
(Answers on p. 315)

Given the following data on a property, calculate the net operating income.

- Gross potential rental income: $500,000
- Estimated vacancy rate: 10%
- Maintenance: $25,000
- Property related taxes and insurance: $5,000

(A) $420,000
(B) $423,000
(C) $470,000

This is a very short reading on commodities.

Learning outcome statements

Application LOS	Knowledge LOS
67a **Explain** the relationship between spot rates and expected future prices in terms of contango and backwardation	67c **Explain** why a commodity index strategy is generally considered an active investment
67b **Describe** the sources of return and risk for a commodity investment and the effect on a portfolio of adding an allocation to commodities	

Application learning outcome statements

67a Explain the relationship between spot rates and expected future prices in terms of contango and backwardation

The definition of a futures contract and futures price should be familiar from the derivatives reading. The new terms contango and backwardation will need to be learned and explained.

The term contango refers to a situation where futures prices are higher than the spot price and often occurs when a commodity's price is high and volatile. The amount of contango is limited by arbitrage, as when the futures price is too high a trade could buy in the spot and sell the futures contract in a "cash and carry" arbitrage trade.

Backwardation occurs when the futures price is below the spot price. Natural backwardation occurs when large producers are concerned about price falls and are willing to sell at a locked-in futures price below the spot to avoid the risk.

67b Describe the sources of return and risk for a commodity investment and the effect on a portfolio of adding an allocation to commodities

There are three sources of return which need to be described:

- Collateral yield – the risk-free return on the collateral used as a margin to take long derivatives exposure
- Roll yield – this is the convergence between the futures price and the spot price. It will be positive if the market is in backwardation, as the futures price will rise up to the spot. It will be negative in contango markets as the futures price will fall to the spot

- Price return – the roll yield ignores any movement in the spot price. If the spot price does move it will drag the futures price with it and cause gains or losses. This return is positive or negative depending on the direction of spot price movements

Knowledge learning outcome statements

67c Explain why a commodity index strategy is generally considered an active investment

Because weightings in a commodity portfolio must be constantly rebalanced, and the collateral consistently rolled over into new futures contracts, hence Reading 67 defines even trying to match a commodity index as an active strategy.

Reading 67 sample question
(Answers on p. 315)

A commodities market is described as being in contango where the:

(A) Spot price is lower than the futures price
(B) Spot price is higher than the futures price
(C) Spot price is the same as the futures price

ANSWERS TO SAMPLE QUESTIONS

READING 1

Correct: C

The Standard does not require that analysts always show at least ten years of historic information in their reports, although this would be required under GIPS once a composite had been in existence for ten years.

READING 2

Correct: B

A discretionary equity fund manager can park funds in T-bills if he is attempting to enter the market at the best possible time. This is consistent with Standard III (A): Loyalty, Prudence, and Care.

READING 3

Correct: C

While verification is not mandatory under GIPS, Abraham Management is in violation of GIPS because the firm cannot provide its own verification; this should be done by an independent third party. By claiming that its compliance is verified, it has violated GIPS.

READING 4

Correct: C

The definition of a firm under GIPS includes the broadest possible definition of the firm. This includes all subsidiaries and branches, regardless of the name of the individual investment management company.

READING 5

1. Correct: C

Press 2nd FV – this clears the TVM data stored in the BAII Plus calculator.
Enter the following values using the TVM buttons:

20	>	N
0	>	FV
6.5	>	1/Y
–120,000	>	PV
CPT	>	PMT = 10,890.76

2. Correct: A

Press 2nd FV – this clears the TVM data stored in the BAII Plus calculator.
Step 1: work out the annual instalments PMT

25	>	N
0	>	FV
6	>	1/Y
10,000	>	PV
CPT	>	PMT = 782

Annual instalments PMT = $782

Step 2: work out the interest due and the loan amount outstanding for Year 2

Year 1: 10,000 + 600 (interest @ 6%) – 782 (instalment) = 9,818 year 1 end balance
Year 2: 9,818 + 589 (interest @ 6%) – 782 (instalment) = **9,625**

READING 6

1. Correct: C

The money market yield is equivalent to the annualized holding period based on a 360-day year.

Money market yield = ((Face value – Purchase price) / Purchase price) × (360 / number of days to maturity)

(1,800 / 98,200) × (360 / 130) = 0.0508 or 5.08%

2. Correct: A

Bank discount yield = (r) = ((Face value – Purchase price) / Face value) × (360 / t) r = 0.03, Face value = \$100,000, t = 120 and let the price be X

0.03 = ((100,000 − X) / 100,000) × (360 / 120), therefore X = \$99,000.

Rather than rearrange the above formula to solve for X, insert the given answers until it matches the required yield of 3%.

But here it is anyway:

$$-0.03 = ((100{,}000 - X) / 100{,}000) \times (360 / 120)$$

$$0.03 / (360 / 120) = (100{,}000 - X) / 100{,}000$$

$$0.01 \times 100{,}000 = 100{,}000 - X$$

$$100{,}000 - 1{,}000 = X = 99{,}000$$

READING 7

1. Correct: B

Note that the question says LOSSES, hence the returns (r) are negative.

$$\text{Geometric mean} = (((1+r) \times (1+r) \times (1+r) \times (1+r))^{\wedge}(1)) - 1$$

$$(0.8 \times 0.9 \times 0.89 \times 0.85)^{\wedge}0.25) - 1$$

Geometric mean = −14.1%

2. Correct: C

Negatively skewed data is where there is a chance of a very low value, creating a long tail on the left-hand side.

The mean will be most affected by this very low value, and the mode the least affected. Therefore the mode will be greater than the median which will be greater than the mean.

READING 8

1. Correct: C

This is a combination question, asking for the number of possible combinations of three directors out of a pool of 12. (12!/9!×3!) = 220 groups. Using the combination function on the calculator, [nCr], Press 12 [2nd] [+] 3 and then equals. The answer is 220.

2.   Correct: A

Covariance / (SD Canadian wheat × SD Kansas wheat) = Correlation coefficient

$$36 \div (9 \times 16) \boxed{=} 0.25$$

READING 9

Correct: B

The probability stays the same with each trial as the trials are independent of one another.

READING 10

Correct: C

Standard error = sample standard deviation / SQRT(n) = SQRT(92.73690) / SQRT(70) = 1.15101

SQRT = square root

The sample size is more than 30 so we can assume the 1.645 reliability estimate from the normal distribution. This is based on the Central Limit Theorem, which states that if a population is normally distributed and the sample size is large (at least 30 observations), the distribution of the sample mean will also be normally distributed.

Confidence interval is calculated as:

Mean +/– (Standard error × reliability factor)
14.6 +/– (1.15101 × 1.645) = 12.7066 – 16.49340

Answer B has wrongly used the 1.96 reliability estimate for 95% confidence.

READING 11

Correct: C

The test statistic would be calculated as follows:

(observed value – hypothesized value) / standard error

(16.5 – 15) / (7 / SQRT 40)

= 1.36

Note: standard error = standard deviation / SQRT(n)

READING 12

Correct: A

The same would hold for resistance levels; once breached, they become support levels.

READING 13

Correct: C

If the number of luxury items demanded decreases from 100 to 50 when the price increases from $500 to $800, the percentage change in quantity is $(50 - 100) / [(50 + 100) / 2] = -66.67\%$ and the percentage change in price is $(\$800 - \$500) / [(\$800 + \$500) / 2] = 46\%$. Therefore, price elasticity of demand $= -66.67\% / 46\% = -1.45$.

READING 14

Correct: B

The substitution effect explains why there is an inverse relationship between price and quantity demanded. When the price of a good rises, other goods become relatively cheaper and therefore other goods are substituted for this good.

The income effect describes the idea that when the price of a good declines, one has more real income (more money left over), which could be used to buy more of this good. For a normal good, if income increases, there is a higher quantity demanded.

READING 15

Correct: A

Marginal revenue is the addition to total revenue from adding one more unit of output. When the fifth unit is sold, total revenue is $90 ($18 × 5) compared with $80 for four units (4 × $20), so marginal revenue is $10 ($90 – $80).

READING 16

Correct: C

When new entrants enter the market the firm will continue to produce in the short run at a loss as long as average variable costs are covered.

READING 17

Correct: B

Aggregate demand is the amount that households and firms intend to spend on output at each level of income. Answers A and C would all lead to an *increase* in spending, which in turn would lead to an increase in aggregate demand.

READING 18

Correct: C

At the beginning of a downturn, sales decrease and companies will have excess inventory, therefore increasing the inventory–sales ratio (Inventory / Sales).

READING 19

Correct: C

The short-run impact of an unanticipated increase in the growth rate of the money supply is reduced real interest rates, an increase to aggregate demand, and an increase in quantity supplied (a shift along the supply curve), reducing unemployment. However, the over-employment level will, in the long run, lead to inflation, causing a leftwards shift to the supply curve, output and employment will decline to the full-employment level, but at higher prices.

The real rate of interest is a function of the supply versus demand for funds. If the supply increases (due to higher money supply) then interest rates (both nominal and real) will fall. This results in higher AD caused by higher consumption and investment and this shifts the AD to the right. Since we are told we started at full employment, this rise in AD produces an inflationary gap. Over time, wages and other costs adjust upwards, causing the short-run AS to shift upwards/to the left until we get back to full employment equilibrium but at the "cost" of a higher price level.

READING 20

Correct: B

The current account measures the flows of goods and services. Tourism, transportation, and business services will be recorded in the services sub-account of the current account in the BOP.

READING 21

Correct: B

GBP is the base currency in the USD/GBP quote and it is expected to increase over the year, which means GBP is expected to appreciate against USD over the next year.

$$(1.5752–1.5705) / 1.5705 = 0.3\%$$

READING 22

Correct: B

The income statement shows a company's profitability for a given time period. It shows the company's revenues minus its expenses = net income or net profit. The cash flow statement and statement of owner's equity give a lot of useful information, but not necessarily about profitability.

READING 23

Correct: A

Tax payments are part of operating cash flow and not investing.

READING 24

Correct: B

FASB is currently responsible for drafting the US Financial Accounting Standards.

The Financial Services Authority is the UK financial markets regulator, and the Public Company Accounting Oversight Board produces the standards which US auditors adhere to.

READING 25

Correct: A

$$\text{Basic EPS} = 300,000 / 100,000 = 3.00$$

$$\text{Adjusted interest net of tax} = (500,000 \times 0.1) \times (1–0.4) = 30,000$$

$$\text{No. of shares on conversion} = 5,000$$
$$\text{Total number of shares on conversion} = 105,000$$
$$\text{Net income including adjusted interest} = 330,000$$

$$\text{"Diluted" EPS} = 330,000 / 105,000 = 3.14$$

Since EPS has increased on conversion of securities it is anti-dilutive and so will not be reported.

READING 26

Correct: A

Financial assets that are classified as either available for sale or held for trading are reflected on the balance sheet at fair value, whereas financial assets classified as held to maturity will be reflected at amortized cost.

READING 27

1.   Correct: B

Dividends paid are treated as financing cash flows. Dividends received are treated as operating cash flows. These are the rules per US GAAP. It may seem more logical to include dividends received in CFI. However, US GAAP specifies that they are operating cash flows. Under IFRS, dividends paid are treated as operating cash flows and dividends received are treated as investing cash flows.

2.   Correct: C

$$
\text{Cash flows from operations (CFO)} =
$$
$$
\text{Net income}
$$
$$
+ \text{ Non-cash expenses}
$$
$$
- \text{ Non-cash revenues}
$$
$$
+ \text{ Decreases in accounts receivables / inventories}
$$
$$
- \text{ Increase in accounts receivables / inventories}
$$
$$
+ \text{ Increase in accounts payable / tax payable / interest payable}
$$
$$
- \text{ Decrease in accounts payable / tax payable / interest payable}
$$
$$
- \text{ Gain on disposal of an asset}
$$
$$
+ \text{ Loss on disposal of an asset}
$$

Cash flow from operations = Net Income + Increase in accounts payable + Deferred tax expense − Profit on sale of equipment. CFO = 50(NI) + 40(AP) + 10(Def Tax) − 30(Equip Profit) = $70.

The profit on sale of equipment is not a cash flow. The proceeds from the sale are and they are included in CFI. The profit is deducted to remove it from net income. The deferred tax is removed because it is not a cash flow.

READING 28

Correct: A

Current ratio is current assets to current liabilities. If the cash is used to pay back a current liability then both the numerator and denominator will decrease. However, because the current ratio is *less* than 1, it will have a bigger impact on the numerator than the denominator, so the current ratio decreases. Asset turnover is sales over assets, sales will be unaffected, but assets will fall. Therefore asset turnover ratio will increase.

READING 29

1.   Correct: C

$$\text{FIFO cost of sales} = (1,418)(\$4/\text{unit}) + (1,918 - 1,418)(\$12/\text{unit}) = \$5,672 + \$6,000 = \$11,672$$

$$\text{Sales} = (1,918 \text{ units})(\$26/\text{unit}) = \$49,868$$

$$\text{EBIT} = \text{Sales} - \text{cost of sales} - \text{Expenses}$$

$$= 49,868 - 11,672 - 5,298 = \$32,898$$

2.   Correct: C

Results in a lower inventory balance which results in lower current ratio during periods of rising prices.

READING 30

1. Correct: C

The profit on disposal is calculated by taking the proceeds – carrying amount. The asset has been depreciated for three years using annual depreciation of $5,000 and so the carrying value on sale is $10,000. $15,000–$10,000 results in a profit of $5,000.

2. Correct: C

Westford would have a lower net income and lower shareholder's equity than Northwood because there would be a higher expense deducted from profits. As net income is a component of shareholder's equity, if net income is lower then shareholder's equity will also be lower.

READING 31

Correct: B

If the revenue is included in the accounts before it has been taxed, then the financial statements should reflect that there will be an obligation to pay tax in the future. This obligation is the deferred tax liability.

READING 32

1.   Correct: A

$$\text{Capital lease obligation} = \text{PV of lease} - \text{1st year's repayment of capital}$$

The PV is calculated using the TVM function on the calculator. N = 5, PMT = $5,000, I/Y = 10%, CPT PV = $18,954.

PV of lease = $18,954, interest in year = $18,954 × 10% = $1,896, capital repayment = $3,104 (annual lease payment of $5,000 less the interest of $1,896 will give the capital repayment of $3,104)

Capital lease obligation = $18,954 − $3,104 = $15,850

2. Correct: B

If the defined benefit pension scheme is underfunded, there is an excess of liabilities. The company has an obligation to make up the shortfall, which meets the definition of a liability and is shown as such on the balance sheet.

READING 33

Correct: A

These involve invoicing for a sale before shipping the goods, or even without doing so at all.

READING 34

Correct: C

Lowering payables implies that cash is being paid to suppliers now with therefore less outflow later.

Reducing receivables securitization leaves more cash to be recovered in future periods.

READING 35

Correct: A

The companies operate in different sectors, but this alone is no reason to adjust the accounts. If companies have different accounting policies or use different accounting rules, then adjustments will be required in order to do a like-for-like comparison.

READING 36

Correct: A

Using the BA II Plus calculator press CF to access the cash flow function then input:

$$CF_0 = -\$10m$$

$$CF_1 = -\$0.7m$$

$$CF_2 = \$2.8m$$

$$CF_3 = \$6.3m$$

$$CPTIRR = -5.97\%$$

READING 37

1. Correct: C

The required rate of return is dividend yield + growth rate. The dividend at time 1 needs to be used.

$$r = (\,[\$1.50(1 + 0.07)]\,/\,\$25\,) + 0.07 = 0.1342 \text{ or } 13.42\%$$

2. Correct: C

Using the capital asset pricing model:

Required rate of return = Risk-free rate + beta (market risk premium)

$$k = 5.5\% + (1.4 \times 10\%) = 19.5\%$$

We do not deduct the risk-free rate because the question quotes the market risk premium which is Rm–Rf.

READING 38

Correct: B

$$\text{Contribution per mop} = \$10 - \$6 = \$4$$

$$\text{Fixed cost / Contribution margin per unit} = \text{operating breakeven point}$$

$$\$2,000,000\,/\,\$4 = 500,000 \text{ units}$$

$$\text{Breakeven quantity} = F\,/\,(P{-}V)$$

$$\$2m/(\$10{-}\$6) = 500,000 \text{ units}$$

READING 39

Correct: A

After a share repurchase:

BVPS will increase if BVPS was greater than market price per share before the repurchase.

Total book value decreases by the dollar repurchase amount, but the shares purchased were less expensive than BVPS, so shares outstanding decreases by a larger proportion than total book value and BVPS increases.

READING 40

Correct: B

Current ratio = Current assets/200 = 5.0 Hence, CA = 1,000 Quick ratio = (1,000 − Inventory)/200 = 3.0 Hence, Inventory = 400.

READING 41

Correct: A

If the independent board members have a lead member, this lead member can facilitate non-executive meetings and candid discussions about management and chief executive performance.

READING 42

Correct: B

Open-end mutual funds trade at the NAV. ETFs and closed-end funds may trade at a premium or discount to NAV.

READING 43

1. Correct: B

$$HPR = (\$185 - \$192 + \$14)/\$192 = 3.64\%$$

2. Correct: A

$$= (0.60)^2 (0.65)^2 + (0.40)^2 (1.20)^2 + 2(0.60)(0.40)(0.65)(1.20)(-0.5)$$

$$= (0.3600)(0.4225) + (0.1600)(1.4400) + (-0.1872)$$

$$= 0.1521 + 0.2304 + -0.1872$$

$$= 0.1953$$

READING 44

1. Correct: C

CAPM expected return of stock $= 4 + 1.5(15 - 4) = 20.5\%$. Estimated return of Stock $= 50 - 40 / 40 = 25\%$. Since the estimated return is more than the required rate, the investor should purchase the stock.

2. Correct: B

CovA,B = the sum of the product of the differences between actual returns and mean returns for each stock. If one of the stocks is the risk-free asset then the difference is zero.

READING 45

Correct: B

The investor is willing to take high risk in return for a high level of long-term returns.

READING 46

Correct: A

This order is a stop loss order. It is designed to prevent excessive losses if the price on a short position increases and is therefore a loss-making position.

READING 47

Correct: C

Equal number of shares in each component will provide an effective track.

READING 48

Correct: B

The semi-strong form of the Efficient Market Hypothesis states that security prices reflect all publicly available information but do not include the privately available information.

READING 49

Correct: C

Preference shares do not usually carry voting rights.

READING 50

Correct: A

Justification:
Charting is used by technical analysis, e.g. looking at moving averages for a company's share price.

As well as market and industry analysis, fundamental analysis would include reviewing a company's financial statement.

READING 51

1. Correct: A

The value of preferred stock is calculated as dividend / required rate of return, $3.50/0.07 = $50. The growth rate is ignored as this is preferred stock that pays a fixed dividend.

2. Correct: A

The answer is a three-step procedure.

Step 1. Calculate the stock's dividends in the first three years, i.e. Div1, Div2, and Div3 using Div1 = Div0$(1+g)^n$ for all three dividends.

Div at time 1 = $1.10 × 1.15 = $1.265
Div at time 2 = $1.10 × 1.15^2 = $1.4548
Div at time 3 = $1.10 × 1.15^3 = $1.672
Div at time 4 = $1.672 × 1.05 = $1.75661. Note in the fourth year we use the sustainable growth rate of 5%.

Step 2. Calculate the stock's price in the third year, i.e. P3, using constant growth DDM, using P3 = Div4/(r–g).

$$\$1.7566 / (0.1 - 0.05) = \$35.13$$

Step 3. Discount each of the cash flows using 10% cost of equity, i.e. P = [Div1/(1 + r)] + [Div2/[(1 + r)^2] + [(Div3 + P3)] / [(1 + r)^3]

Div1 is $1.265 (PV = $1.15), Div2 is $1.4548 (PV = $1.20), Div3 is $1.673 (PV = $1.26), and Div4 is $1.7566.

Using Div4, Price3 is $35.13 as per stage 3 (PV = $26.39).

The sum of these present values leads to price of $30.

READING 52

1. Correct: C

As interest rates fall, bond prices rise. The investor must have purchased the bond at a discount and is now selling it at par (face value) for a capital gain. The other answers reflect a purchase price.

2. Correct: C

A call option will benefit the issuer as the issuer has the right to redeem the bond when the price rises. Caps on floating rate bonds will limit the cash flows the bond holder receives.

Both put and convertible bonds benefit the bondholder, allowing them to redeem the bond if the price falls and convert to equity shares if they are worth more than the maturity value.

READING 53

1. Correct: B

We need to use the effective duration formula below:

$$\text{Duration} = (\$109.405 - \$105.509) / (2 \times \$107.434 \times 0.005)$$

$$\text{Duration} = 3.626$$

2. Correct: A

If the bond is above par, investors will suffer a capital loss if they hold the bond until it is redeemed for par at maturity. Therefore its yield must be below coupon. The coupon is set at issue and you assume it is issued at par of 100.

READING 54

Correct: C

Both statements are accurate. Treasury inflation-protected securities (TIPS) make semi-annual coupon payments at a rate fixed at issuance of the bonds. TIPS coupons are paid semi-annually as a percentage of the inflation-adjusted face value of the bond.

READING 55

Correct: C

Both statements are inaccurate. The normal yield curve is upward sloping whereas the inverted one is downward sloping.

READING 56

Correct: A

The question asks for the price of a three-year bond. You only need the first three spot rates in the series to value each coupon and the principal.

$$80 / (1 + 0.085) + 80 / (1 + 0.0775)^2 + 1{,}080 / (1 + 0.0725)^3 = \$1{,}018.09$$

READING 57

Correct: C

If coupons are reinvested at the YTM, the realized yield and YTM will be the same.

The yield must be above 10% due to the discount but will be beneath 12% as the YTM assumption (that coupons are reinvested at the YTM) is not satisfied.

READING 58

Correct: C

Effective duration estimates the % price change for a 1% change in yield.

Effective duration = (Price when yield falls – Price when yield rises) / (2 × Initial price × Change in yield)

Effective duration = ($1,300 – $900) / (2 × $1,100 × 0.015) = 12.12%

This question is asking for the effective duration. It does not matter that the duration calculation in this instance uses a 150bp change. The formula will still give you the % change in price for a 1% change in yield.

READING 59

Correct: C

$$\text{Return impact} = -(\text{Mdur} \times \Delta\text{Spread}) + 0.5\text{Cvx} \times (\Delta\text{Spread})^2$$

$$= -(8.3 \times 0.0075) + (0.5 \times 74.9) \times (0.0075)^2$$

$$= -0.06225 + (37.45 \times 0.00005625)$$

$$= -0.0601 \text{ or } -6.01\%$$

READING 60

1. Correct: B

The forward price should be the current spot price x $(1 + r)$ where r is the appropriate interest rate.

Here 300×1.015 as the 6% annual risk-free rate needs to be taken down to a quarterly rate (using money market yields).

Answer A is the current market price – if investors could buy silver in three months' time for $300 they would sell silver today for the current spot price (=$300), deposit the $300, and have $304.50 in three months' time to buy back the silver initially sold and be left with a $4.50 risk-free gain.

Answer C wrongly uses the full annual rate.

2. Correct: C

Contingent claims are derivatives in which the payoffs occur if a specific event happens. Essentially a degree of optionality is contained within the financial instrument. Futures represent commitments rather than choice to buy or sell.

READING 61

Correct: A

As PB Industries are due to receive a cash flow, they will be concerned about interest rates falling. Therefore they will sell a FRA, receive fixed, and pay floating. An increase in interest rates results in PB Industries making a payment under the contract.

LIBOR at the start of the period was 0.1% (or 10 basis points) higher than the amount contracted in the FRA, so PB Industries will be having to *pay* (either answer A or B) out the excess interest they would be receiving on the deposit to the buyer of the FRA.

The amount of interest is $90 / 360 \times \$10m \times 0.001 = \$2,500$ and this needs to be discounted by 90 days of LIBOR at $5.85\% = 2,500 / 1.01463 = \$2,463.96$

Answer B has omitted to deal with the issue of the payment of the FRA happening at the start of the period.

READING 62

Correct: B

First, it's a loss. The seller sold for less than he could buy it back for now, so that eliminates answer A. How big is the loss? $94.75 - 94.87$ equals a loss of 12 full ticks. The Eurodollar contract is worth $25 per full tick. And the seller sold 10 contracts. $-12 \times \$25 \times 10 = -\$3,000$.

READING 63

1. Correct: A

If interest rates rise, investors will gain exposure to share prices through buying call options rather than buying the underlying share. It requires a much smaller outlay than buying the underlying directly, and the excess cash can be placed in an interest-bearing account at the current interest rate. As a result, the demand for call options increases and premiums rise. The opposite is true for puts. When interest rates rise, the opportunity cost of holding the put increases, which exerts downward pressure on the put's value.

2. Correct: C

Using put–call parity:

$$Co + PV(x) = So + Po$$

Therefore:

$$Po = Co + PV(X) - So$$

$$= 15p + 250p / 1.08^{\wedge}(250 / 365) - 200p$$

$$= 15p + 250p / 1.054127 - 200p$$

$$= 15p + 237.16p - 200p$$

$$= 52.16$$

READING 64

Correct: B

1. ABC Inc. owes the dealer ($1,000,000)(0.09)(90 / 360) = $22,500.
2. XYZ Inc. owes ABC Inc. ($1,000,000)(0.11)(90 / 360) = $27,500.
3. Payments in interest rate swaps are paid net, i.e. $27,500 – $22,500 = $5,000.

READING 65

Correct: B

A is incorrect as the writer of an option receives a premium. C is incorrect as it is the writer, not the holder, that has unlimited downside potential.

READING 66

Correct: A

$$NOI = \$500,000 \text{ gross rental income} \times (1 - 0.1) - \$5,000 \text{ property-related taxes and insurance}$$
$$- \$25,000 \text{ maintenance} = \$420,000$$

0.1 in the calculation is the estimated vacancy rate given in the question.

READING 67

Correct: A

A contango market exists where the spot price is lower than the futures price.

a priori probability 28
absolute advantage 85
accounting equation 18, 99–100, 101
accounting profit 58
accounting warning signs 154
accounts payable 121, 177
accounts receivable 121, 177
accruals 100, 110
activity ratio 124
ADR *see* American Depositary Receipts
after-tax cash flow (ATCF) 291
aggregate demand and supply 54, 70–1, 72
aggregate output 69–72
    sample question/answer 73, 301
alternative hypothesis 41
alternative investments 289
    benefits 292
    categories 292
    commodities 293
    compared with traditional investments
        291
    hedge funds 293
    overview 290
    private equity 293
    real estate 293
    risk management 292
    sample question/answer 294, 315
American Depositary Receipts (ADR) 216
American options 279, 280–1
amortization 137
annual interest rate 15–16
annual pay bond 254
annual report 97
annuity 14, 16, 17
arbitrage 280–1
    definition/role 269
    profit 249–50
arbitrage-free value 226, 249–50
arithmetic mean 22
asset-backed security 237–8
asset-based valuation models 223
asset/s 98, 115
    allocation 46, 197
    classes 197
    current/non-current 116
    leasing/purchasing 147
    prices 36
    tangible/intangible 136, 137–8
    values 137–8
ATCF *see* after-tax cash flow

auctions
    types 54
    winning price 54
audits 97, 181
average cost 59
average product 59
average revenue 59

backwardation 294
balance of payments (BOP) 87
balance sheet 96, 100, 114–17
    assets 116
    common-size 114–15
    elements 115
    formats 115–16
    liabilities 116
    limitations 115
    liquidity/solvency ratios 115
    sample question/answer 117, 303
    shareholder equity 116–17
balancing adjustment 100
bank discount yield 14, 20
banker's acceptances 239
barter transactions 110
Bayes' formula 27–8
Bernoulli random variable 34, 36, 299
beta calculation 167, 193
bias 39
binomial random variable 34
binomial trees 34
bond equivalent yield 14, 20–1, 177, 254
bond sectors and instruments 236–9
    asset-backed security 237–8
    corporate debt 239
    coupon/principal strips 236–7
    government securities 238
    mortgage-backed securities 237
    primary/secondary markets 239
    sample question/answer 240, 311
Bond-Yield plus Risk Premium method
    167
bonds
    accrued interest, full price, clean price
        229
    affirmative/negative covenants 229
    arbitrage-free value 226
    call options 234
    callable/prepayable security
        disadvantages 233
    coupon rate 227, 231, 232

deferred coupon 228
duration/dollar duration 234, 258
embedded option 226, 228
exchange rate risk 235
expected cash flow estimation 250
indentures 229
inflation risk 235
institutional investors 229
interest rate risk 232–3
investment risk 226, 234
liquidity risk 234–5
margin buying/repurchase agreements
    229
maturity 250
measurement of interest rate risk
    257–61
non-amortizing 229
par value 227
price 227
price relative to par value 231, 232
redemption/retirement 229
reinvestment risk 233
risks 231–5
sample questions/answers 235, 240, 311
sovereign/event risk 235
spot/forward rates 226
step-up notes 228
taxable/tax-exempt 242
valuation 226, 247–50
yield 231, 232
yield measures 252–3
yield volatility 233
yield-curve risk 233
zero coupon 228
book value of equity 217, 222
book value per share 172
bootstrapping 254
BOP *see* balance of payments
borrowed costs 136
breakeven point of production 60
breakeven price of option 288
breakeven quantity of sales 171
budget constraint 56, 57
business cycles 73–5
    sample question/answer 76, 301
business risk 170

CAL *see* capital allocation line
calculators 17
callable bonds 233, 258

capital allocation line (CAL) 184, 189, 190, 192–3
capital asset pricing model (CAPM) 166, 184, 193–4
capital budgeting 161–4
    calculating 161–2
    evaluation/selection of projects/ methods 163
    NPV, company value, share price relations 164
    popularity of methods 164
    principles 162–3
    process/categories 162
    sample question/answer 164, 306
capital estimation 165–9
    sample questions/answers 169, 306–7
capital gain or loss 256
capital market line (CML) 192–3
capital rationing 163
CAPM see capital asset pricing model
cash dividend 173
cash flow 14, 17, 18
    effect on options 280–1
    effects on net daily cash position 178
    estimation 162–3
    present-value model 222
cash flow statements 96, 101
    accounting shenanigans 155
    CFO, CFI, CFF 118–19
    common-size 122
    direct/indirect 119–21
    firm, equity, performance ratios 121–2
    non-cash investment/finance activities 122
    sample questions/answers 122–3, 155, 303–4, 306
cash settlement 270–1
CBOs see collateralized bond obligations
CDOs see collateralized debt obligations
central banks
    inflation, interest rate, exchange rate 79
    qualities 80
    role/objectives 80
central limit theorem 37–8
central tendency, measures of 22
certificate of deposit (CD) 239
CFA Institute 3
chart patterns, common 46
Chebyshev's inequality 23
clean price 229
closed-end fund 290
closely held companies 293, 294
CML see capital market line
CMO see collateralized mortgage obligations
Code of Ethics 3–5, 8, 182
    difference with Standards of Professional Conduct 2
    ethical responsibilities 5
    fundamental to values of CFA Institute 3
    key points 2
    reciting/understanding 1–2
    sample questions/answers 7, 297
    six components 3–4

violations/sanctions 3
    see also ethics; Standards of Professional Conduct
coefficient of variation 23
collateral yield 294
collateralized bond obligations (CBOs) 239
collateralized debt obligations (CDOs) 239
collateralized mortgage obligations (CMO) 237
combination notation 29
commercial paper 239
commodities 208, 290
    collateral yield 294
    price return 295
    roll yield 294
    sample question/answer 295, 315
    sources of return and risk 294
    spot rates/expected future prices 294
commodity index strategy 295
common markets 87
common stock 215
common-size balance sheet 114–15
common-size cash flow statement 122
common-size income statement 111
company analysis see industry and company analysis
company comparisons 157–8
company disclosures 106
company value 164
comparable method 294
comparative advantage 85
compensation 181
compliance
    benefits 9
    claiming 8–9
composites 9
compound rate 16
comprehensive income 113
concentration measures 66
conditional/unconditional probability 28
confidence interval
    estimate 37, 38–9
    relation with hypothesis test 41
constant-cost 61
consumer choice theory 56
consumer demand 56–7
    sample question/answer 30, 57
contango 294
contingent claim 269
continuous compound rates of return 36
continuous random variable 35
continuous uniform distribution 35
convexity 257–8, 260
    modified/effective 261
corporate bonds 239, 262, 263
corporate debt 263
corporate finance 159
    capital budgeting 161–4
    cost of capital estimation 165–9
    dividends/share repurchases 172–4
    financial statement analysis 180–79
    governance of listed companies 180–2

measures of leverage 170–1
    overview 160
    sample questions/answers 164, 169, 171, 174, 179, 182, 306–8
    working capital management 175–9
corporate governance of listed companies 180–2
    board independence 181
    code of ethics 182
    definition 181
    evaluation of committees 181
    qualifications of board members 181
    rules 180–1
    sample question/answer 182, 308
    shareowner perspective 182
corporate issuer credit ratings 264
correlation 28, 29, 34
cost method 291, 294
costs 59–61
    borrowing 136
    capitalized/expensed difference 135–6
    inventories 131–2, 134
    long-lived assets 135–6
counting problems 29
    sample question/answer 29, 299
country risk premium 168
coupon paying 248
coupon rates 227–8, 231, 232
coupon strips 236–7
covariance 28–9, 188
covenants, affirmative/negative 229
covered call 287–8
credit analysis 262–4
    high yield, sovereign, municipal debt issuers/issues 263
    level/volatility of yield spreads 264
    quality of corporate bond issuer/bond issued 262, 263
    ratios 125–6, 262
    return impact of spread changes 263
    seniority rankings 263
    traditional components 264
credit ratings 234, 264
credit ratings agencies 262, 264
credit risk 234, 263, 274, 275
credit spread 242
creditors 147
cross-price elasticity of demand 53
cross-rate 89
cross-sectional data 39
cumulative relative frequency 24
currency exchange rates 88–90
    sample question/answer 90, 302
currency forward contract 273
currency swap 285
current/non-current assets 116
customer bargaining power 219
cycles 46

data set 24
data-mining bias 39
dealer 272
debt 93
    break-points 169

corporations 239
covenants 147
de-recognition 147
financial statement presentation/
  disclosure 147
investment 157
obligations 239
debt securities 227–9
  bonds, coupon rate structures, floating-
    rate 227–8
  embedded options 228
  features 227–30
  sample question/answer 230, 251, 311,
    312
  valuation 247–50
debt-rating method 166
deciles 24
decision making 57, 86
decision rule 41
declaration date 173–4
decreasing-cost 61
deferred tax assets/liabilities 142–3
defined benefit pension plans 148, 149
defined contribution 148, 149
deflation 75
demand and supply
  aggregation 54, 70–1
  application of LOS 51–4
  auctions 54
  consumer demand 56–7
  curves 52, 54, 70–1
  elasticities 53, 63, 66
  equilibria 54
  excess 52
  the firm 58–61
  government regulation/intervention 54
  inverse 52
  knowledge LOS 51, 54
  market interference 52–3
  market types 54
  principles 51
  sample questions/answers 55, 57, 61,
    300–1
  theories of money 79
depositary receipts 216
depreciation 112, 120
  calculation 136–7
derivatives
  definitions 267
  forwards 266, 270–3
  futures 266, 274–5
  instruments 267–9
  options 266, 278–82
  overview 265–6
  purposes/criticisms 268
  risk management of option strategies
    287–8
  sample questions/answers 269, 273,
    277, 283, 286, 312–14
  swaps 266, 284–5
descriptive statistics 24
developing market 168
dilutive/anti-dilutive securities 111
diminishing marginal returns 59

direct/indirect foreign exchange 88–9
dirty price 229
disclosures 134, 138, 143, 148
discount rate 17, 249, 250
discount-basis yield 177
discounted cash flow 19–21
  sample question/answer 21, 298
discounted payback period 162
discrete compound rates of return 36
discrete random variable 35
discrete uniform random variable 34
disinflation 75
Dividend Discount Model 167, 222
dividend growth models 223
dividends/share repurchases 172–4
  book value per share 172
  cash dividends equivalence 173
  comparison of methods 174
  definitions 173
  earnings per share 172
  payment chronology 173–4
  sample question/answer 174, 307
dollar duration of a bond 234
DuPont formula 125
duration of a bond 234
  definitions 261
  effective 261
  measurement 258–60

earnings per share (EPS) 110–11, 172
EBIT (or operating profit) 112
economic growth 69
  input growth vs. growth of total factor
    productivity 73
  production function approach 73
economic indicators 75
economic profit 58
economic rent 59
economic unions 87
economics
  aggregate output 69–72
  business cycles 73–6
  currency exchange rates 88–90
  demand and supply 51–61
  economic growth 69–73
  firm/market structures 62–6
  international trade/capital flows 85–7
  macroeconomics 50
  microeconomics 50
  monetary/fiscal policy 78–82
  overview 50
  prices 69–72
  sample questions/answers 55, 57, 61,
    66, 73, 76, 80, 87, 90, 300–2
economy well-being 242
effective annual yield 20
efficient frontier 190
Efficient Market Hypothesis 269
  market pricing anomalies 210
  market value/intrinsic value difference
    210
  psychological factors 211
  sample question/answer 211, 309
  weak, semi-strong, strong 209–10

elasticities 53, 63, 66
Elliott Wave Theory 46
embedded options 226, 232, 242
empirical probability 28
end user 272
EPS see earnings per share
equilibrium 54, 57, 63, 66, 72
equity 98, 101, 199, 213
  analysis 125–6, 206–11, 213, 215–17
  balance sheet 115, 116, 117
  comparisons, calculations,
    interpretations 202–4
  financial intermediaries 202
  forward contract 272
  functions/characteristics of financial
    system 201–2
  indices 208
  industry/company analysis 200, 218–20
  investment 157, 292
  markets 200
  overview 200
  ratio 121
  real estate 293
  sample question/answer 205, 309
  securities 200
  shareholders' 116
  statement of changes in 96
  valuation 200, 221–4
equity markets and analysis 206
  index construction/management 206–7
  market efficiency 209–10
  psychological factors 211
  rebalancing/reconstitution of index 207
  sample questions/answers 208, 211, 309
  security market index calculation/
    interpretation 206, 208
  types of indices 208
equity securities
  characteristics/role 215
  market value/book value difference
    216–17
  non-domestic 216
  public/private 215–16
  risk/return characteristics 216
  sample question/answer 217, 310
equity swap 285
equity valuation
  asset-based valuation models 223
  cash flow models 222
  categories 223
  concepts/basic tools 221–4
  dividend discount model 220
  estimations 223
  multiplier model 222–3
  non-callable/non-convertible preferred
    stock 224
  peer group 220
  sample question/answer 224, 310–11
estimation 37–9
estimator 37
ETFs see Exchange Traded Funds
ethics, importance of 1
  see also Code of Ethics; Standards of
    Professional Conduct

Euribor 272
Eurodollar 272
European options 279, 280–1
event risk 235
events 28
    exhaustive 28
    (in)dependent 28
    joint probability 28
    mutually exclusive 28
    probability of for/against 28
ex-dividend date 173–4
exchange rate, contrast with inflation/interest rate 79
exchange rate risk 235
Exchange Traded Funds (ETFs) 292
exchange-traded derivatives 267
exchange-traded options 281
expense recognition 112
expenses 98, 131
external credit enhancements 237–8
external efficiency 202

factorial notation 29
factors of production 60
FASB see Financial Accounting Standards Board
FCFF see free cash flow to the firm
Fibonacci numbers 46
FIFO (first in, first out) 132, 134
Financial Accounting Standards Board (FASB) 104
financial analysis techniques 124–7
    sample question/answer 127, 304
financial information 105
financial leverage 171
financial notes/supplementary information 96
financial ratios 92, 111, 262
financial reporting and analysis 91, 96, 109, 151
    balance sheets 114–17
    cash flow statements 118–23, 155
    financial statements 91, 92, 95–7
    income statements 92, 109–13
    income taxes 140–3
    inventories 131–4
    long-lived assets 135–9
    mechanics of reporting 98–102
    non-current (long-term) liabilities 144–9
    overview 92
    quality 93, 153–4
    red flags/accounting warning signs 153–4
    sample questions/answers 102, 154, 302, 306
    specific accounting issues 92–3
    standards 103–6
    techniques 124–7
financial reporting standards 103
    company disclosures 106
    comparison of concepts 105
    framework characteristics 105–6
    global convergence/barriers 104–5

importance 104
    intangible assets 136
    monitoring developments 106
    requirements 105
    roles/attributes 104
    sample question/answer 106, 303
financial risk 170
financial statement analysis 95–7, 156–8
    accounting equation 99–100
    accruals/adjustments 100
    balance sheet statement 180–79
    cash flows/owners' equity link 101
    comparisons with another company 157–8
    credit quality of potential debt investment 157
    five elements 98–9
    future net income/cash flow 157
    income/balance sheet link 101
    intangible assets 138
    inventories 134
    past performance 156
    sample questions/answers 97, 158, 302, 306
    screening potential equity investments 157
financial system 201–2
The Firm
    costs 59, 61
    demand and supply 58–61
    diminishing marginal returns 59
    diseconomies of scale 60
    exit/entry 66
    labor 59
    market structures 62–6
    output 60
    production 60
    profit 58, 61
    resources 60
    revenue 59
    sample questions/answers 61, 66, 301
firm ratio 121
fiscal balance 69–70
fiscal policy 78–82
    arguments for/against size of deficit 81
    implementation 81
    interaction with monetary policy 82
    sample question/answer 80, 301–2
    tools 81
Fisher effect 80
fixed income 225, 227–9, 245
    bond sectors/instruments 236–9
    debt securities 227–30
    forward rates 252–6
    interest rate risk 257–61
    overview 226
    risk associated with bond investment 231–5
    risks 226
    sample questions/answers 230, 235, 240, 244, 251, 256, 261, 311–12
    spot rates 252–6
    valuation of debt securities 247–51
    yield measures 252–6

yield spreads 241–3
fixed income indices 208
fixed rate bonds 252–3
fixed rate debt capital 166
float-adjusted market capitalization weighting 207
floating rate securities (or variable rate securities) 228
flotation costs 169
flow-of-funds indicators 45
forward commitments 268
forward contract 268
forward discount (or premium) rate 89–90
forward exchange rate 88, 89, 90
forward rate 226, 255–6
forward rate agreement (FRA) 270, 271, 281–2
forwards 266
    contract 272
    dealer/end user difference 272
    default risk 270–1
    definition 268
    delivery/settlement 270–1
    equity forward contract 272
    sample question/answer 273, 313
fraud 153–4
free cash flow to the firm (FCFF) 121–2
free and clear equity 293
frequency distribution 24
frequency polygon 24
full employment 72
full valuation method 260–1
fund of funds 293
future net income 157
future value (FV) 14, 16
futures 266
    characteristics 274
    definition 268
    margin 274, 275–6
    sample question/answer 277, 313
    termination at or prior to expiration 275–6
futures contract 268
FV see future value

GDP see gross domestic product
geometric mean 20, 22, 23
    sample question/answer 25, 298
Giffen goods 57
GIPS see Global Investment Performance Standards
Global Depositary Receipts (GLR) 216
Global Investment Performance Standards (GIPS)
    basic idea 2
    beneficiaries 2
    benefitting from compliance 9
    characteristics, scope, implementation 11
    claiming compliance 8–9
    composites 9
    key elements 2
    knowledge LOS 8–10
    nine major sections 11

Index

reasons for creation 8
sample questions/answers 10, 12, 297
verification 9
GLR *see* Global Depositary Receipts
good-till-cancelled (GTC) vs. time limited
    orders 204
goodwill 136
Gordon's Growth Model 167, 222
governance, corporate *see* corporate
    governance of listed companies
government regulation/intervention 54
government securities 238
gross domestic product (GDP) 50, 72, 86
gross national product (GNP) 86
gross profit 132–3
gross return 188
gross vs. net reporting 110
GTC *see* good-till-cancelled

harmonic mean, median, mode 22, 23
head and shoulders reversal 46
Heckscher–Ohlin model 85
hedge funds 208, 293
hidden orders 204
high yield issues 263
histogram 24
historical simulation 36
holder-of-record 173–4
holding period return 20, 36
holding period yield 14, 20
hypothesis testing 40–4
    population means 42–3
    relation with confidence interval 41
    sample question/answer 44, 300

IASB *see* International Accounting
    Standards Board
IFRS *see* International Financial
    Reporting Standards
impairment of assets 137–8
income effect 56
income elasticity of demand 53
income method 291, 294
income statements 92, 109, 110–13
    sample question/answer 113, 303
income taxes 92, 140–3
    calculation 141
    deferred items 142
    deferred liabilities 141
    disclosures 143
    key provisions under IFRS/US GAAP
        143
    key terms 142
    profit/taxable income difference 142
    sample question/answer 143, 305
    tax base of assets/liabilities 141
    tax rate changes 142
    temporary/permanent pre-tax
        accounting/taxable income 142
    valuation allowance 143
indices 73
indifference curves 57, 189
industry and company analysis 218
    business cycle 219

classifications 219, 220
elements/characteristics 219
external factors 220
internal factors 219
life cycle phase 219
sample question/answer 220, 310
stage of life 220
uses of/relation to company analysis
    219
inferential statistics 24
inferior goods 57
inflation 75
    calculating 73
    contrast with interest rate/exchange rate
        79
    premium 17
    risk 235
initial margin 275–6
input growth 73
input level 59
installment sales 110
interest rate
    caps, floors, collars 281–2
    contrast with inflation/exchange rate 79
    options 279
interest rate risk 232–3
    measurement 257–61
interest rate swaps 284–5
intermarket analysis 46
internal control 97
internal efficiency 202
internal rate of return (IRR) 14, 19, 160,
    161, 163, 164
internally developed intangible assets 136
International Accounting Standards Board
    (IASB) 104–5
International Financial Reporting
    Standards (IFRS) 92, 104, 105, 111,
    122, 136, 138, 143
International Monetary Fund (IMF) 87
International Organization of Securities
    Commissions (IOSC) 104
international trade 85–7
    sample question/answer 87, 302
intrinsic value 210, 282
inventories 92, 121, 177
    closing (or ending) 132
    cost formulas 132, 134
    costs included/costs as expenses 131–2
    financial statement presentation/
        disclosure 134
    impairment 133
    levels 74
    measurement 133
    perpetual/periodic systems 132
    ratios 133
    sample question/answer 134, 304
    valuation methods 132–3
investment 69–70
    constraints 197
    debt 157
    equity 157
    portfolio method 185
    property 138–9

short-term policy guidelines 176–7
    strategies 177
investment policy statement (IPS) 196,
    197
investments savings (IS) curve 70
Investor Relations statement 97
investors 185–6
    bond market 229
    evaluation of board members 181
    major asset classes 190
    positions in an asset 202
    psychological behavior 211
    risk-averse 188, 193
IPS *see* investment policy statement
IRR *see* internal rate of return
IS curve *see* investments savings (IS)
    curve
issue credit ratings 264

joint probability function 28

kurtosis 24, 188

leases 93
    advantages 147
    disclosure 148
    finance/operating 148
leverage, measures of *see* measures of
    leverage
leveraged equity 293
leveraged returns 188
liabilities 98, 100, 115
LIBOR 243, 271–2
life cycle models 219
LIFO (last in, first out) 132, 134
limit order 204
liquidity 197, 202, 239
    measures 175
    preference theory 243
    ratio 115, 124
    risk 234–5
    sources 178
liquidity/money supply (LM) curve 70
listed company governance *see* corporate
    governance of listed companies
LM curve *see* liquidity/money supply
    (LM) curve
lognormal distribution 36
long position 202–3, 270–1
long-lived assets
    amortization methods 137
    capitalized/expensed costs difference
        135–6
    de-recognition 138
    depreciation 136–7
    financial statement presentation 138
    impairment 137–8
    intangible assets 136
    investment property 138–9
    revaluation model 137
    sample question/answer 139, 305
long-run equilibrium 65–6
long-term contracts 110
look-ahead bias 39

Macaulay duration 261
macroeconomics 50
MAD *see* mean absolute deviation
maintenance margin 275–6
major asset classes 190
Management Discussion and Analysis
    statement 97
margin 274
   buying 229
   securities market/future market
     difference 275–6
marginal cost of capital (MCC) 168, 169
marginal product 59
marginal revenue 59
mark to market accounting 137, 275
market
   interference 52–3
   model 194
   order 203
   regulation 204
   returns 22–5
   types 54
   value 210
market efficiency *see* Efficient Market
    Hypothesis
market pricing anomalies
   calendar effects 210
   closed-end investment fund discounts
    210
   momentum and overreaction 210
   size/value effect 210
market segmentation theory 243
market structures 50
   characteristics 62–3
   concentration measures 66
   long-run equilibrium 65–6
   monopolistic competition 64
   monopoly 65–6
   oligopoly 64–5
   optimal price and output 63
   perfect competition 63
   pricing strategy 66
   sample question/answer 66, 301
   supply function 64–5
market value-weighted indices 207
MCC *see* marginal cost of capital
mean absolute deviation (MAD) 23
mean of asset returns 188
meaningful result 43
measurement scales 24
measures of central tendency 22
measures of leverage 170–1
   calculating/interpreting 171
   definition/explanation 170
   effect of financial leverage 170–1
   sample question/answer 171, 307
medium term notes (MTN) 239
microeconomics 50
minimum-variance portfolio 189
momentum oscillator indicators 45
   ROC, RSI, MACD 45
monetary policy 78–82
   functions/definitions of money 79–80
   implementation 79

interaction with fiscal policy 82
   limitations 81
   money creation process 79
   sample question/answer 80, 301–2
money, time value of *see* time value of
    money
money-market yield 14, 20, 177
money-weighted rate of return (MWRR)
    14, 20
monopolist 66
monopolistic competition 64
   pricing strategy 66
monopoly 65–6
   pricing strategy 66
Monte Carlo simulation 36
mortgaged-backed securities 237
mortgages 293
MTN *see* medium term notes
multi-factor models 194
multiplier model 222–3
multivariate distribution 34
municipal debt 263
mutual funds 186
mutually exclusive projects 163
MWRR *see* money-weighted rate of return

national income identity formula 86
NAV *see* net asset value
negotiable CDs 239
net asset value (NAV) 290
net operating cycle 176
net operating income (NOI) 291
net present value (NPV) 14, 19, 160, 161,
    163, 164, 292
net realizable value 133
net return 188
new entrants 219
NOI *see* net operating income
nominal exchange rate 88
nominal spread 254
non-callable/non-convertible preferred
    stock 166, 224
non-current (long-term) liabilities 92, 144
   debt 147
   defined contribution/benefit pension
    plans 148–9
   interest rate of bonds 145–6
   leasing assets 147–8
   leverage/coverage ratios 146
   measurement of bonds 145
   sample question/answer 149, 305
non-domestic equity securities 216
non-equilibrium price 52
non-recurring items 112
normal distribution 34
normal goods 57
normal profit 58
notching 264
NPV *see* net present value
null hypothesis 41

OAS *see* option-adjusted spread
oligopoly 64–5
   pricing strategy 66

one-tailed tests of hypothesis 41
open position 275
open-end fund 290
operating leverage 171
operating profit (or EBIT) 112
operating risk 170
operating/non-operating income statement
    112
opportunity cost 17
opportunity sets 57
optimal portfolio 190
optimal price and output 63
option-adjusted spread (OAS) 254–5
option-free bonds 258
options 269
   cost 255
   definition 268
   European and American 279, 280–1
   exchange-traded cf over-the-counter
    281
   interest rate 279
   moneyness 279
   payoffs 279
   put–call 278, 279
   risk management application of
    strategies 287–8
   sample questions/answers 283, 314
   synthetic 280–1
   value estimates 278
options, embedded
   accelerated sinking fund 228
   call and refunding 228
   cap on a floater 228
   conversion 228
   floor on a floater 228
   prepayment 228
   put provision 228
order, types of 203–4
outcome 28
over-the-counter (OTC) derivatives 267
over-the-counter (OTC) options 281

p-value 43
parameter 24
parametric/non-parametric tests 44
past financial performance 156
payback period 162
payment date 173–4
payoff 271
peer group 220
pensions 93, 148, 149
percentiles 24
perfect competition 63
   pricing strategy 66
performance ratio 121
permutation notation 29
perpetual/periodic systems 132
PI *see* profitability index
plain vanilla interest rate swap 284
point estimate 37
polarity, change in 46
population 23, 24
population mean 22, 43–4
population variances 42–3

portfolio
  duration 259–60
  performance 20
  rates of return 20, 22
  standard deviation 189
portfolio management 183
  investment approach 185
  investors 185–6
  mutual funds 186
  overview 184, 185–6
  passive 210
  planning and construction 196–8
  process 186
  risk and return 184, 187–95
  sample question/answer 186, 308
portfolio planning and construction
  asset allocation 197
  investment constraints 197
  IPS 196
  principles 197
  risk/return objectives 197
  sample question/answer 198, 309
power of a test 41
preference stock 215
prepayable bonds 258
prepayable security 17
present value (PV) 14, 16
price 69–72
  discrimination 66
  levels 75
  return 206, 296
  role of arbitrage 269
  strategy 66
  target 46
price earnings model (P/E ratio) 222
price elasticity of demand 53
price floor or ceiling 52–3
price return 295
price value of a basic point (PVBP) 260
price-based indicators 45
  Bollinger Bands 45
  moving averages 45
price-weighted indices 207
primary market 204, 239
principal strips 236–7
private equity 293
probability concepts 26–9
  sample question/answer 29, 299
probability distribution 33–6
  sample question/answer 36, 299
product of labor 59
product markets 50
production 60
production function 73
profit 58
profit metrics 112
profit-maximization
  the Firm 63, 64, 65
  level of output 35
  short-run/long-run 61
profitability index (PI) 162
profitability ratio 124
project sequencing 163
protective put 287–8

psychological behavior 211
public/private equity 215–16
purchased intangible assets 136
pure expectations theory 243
put–call parity 278, 280–1
putable bonds 258
PVBP see price value of a basic point

quantitative methods 187–8, 189
  application 31, 33–47
  basic concepts 13–29
  discounted cash flow applications
    19–21
  market returns 22–5
  overview 13–14
  probability concepts 6–9
  sample questions/answers 25, 298–9
  statistical concepts 14, 22–5
  technical analysis 14
  time value of money 15–18
quartiles 24
quintiles 24

random variable 28, 34
rate of return 14, 17
  discrete/continuous compound 36
rates of exchange see currency exchange
    rates
ratios
  activity 124, 125
  classify, calculate, interpret 124–6
  equity 121
  financial 92, 111
  firm 121
  gross profit margin 133
  inventory 133
  leverage/coverage 146
  liquidity 124, 125, 175–6
  model/forecast earnings 126–7
  performance 121
  price/earnings (P/E) 222
  profitability 124, 125
  relationship among 125
  Roy's safety-first ratio 35
  Sharpe ratio 23, 189
  solvency 124, 125
  valuation 124, 125
real estate 208
  investment 293
real exchange rate 88
reinvestment risk 233
REITs see real estate investment trusts
relative frequency 24
RELPs see real estate limited partnerships
reported cash flow statement 122
repurchase agreements 229
resistance lines 46
resources 60
return on equity (RoE) 170–1
return-generating models 194
revaluation model 137
revenue 59, 98, 100
revenue recognition 110
Ricardian model 85

risk
  bond investment 226, 231–5
  credit 263
  definitions 170
  mortgage-backed securities 237
  premium 17
  systematic/non-systematic 193
risk management 266
  alternative investments 292
  option strategies 287–8
  sample question/answer 288, 314
risk and return 187–90, 192–4
  commodity investment 294–5
  equity securities 216–17
  objectives 197
  overview 184
  sample questions/answers 190–1, 195,
    308, 309
risk-averse 188, 188–9, 193
risk-free assets 192–3
risk-free rate 17
risk-neutral 188
risk-seeking 188
rivalry 219
roll yield 294
Roy's safety-first ratio 35

safety-first ratio 35
sample 23, 24
  mean 22
  selection bias 39
  skewness 24
  statistic 24
  variance 23
sampling 37–9
  distribution 39
  error 39
  question/answer 39, 299–300
saving 69–70
scenario analysis method 260–1
SEC see Securities and Exchange
    Commission
secondary market 204, 239
Securities and Exchange Commission
    (SEC) 104, 105
security analysis 102, 104
  callable/prepayable security 233
  overvalued, fairly valued, undervalued
    223
  reinvestment risk 233
security market index
  choices/issues in construction/
    management 206–7
  rebalancing/reconstitution 207
  sample question/answer 208, 309
  types 208
  uses 208
  value, price return, total return 206
  weighting methods 207
security market line (SML) 184, 193–4
segment analysis 125–6
semiannual pay bond 254
sentiment indicators 45
  margin debt 45

sentiment indicators (*continued*)
  options volatility index (VIX) 45
  put/call ratio 45
  shorting interest 45
share price 164
share repurchases *see* dividends/share
  repurchases
shareholders' equity 116
shareholders' wealth 173
Sharpe ratio 23, 189
short position 203, 270–1
short run macroeconomic equilibrium 72
short-term funding 178
shortfall risk 35
shutdown point of production 60
significance level 41
simple random sampling 39
skewness 24, 188
  sample question/answer 25, 299
SML *see* security market line
solvency ratio 115
sources of return 256
sovereign debt 263
sovereign risk 235
special purpose vehicle 237–8
spot exchange rate 88
spot rate 226, 243, 255–6
spread changes 263
standard deviation 23
standard error of the mean 37
Standards of Professional Conduct 3–5, 8
  difference with Code of Ethics 2
  ethical responsibilities 5
  fundamental to values of CFA Institute 3
  key points 2
  reciting/understanding 1–2
  sample questions/answers 5, 297
  seven components 4
  violations/sanctions 3
  see also Code of Ethics; ethics
statistical concepts 14, 22–5
  sample questions/answers 25, 298–9
statistical result 43
stock price 164
stocks 190, 193
stop 204
strategic analysis
  external factors 220
  internal factors 219
stripped Treasury securities 236–7
structured notes 239
Student's t-distribution 38–9
subjective probability 28
substitution effect 56, 219
supplier bargaining power 219
support 46
survivor bias 39
swaps 266
  characteristics 284

currency swap 285
  definition 268
  equity swap 285
  interest rate swaps 284–5
  sample question/answer 286, 314
  termination 284
synthetic options 280–1

T-accounts 101
T-bills 190
tangible/intangible assets 136, 137
tax/es 93, 197
  cost of capital 167
  payable 142
  real estate 292
technical analysis 13, 14, 45–6
  cycles 46
  indicators 45
  intermarket analysis 46
  principles 45
  sample question/answer 47, 300
term structure 242–3
test statistic 41
time deposit market 272
time horizon 197
time value 282
time value of money 14, 15–18
  annual rate 15–17
  frequencies of compounding 16
  sample questions/answers 18, 298
  timeline 18
time-period bias 39
time-series data 39
time-weighted rate of return (TWRR)
  14, 20
TIPS *see* Treasury inflation protected
  securities
total cost 59
total factor productivity 73
total leverage 171
total probability rule 28
total product 59
total return 206
total revenue 59
trade balance 69–70
trading blocs 87
transparency 202
Treasury bills 238
Treasury bonds 238
Treasury inflation protected securities
  (TIPS) 238
tree diagram 27
trend 46
trial balance 101
two-tailed tests of hypothesis 41
TWRR *see* time-weighted rate of return
Type I and Type II errors 41

uncertainty 13

unemployment 75
unimodal, nonsymmetrical distribution
  24
univariate distribution 34
unweighted indices 207
US Department of the Treasury 238
US GAAP (US generally accepted
  accounting standards) 92, 102, 104,
  111, 122, 133, 136, 137, 139, 143
utility 188–9
  analysis 57
  theory 56

valuation 13
  allowance 142–3
  ratio 124
variable cost 59
variance 23
  population means 42–3
variance of asset returns 188
variation margin 275
Veblen goods 57
venture capital investment 292
verification 9
voting rights 215

WACC *see* weighted average cost
weighted average cost (WACC) 132, 134,
  166, 168
weighted average or mean 22, 23
working capital management 175–8
  sample question/answer 179, 307–8
World Bank 87
World Trade Organization (WTO) 87

yield 14
  curve 242–3
  curve risk 233
  measures 252–3
yield spreads 241, 241–3
  central bank interest rate policy 242
  credit spread 242
  embedded options 242
  level/volatility 264
  LIBOR 243
  liquidity/issue size 243
  measures 241
  sample question/answer 244, 312
  spot rate 243
  taxable/tax-exempt bonds 242
  yield curve 242–3
yield to call (YTC) 253
yield volatility 233, 261
yield-to-maturity (YTM) 166, 253–4
YTC *see* yield to call
YTM *see* yield-to-maturity

zero coupon bond 243, 248
zero-volatility spread (z-spread) 254–5